D0015961

T H E
Secretary's Handbook

THE
Secretary's Handbook

TENTH EDITION

Sarah Augusta Taintor
and
Kate M. Monro

Revised by
Margaret D. Shertzer

MACMILLAN PUBLISHING COMPANY
NEW YORK
COLLIER MACMILLAN PUBLISHERS
LONDON

Macmillan Publishing Company
866 Third Avenue, New York, NY 10022
Collier Macmillan Canada, Inc.

Library of Congress Cataloging-in-Publication Data
Taintor, Sarah Augusta.
    The secretary's handbook / Sarah Augusta Taintor and Kate M.
Monro.
        p.   cm.
    Includes index.
    1. Office practice.   I. Monro, Kate M.   II. Shertzer, Margaret D.
III. Title.
HF5547.5.T29   1988
651.7'402—dc19   87-24960
ISBN 0-02-610211-0   CIP

Macmillan books are available at special discounts for bulk purchases for
sales promotions, premiums, fund-raising, or educational use. For
details, contact:
    Special Sales Director
    Macmillan Publishing Company
    866 Third Avenue
    New York, NY 10022

Designed by Nancy Sugihara

10 9 8 7 6 5 4 3 2 1

Printed in the United States of America

Contents

PART ONE

PART TWO

Preface to the Tenth Edition

In revising *The Secretary's Handbook* I have kept in mind the intent of the previous authors, namely, to provide useful information for secretaries, with an emphasis on grammar and good English usage.

The new chapters provide guidance in the areas of goals and attitude toward one's job, as well as information about the equipment used in today's offices. The other chapters have been rewritten and updated in order to provide information in the areas of greatest interest to most secretaries.

I have been fortunate in having the advice and suggestions of the following persons and corporations:

Elmer A. Richards, Sabine G. Yepes, Anne Spencer, and Tangul Jalbert; Anita Baron of Olin Corporation; Joyce Bidwell, Joan Carley, and Lisa Heinzmann of GTE; Barbara Freeman of IBM Corporation; Mary Ward of Happy Holidays, Inc.; Lehti Laan of Richardson-Vicks, USA; Mary Napier of Occidental Chemical Corp.; Susan Nelson of Learning International, Inc.; The Aetna Institute for Corporate Education, Hartford, Connecticut; Beiersdorf Inc.; Katharine Gibbs School, Inc.; The Gorham Press; and GTE Telenet Communications Corp.

I wish to thank the reference librarian at GTE, Theresa Smith, for her encouragement and advice; and also the reference staffs at the Norwalk and Darien, Connecticut, libraries for their assistance.

Most of all I am indebted to George E. Shertzer for his suggestions, advice, and patience, particularly with regard to the computer.

MARGARET D. SHERTZER

PART ONE

CHAPTER ONE

Recognizing Good Grammar

Grammar may be defined as a system of rules for the use of language, or as a study of what is preferred and what is to be avoided in effective speech and writing.

We all speak and write whether or not we are able to state rules governing the words we use. To be effective we must achieve clarity of expression. We need to know how to present ideas forcefully, without confusion or unnecessary words, by choosing language suited to our purpose.

A speaker may say, "It's me. I ain't the one that come first, but I'm gonna speak for all us boys." The intent is clear, but the choice of words is crude. While informal speech commonly uses colloquial expressions, few people wish to appear illiterate in their speaking or writing.

In order to use English correctly and gracefully, it is necessary to recognize and to practice using good grammar. Listening to speakers who are accustomed to speaking grammatically helps to train the ear to recognize correct usage. Simple, idiomatic English is desirable for both writing and speaking, but it is not effortless.

Good habits of speech will improve one's writing, but the best training may be to read examples of effective writing. Whether the subject is a news report, a humorous anecdote, a comment on today's events, a description of an exciting happening, or a romantic novel—any of these kinds of writing can be satisfying to read and instructive to study. The following are examples of various styles of English composition, each the work of a writer who has mastered his craft.

. . . To regard the people of any time as particularly obtuse seems vaguely improper, and it also establishes a precedent which members of this generation might regret. Yet it seems certain that the economists and those who offered economic counsel in the late twenties and early thirties were almost uniquely perverse. In the months and years following the stock market crash, the burden of reputable economic advice was invariably on the side of measures that would make things worse.

JOHN KENNETH GALBRAITH, *The Great Crash 1929*

Big money in turn has brought big emotional trouble. Envy is the new worm in the apple of sport. To read about the New York Yankees as they bickered through the summer of 1977, when Reggie Jackson had arrived toting his monetary bundle, was like reading Ann Landers. The game was secondary; first we had to learn whose feelings were hurt, whose pride was wounded. In once-sedate tennis, the pot of gold is now enormous and the players are strung as tightly as their rackets. In football and basketball the pay is sky-high, and so is the umbrage.

WILLIAM ZINSSER, *On Writing Well*

. . . Dick goes out on the leveled stream and lays down harnesses in the snow. The sled is packed, the gear lashed under skins. Everything is ready for the dogs. They are barking, roaring, screaming with impatience for the run. One by one, Donna unchains them. Out of the trees they dash toward the sled. Chipper goes first and, standing in front, holds all the harnesses in a good taut line. Abie, Little Girl, Grandma, Ug—the others fast fill in. They jump in their traces, can't wait to go. If they jump too much, they get cuffed. Wait another minute and they'll have everything so twisted we'll be here another hour. Go! The whole team hits at once. The sled, which was at rest a moment before, is moving fast. Destination, Eagle; time, two days.

JOHN McPHEE, *Coming into the Country*

A good laboratory, like a good bank or a corporation or government, has to run like a computer. Almost everything is done flawlessly, by the book, and all the numbers add up to the predicted sums. The days go by. And then, if it is a lucky day, and a lucky laboratory, somebody makes a mistake; the wrong buffer, something in one of the blanks, a decimal misplaced in reading counts, the warm room off by a degree and a half, a mouse out of his box, or just a misreading of the day's protocol. Whatever, when the results come in, something is obviously screwed up, and then the action can begin.

The misreading is not the important error; it opens the way. The next step is the crucial one. If the investigator can bring himself to say, "But even so, look at that!" then the new finding, whatever it is, is ready for snatching. What is needed, for progress to be made, is the move based on the error.

LEWIS THOMAS, *The Medusa and the Snail*

CHAPTER TWO

Some Grammatical Terms

The terms used in grammar help to explain the function and relationship of the words in sentences.

1. A *noun* is the name of a person, place, thing, or idea. Common nouns refer to any person, place, thing, idea, and so forth.

   boy   house   water   town   religion   despair

   Proper nouns refer to particular places, persons, objects, ideas, and so forth.

   George   the White House   Yokohama   Christian Science

   Nouns are used as the subjects of sentences, and as the objects of verbs and prepositions. (*See also* Recognition of the Subject, pp. 22–24, and Agreement of Adjective and Noun, p. 37.)

2. A *pronoun* can take the place of a noun.

   John called *his* mother as soon as *he* returned from work.
   The cat sat by *her* dish, waiting to be fed.

   (*See* Pronouns, pp. 15–21.)

3. *Case* refers to the form of a noun or pronoun, which shows its relationship to other words in a sentence. In English there are three cases: nominative (used for the subject of the sentence or clause), possessive (showing who owns something), and objective (receiving

the action of the verb or preposition). Nouns do not change their form except in the possessive case, when *'s* is added. Pronouns have different forms for each case. (*See* Pronouns, pp. 15–21.)

4. A *verb* shows the action or state of being, and it also indicates the time of action or being.

He *waived* his right to appeal. (past)
I *need* your report now. (present)
You *will enjoy* your trip to Norway. (future)

(*See* Verbs, pp. 21–33.)

5. *Adjectives* are words that describe nouns and specify size, color, number, and the like. This quality is called modifying, and an adjective is a modifier.

A *small* light showed in an *upper* window of the *old* factory.
The *two old* women lived in the *big stone* house.

(*See* Adjectives and Adverbs, pp. 33–38.)

6. *Adverbs* are words that describe verbs, adjectives, and other adverbs. They specify in what manner, when, where, and how much.

The child screamed *loudly* as the doctor prepared an injection.
It is *much* later than I thought.

(*See* Adjectives and Adverbs, pp. 33–38.)

7. *Prepositions* show how a noun or pronoun is related to another word in a sentence.

The dog came bounding *into* the room.
He parked *behind* the truck.
In this instance, I believe you are mistaken.

When used with a verb, the combination of verb and preposition usually has a meaning different from the verb alone.

They *laughed at* the very idea.
I must *look into* the proposal before I decide.
Have you *come to* any conclusion?

(*See* Prepositions, pp. 38–42.)

8. *Conjunctions* join words, phrases, or clauses. Coordinating conjunctions connect sentence elements of the same value: single words,

phrases, or clauses. These conjunctions are *and, but, for, or, nor, either, neither, yet, so,* and *so that.* (*Yet* and *so* are also used as adverbs.)

Subordinating conjunctions join two clauses, the main one and the dependent (or subordinate) one. The conjunctions used with dependent clauses are *although, because, since, until, while,* and others that place a condition on the sentence. (*See* Conjunctions, pp. 42–43, and Subordinate Clauses, pp. 43–44.)

The Parts of a Sentence

1. *Subject and predicate.* A sentence expresses a complete thought and consists of a subject and a predicate. (If either the subject or predicate is not expressed, it must be readily understood from sentences that precede or follow.)

The subject of a sentence is the person, object, or idea being described. The predicate is the explanation of the action, condition, or effect of the subject.

The after-Christmas sale is nearly over.
Getting a job can be a difficult process.

In the examples above, the subjects are in italics; the rest of the sentences are the predicates.

Subjects are nouns, pronouns, or phrases used as nouns. Predicates are verbs and the words used to explain the action or condition. (*See* Recognition of the Subject, pp. 22–24.)

2. *Phrases.* A phrase is a group of words that are closely related but have no subject or predicate. A phrase may be used as a noun, verb, adjective, or adverb.

Noun: *Waiting for a telephone call* has kept me at home all morning.
Verb: That work *could have been done* earlier.
Adjective: The building *with the satellite dish on the roof* has been converted to a condominium.
Adverb: The price is higher *out of season.*

A phrase that is essential to the meaning of the sentence is called restrictive. A phrase that is actually a parenthetical comment is called nonrestrictive and is usually set off by commas.

Restrictive: The computer *in my office* is used *by several people.*
Nonrestrictive: I wonder, *by the way,* who will be named director.

(*See* Prepositions, pp. 38–42.)

3. *Clauses.* A clause is a group of words that has a subject and a predicate. A main clause can stand alone as a sentence. A subordinate clause is incomplete and is used with a main clause to express a related idea.

Main clause: *This is the man* who sold me the dog.
I enjoy walking our dog when the weather is good.
Subordinate clause: I enjoy walking our dog, *which we bought last week.*
When I have time, I like to work out at the gym.

(*See* Relative Pronouns, pp. 18–19; Correlative Conjunctions, pp. 42–43; Subordinate Conjunctions, p. 43; and Subordinate Clauses, pp. 43–44.)

CHAPTER THREE

Points of Grammar

Formation of Noun Plurals

1. Most nouns form the plural by adding *s* to the singular.

   banks   chemists   hospitals   letters

2. Nouns ending in *f*, *fe*, and *ff*:

   (1) Some nouns ending in *f*, *fe*, and *ff* form their plurals regularly by adding *s* to the singular.

   briefs   giraffes   proofs   sheriffs
   chiefs   plaintiffs   scarfs   tariffs

   (2) Some nouns ending in *f* and *fe* change these letters to *v* and add *es* to form the plural.

   halves   leaves   selves   thieves
   knives   lives   shelves   wives

3. Common nouns ending in *s*, *sh*, *ch*, *x*, and *z* form their plurals by adding *es* to the singular if an extra syllable is needed in pronouncing the plural.

   annexes   churches   lunches   waltzes
   brushes   dishes   quartzes   waxes
   businesses   dispatches   sixes   witnesses
   chintzes   hoaxes   taxes   yeses

But: buses *or* busses

4. Nouns ending in *y:*

(1) Nouns ending in *y* preceded by a consonant form their plurals by changing *y* to *i* and adding *es.*

armies	diaries	families	quantities
authorities	discoveries	industries	skies
cities	duties	ladies	utilities
companies	fallacies	parties	vacancies

(2) Nouns ending in *y* preceded by a vowel, except those ending in *quy,* form their plurals in the usual way by adding *s* to the singular.

attorneys	journeys	keys	valleys

5. Nouns ending in *o* form their plurals by adding *s* or *es,* but there are many exceptions and alternatives to the following generalizations, so that it is advisable to consult a dictionary when in doubt.

(1) Most common nouns ending in *o* preceded by a vowel form their plurals by adding *s* to the singular.

cameos	patios	radios	rodeos
curios	portfolios	ratios	studios

(2) Most common nouns ending in *o* preceded by a consonant form their plurals by adding *es* to the singular.

embargoes	Negroes	torpedoes	vetoes
heroes			

But: cantos, pianos, solos, sopranos, tobaccos

(3) Some nouns ending in *o* form their plurals by adding either *s* or *es* to the singular.

cargos *or*	mottos *or* mottoes	provisos *or*
cargoes	mulattos *or*	provisoes
manifestos *or*	mulattoes	zeros *or*
manifestoes	nos *or* noes	zeroes

6. Some nouns form their plurals by a change in an internal vowel.

feet   geese   men   mice   teeth   women

7. Some nouns have the same form in the plural as in the singular.

aircraft	deer	salmon

| chassis | grass | series |
| corps | moose | sheep |

Some of these nouns are pluralized when they represent several species.

the deers of North America   grasses found on the prairies

8. Some nouns are always plural. They have no singular form in the same sense.

annals	earnings	scales
assets	goods	scissors
auspices	headquarters	trousers
ceramics	pants	
credentials	proceeds	

9. Certain nouns may be used as singular or as plural according to their meaning.

Acoustics (the science) is studied by architects.
The acoustics (acoustic qualities) of the hall are poor.
Athletics (athletic training) is part of the school program.
Athletics (sports) are popular with our students.
Politics (in a general sense) was behind his appointment.
Her politics (opinions) need not concern us here.

10. Some nouns have two plurals differing in meaning.

brothers (kin)	brethren (class or society)
cloths (kinds of cloth)	clothes (wearing apparel)
indices (in mathematics)	indexes (in books)

11. Some nouns plural in form are singular in use and therefore take a singular verb.

| aeronautics | economics | molasses | physics |
| civics | measles | news | whereabouts |

12. Most compound nouns form the plural by pluralizing the fundamental part of the word.

adjutants general	trade unions
governors general	vice presidents
spelling matches	

(1) When the compound is made up of a noun and a preposition,

a noun and a prepositional phrase, or a noun and an adverb, the noun is usually pluralized.

bills of lading	fillers-in	runners-up
brothers-in-law	listeners-in	works of art
commanders in chief	lookers-on	

(2) When compounds are written as one word (solid), their plurals are formed according to the usual rules for nouns.

businessmen	cupfuls	undersecretaries
bylaws	stockholders	weekends

(3) When the first element of a compound is derived from a verb, the plural is formed on the last element.

castaways	leftovers	runaways
go-betweens	letdowns	shut-ins
handouts	makeups	strikeovers

13. Nouns that retain their foreign endings form their plurals as follows: those ending in *a* change to *ae;* those ending in *us* change to *i;* those ending in *um* change to *a;* those ending in *on* change to *a;* those ending in *is* change to *es.*

Many nouns retain their foreign plurals for formal and scientific material and use the English plurals in nontechnical or informal writing.

a to *ae*   alumna-alumnae (f)
antenna-antennae-antennas (radio)
formula-formulae-formulas
larva-larvae-larvas
minutia-minutiae
vertebra-vertebrae-vertebras

us to *i*   alumnus-alumni (m)
cactus-cacti-cactuses
focus-foci-focuses
fungus-fungi-funguses
genius-genii-geniuses
gladiolus-gladioli-gladioluses
nucleus-nuclei-nucleuses
radius-radii-radiuses
stimulus-stimuli

syllabus-syllabi-syllabuses
terminus-termini-terminuses

um to *a*   addendum-addenda
aquarium-aquaria-aquariums
bacterium-bacteria
curriculum-curricula-curriculums
dictum-dicta-dictums
erratum-errata
gymnasium-gymnasia-gymnasiums
maximum-maxima-maximums
medium-media-mediums
memorandum-memoranda-memorandums
minimum-minima-minimums
planetarium-planetaria-planetariums
referendum-referenda-referendums
residuum-residua-residuums
spectrum-spectra-spectrums
stratum-strata-stratums
ultimatum-ultimata-ultimatums

on to *a*   automaton-automata-automatons
criterion-criteria
phenomenon-phenomena-phenomenons

is to *es*   analysis-analyses
axis-axes
basis-bases
crisis-crises
diagnosis-diagnoses
ellipsis-ellipses
emphasis-emphases
hypothesis-hypotheses
oasis-oases
parenthesis-parentheses
synopsis-synopses
synthesis-syntheses
thesis-theses

The following nouns also retain their foreign forms and in some cases also have an English plural:

appendix	appendices, appendixes
beau	beaux, beaus
château	châteaux, châteaus

dilettante	dilettanti, dilettantes
genus	genera
index	indices, indexes
madame	mesdames
monsieur	messieurs
tableau	tableaux, tableaus

Note that *agenda* and *data*, though plural in form, are usually considered as singular collective nouns.

14. Proper nouns form their plurals by adding *s* to the singular or *es* when the word ends in *s, z, ch, sh,* or *zh.*

(the) Carolinas	Adamses	Lynches
(two) Helens	Busches	Morrises
(the) Kennedys	Joneses	Nashes

Not: the Kennedys'; the Jones'

(1) Some proper nouns representing nationalities have the same form in the plural as in the singular.

Chinese	Japanese

(2) When titles are used with proper nouns, either the title or the proper noun may be pluralized. In informal writing or in speaking, the noun (name) is usually pluralized.

Formal	*Informal*
the Misses Barlow	the Miss Barlows
Mesdames John Penn, Henry Baxter, and William Foster (different names)	Mrs. John Penn, Mrs. Henry Baxter, and Mrs. William Foster
the Mesdames Norton (same name)	the Mrs. Nortons
Messrs. Grant and Howell	Mr. Grant and Mr. Howell

15. Plurals of letters, signs, symbols, figures, and abbreviations used as nouns are formed by adding *s* or an apostrophe and *s.* The omission of the apostrophe is gaining ground, but in some cases it must be retained for clarity, as with letters.

a's, A's	ABCs *or* ABC's	apts.
i's, I's	GIs *or* GI's	depts.
6s and 7s *or* 6's and 7's	IOUs *or* IOU's	mfrs.
	IQs *or* IQ's	nos.

M.D.s *or* M.D.'s
YWCAs

Dot your *i*'s and cross your *t*'s.
She was a woman in her late 30s (*or* 30's).

(1) In financial contexts, the figures identifying certain securities
are written without the apostrophe: *Union Pacific 2½s.*

16. Plurals of words used as nouns are formed by adding *s* if the word
ends with a consonant, and an apostrophe and *s* if with a vowel
sound.

ifs and buts	wherefores	do's
ins and outs	yeas and nays	oh's and ah's
ups and downs		

But: twos and threes

(1) Plurals of contractions used as nouns are formed by adding *s*:
dos and *don'ts.*

Pronouns

Use of Personal Pronouns

Personal pronouns agree with their antecedents (the nouns they represent) in gender and number, but their case depends upon their construction in the clause in which they appear.

1. The nominative case (*I, you, she, he, it; we, you, they*) is used:

(1) as the subject of a verb

I shall finish the report on Tuesday.
You received a fair price for the property.
They always pay their bills promptly.

(2) as a predicate complement; that is, a pronoun following some
form of the verb *to be.* (Note: The verb *to be* takes the same case
after it as it takes before it.)

I think it was *they* who called.
If you were *he*, would you move to California?
Yes, it is *I.*
It was *she* who volunteered to address the circulars.

There is a tendency to use the objective case of pronouns following *to be:* it's *me*, it was *her*, it's *him*, it was *us*. This usage is acceptable in informal speaking and writing but should be avoided in formal writing.

Even in speaking, it is possible to say, "It's I" without being considered pompous. It is a question of formality and preference.

(3) in apposition with the subject of a verb

Several delegates, *he* among them, will state their opposition at the next meeting.
Most of the team, at least *we* from the upper classes, are in favor of holding extra practice sessions.

(4) as the complement of an infinitive. (When the infinitive has no subject, the pronoun following *to be* is in the nominative case to agree with the subject of the sentence.)

Greene seems to be *he* who made the protest.
The speakers are to be *they* who are running for election.

2. The objective case (*me, you, her, him, us, them*) is used:

(1) as the object of a verb

The supervisor trusted *her* to make out the payroll.
The delegates unanimously appointed *him* chairman.
Our lawyer advised *him* and *me* to sign the contract.

(2) as the indirect object of a verb

Last year the company gave *him* a bonus.
The witness told *us* the truth.

(3) in apposition with the object of a verb

The judge fined us, both *me* and my brother.
The chairman asked them all, Bent, Lowell, and *her,* to vote for the repeal.

(4) as subject of an infinitive

The committee invited *him* and *me* to be present (not *he* and *I*).
I wish you would let *him* and *me* finish the checking (not *he* and *I*).

(5) as object of an infinitive

The chairman asked me to invite *him* to the conference.
The buyer asked us to meet *her* at the terminal.

(6) as complement of an infinitive. (If the infinitive *to be* has a subject, that subject is in the objective case. Thus, the pronoun that follows the infinitive must be in the objective case, following the rule that the verb *to be* takes the same case after it as before it.)

The manager took *her* to be *me*.
We thought the applicants to be *them*.

(7) as the object of a preposition

No orders were received from *them* this week.
The outcome depends on *us*.

(8) When a pronoun follows *as* or *than*, it takes the form it would have if the clause were completed.

Jennifer is more competent than *I* (I am).
Charles is not so accurate as *he* (as he is).
The Blakes are better travelers than *we* (we are).
We like his brother as much as *him* (as we do him).
I trust Greene more than *him* (than I do him).

3. The possessive case (*my, mine, your, yours, his, her, hers, its, our, ours, their, theirs*) is used:

(1) to denote possession and to complete the predicate when the noun is omitted. (Note: There is no apostrophe before the *s* in the possessive of personal pronouns.)

This property is *his* (*hers*).
Is this coupon *yours* (*theirs*)?
The plan was *ours*, the details were *his*.

(2) to form a double possessive

This summary of *yours* makes the financial statement clear.
That property of *theirs* lies along the river.

(*See also* Possessive Adjectives, p. 35.)

Compound Personal Pronouns

Compound personal pronouns (*myself, yourself, himself, herself, itself, ourselves, yourselves, themselves*) are used:

4. for emphasis (intensive use)

She *herself* will pay the damages.
The secretary *himself* mailed the letter.

5. for expressing action as turned back upon the subject (reflexive use)

They will hurt *themselves* by such actions.
He convinced *himself* that the scheme would not work.

Compound personal pronouns should not be used as substitutes for personal pronouns.

The principal gave the paper to Holden and *me* (not *myself*).
Lake, Bridges, and *I* bought the building (not *myself*).

Relative Pronouns

A relative pronoun introduces a subordinate clause that modifies a noun or a pronoun occurring earlier in the sentence and connects a dependent clause to the main clause. It is also a substitute word that refers to its antecedent and stands for that antecedent in a subordinate clause.

The most frequently used relative pronouns are *who, that, which,* and *what.*

The association elected Ellen Carr, *who* has had years of experience.
The office *that* we wanted has been rented.
What you say is correct.
The Careful Writer, which you borrowed two weeks ago, is now due.

Who is the only one of the relative pronouns that changes its form to indicate case (*who, whose, whom,* as well as *whoever, whomever*). Before its case can be determined, the function it plays in a sentence must be decided.

Who, whose, and *whom* (as well as *whoever* and *whomever*) refer to persons. *That* refers to animals, persons, or things and is used to introduce restrictive clauses. *Which* refers to lower animals, things, and ideas, and introduces nonrestrictive clauses. (While *that* may refer to persons, many writers prefer to use *who* and *whom.*)

For a discussion of the distinction between restrictive and nonrestrictive clauses, *see* Clauses, p. 8.

A relative pronoun has the following functions in its own clause:

6. In the nominative case:

(1) as subject of the clause in which it stands

The School Board interviewed all the candidates *who* applied.
The dogs *that* appear on television are unusually well trained.
The league will help *whoever* needs help.
Our best wishes go to Homer and Frost, *who*, we are certain, have the best interests of the city at heart.

7. In the objective case:

(1) as object of a verb

We awarded the contract to the Philips Company, *which* we have dealt with in the past.
Dr. Benson is the surgeon *whom* we recommend.

(2) as object of a preposition

All the men with *whom* he worked were experienced.
Maurice nominated the Rev. Gordon Major, for *whom* we all have a high regard.

(3) as subject of an infinitive

We do not know *whom* to invite as next month's speaker.
John asked *her* to play the piano.

Interrogative Pronouns

8. Interrogative pronouns (*who, which, what*) are used in asking questions. *Which* and *what* present no problems of case.

An interrogative pronoun has no antecedent in the sentence; the word to which it refers appears only in the answer.

What caused the explosion?
Whose is it?
Who addressed these envelopes?

Notice that in questions, particularly those in which the pronoun comes first and is separated from the preposition that governs it, *who* is acceptable usage.

Who was the monument named for? *But:* For *whom* was it named?
Who are you going with? *But:* With *whom* are you going?

Note: The possessive *whose* does not have an apostrophe. It should be distinguished from the contraction *who's* (*who is*).

9. The interrogatives *which*, *whose*, and *what* often modify nouns and are then interrogative adjectives.

> *Which* book is due?
> *Whose* letters are ready to be mailed?
> *What* caller left this briefcase?

Indefinite Pronouns

Indefinite pronouns, such as *all, any, both, each, either, everybody, none, one, several, some, someone,* do not refer to specific persons or things. It should be noted, also, that many of these words may be either pronouns or adjectives, depending upon their use in the sentence.

> *Both* of us have been assigned special work. (pronoun)
> *Both* clerks were busy. (adjective)

Indefinite pronouns frequently present problems in number and gender. Following are suggestions for the use of these words.

10. When the indefinite pronoun is the subject of a sentence, it regularly takes a singular verb and the pronoun referring to it agrees with it in number and gender. When gender may be considered as either masculine or feminine, the masculine pronoun often is preferred, but some writers use both.

> *Each* of you must decide for *himself*.
> *Neither* of the candidates has expressed *his* opinion in the matter.

> *Each* of the students raised *his* or *her* hand.
> Has *any* of the saleswomen refused to sign *her* name to the petition?
> *Everybody* has stated *his* views on this subject.

Note: *Everyone* and *everybody* are not always referred to by a singular pronoun. The number of the pronoun following depends upon the meaning of the sentence. Modern usage accepts these words as having plural significance, and they are referred to by a plural pronoun.

> *Everybody* comes, but *they* seldom stay through the meeting.
> *Everybody* has considered the regulations, but *their* opinions differ.

11. As the words *both, few, many, several* are plural in meaning, they take plural verbs and are referred to by plural pronouns.

> *Both* of the accountants sent in *their* reports.

Few cast *their* votes for Thompson.
Many of the delegates presented *their* credentials early.

12. Some indefinite pronouns, such as *all, most,* and *some,* are singular or plural depending on their meaning in a sentence.

All (everything) has been prepared for the reception.
All (the boats) have hoisted their sails.

The modern tendency is to consider *none* as plural except when it is equivalent to *no one* or *not one.* If the meaning is unmistakably singular, use *no one* or *not one.*

None have succeeded in their efforts to change the club constitution.
Not one of the partners has registered a complaint.

13. When *else* is added to a compound indefinite, the possessive is formed by adding an apostrophe and *s* to the word *else.*

Nobody else's decisions are more respected than yours.
Somebody else's plan may prove better than John's.

14. When compound indefinites are formed by adding *body* or *thing* to indefinite pronouns, the words thus formed are written solid: *everybody, something.* When such compounds are formed by adding *one,* they are written solid unless the reference is to each of several persons: *anyone, everyone, someone.*

Everyone listened attentively to the speaker.
Everybody arrived on time.
Can *someone* type this memorandum accurately?

Write the compounds as two words if a prepositional phrase follows:

Every one of the class attended the reunion.
Any one of the officers is willing to serve as chairman.

Verbs

A verb is a word that tells what the subject (noun, pronoun, or clause) does or what is done to it. The verb expresses action, mode of being, occurrence, or condition, and should agree with its subject in person and number.

Recognition of the Subject

1. Compound subjects.

   (1) A subject consisting of two or more nouns or pronouns connected by *and* takes a plural predicate unless the nouns refer to the same person or express a single idea.

   Our merchandise and equipment *are covered* by insurance.
   Weather and unemployment *are cited* as causes of the decline in trade.
   He and I *are* members of the Faculty Committee.
   The sum and substance of the matter *is* that our firm remains prosperous.
     (single idea)
   My friend and adviser *suggests* I take a business course. (one person)

   (2) Singular subjects connected by *or* or *nor* take a singular verb.

   Either the secretary or the treasurer *is* always present at every meeting.
   Neither Black nor Nichols *fears* the court's decision.

   (3) When two subjects differing in number are connected by *either-or* or *neither-nor* and one of the subjects is plural, it should be placed second and the verb should agree with it in number.

   Correct: Neither the *candidate* nor the *voters are* satisfied with the proposal.
   Incorrect: Neither the voters nor the candidate *are* satisfied with the proposal.

2. A verb should agree with its subject, not with a noun placed between the verb and its subject.

   This *list* of addresses *was* prepared by Horton.
   The latest *news* about those accidents *has* just been received.
   The *report* about conditions in the slum areas *was* published last week.

3. Phrases or clauses introduced by such expressions as *together with, as well as, in addition to* are not part of the subject and, therefore, do not affect the number of the verb.

   The *church*, as well as the nearby stores, *was* destroyed by fire.
   The *problem* of building more schools, in addition to paying teachers' salaries for them, *was* discussed by the board.
   All *indications*, as far as we can see, *point* to better business.

4. When the verb precedes the subject, care should be taken to have it agree with its subject in number.

In this catalogue *are* the *requirements* for admission, the courses, and the fees.

Howe stated that there *were reports* on the budget to be considered at the April meeting.

5. The form of plural nouns, especially those ending in *a*, which require a plural verb, should not be mistaken for the singular form: *bacteria, criteria, phenomena.* (*See* pp. 9–15.)

6. With fractions, the verb agrees with the noun in the prepositional phrase.

   Half of the *road was* blocked off.
   Half of the *roads were* blocked off.
   One-third of the *tax goes* to the county.
   One-third of the *taxes go* to the county.

7. When nouns of quantity, distance, time, and amount are thought of as a unit, the verb should be singular.

   Forty pounds *is* enough for the present.
   Twenty dollars *is* still due on John's account.
   Four years *is* usually required for a B.A. degree.
   Two hundred miles *remains* to be driven in the morning.

8. Subjects modified by *each* and *every* are singular and therefore require a singular verb.

   Each boy *gets* an apple.
   Every street in the town *is* well lighted.

9. Collective nouns as subjects.

   A collective noun is a noun that names a group of persons, animals, or things: *committee, herd, furniture.*

   Such nouns may be regarded as singular or plural: singular, if the word denotes a group acting as an individual; plural, if the word denotes the individuals that make up the group.

   The jury *has* (not *have*) agreed upon the verdict.
   The jury *have* (not *has*) disagreed as to their verdict.
   The Community Service Committee *were* (not *was*) divided on *their* (not *its*) understanding of the question.
   When your committee *has* (not *have*) completed *its* (not *their*) work *it* (not *they*) should prepare a report.

   (1) Since the names of associations, boards, companies, corporations, and the like are collective nouns, they should be regarded

as singular if the name denotes a group acting as an individual or as an entity and plural if the name denotes the individuals composing the group. Care must be taken to have the pronouns and the verbs agree with the collective nouns.

The American Association of University Women *has* urged *its* members to contribute to the Scholarship Fund.
The Southeastern Coast Line *is* agreeable to your suggestion. . . . *It has* adopted a progressive public relations program and *is* receiving encouraging support.
The Hall Company *has* scheduled the largest promotional program *it* has ever placed behind any of *its* more than one thousand products.

Some authorities regard a company name with a plural ending or makeup as plural; as, *Haines Brothers, Upjohn Publishers, L. M. Gordon and Sons.* Most firms with such endings, however, regard their titles as singular. This is true, for instance, of *Charles Scribner's Sons* and of *Brooks Brothers.*

Because the use of *it* or *its* to refer to an association, a company, a corporation, or any other entity may seem unsuitable or stilted, the plural pronouns, *they, their, them* may sometimes be preferred. Then, of course, the verb must also be plural.

As the copyright of the book is held by Macmillan Publishing Company, you must have *their* permission to reproduce this extract. If you ask *them, they* are not likely to refuse you.

(2) The article *a* usually precedes a collective noun regarded as plural; the article *the* usually precedes a collective noun regarded as singular.

A number of students *have* signified their intention to take the advanced course.
The number of students in economics *has* increased this year.
A majority of voters *are* opposed to the amendment.
The majority in an assembly *has* the right to decide what the action will be.
A couple of suggestions *were* offered by the audience.
The couple *was* recognized boarding a plane.

Voice of Verbs

The voice of a verb shows whether the subject of the verb has performed the action (active voice) or has received the action (passive voice).

Active voice: Bill *has washed* his car.
Passive voice: The car *is washed* every week.

The subject of the verb (*see* pp. 22–24) may be a noun or pronoun, a phrase, or an entire clause. In all cases, it will provide the answer to *who* or *what*.

Who washed the car?   *What* was washed?

The verb in the passive voice consists of a form of *to be* combined with the past participle of the main verb:

I was eating when I *was called* to the telephone.
You *have been waited on* all your life.
The need for better housing *was discussed* at the workshop.
Everything you could wish for *was given* to you as a child.
This book *will be used* in adult education classes.
The house *was being painted.*

Transitive and Intransitive Verbs

Transitive verbs show action, either upon someone or something. A verb in the active voice shows that an action has passed over to the receiver or object.

The Winterthur Museum *sells* reproductions of its treasures.
Who knows what next year *will bring?*
We each *do* our own laundry.

When action is passed back to the subject, the verb is passive.

Reproductions *are sold* at the Winterthur Museum.
Personal laundry *is done* by each resident.
An action *has been brought* against the owner of the truck.

In another situation, the subject receives the results of the action, again in the passive voice.

The baby *was given* a football by his proud father.
Lyndon Johnson *was sworn* in as President after John Kennedy's assassination.
Our guests *are offered* complimentary drinks on their arrival.

Some verbs of action have no receiver and are intransitive.

The children *played* in the backyard.
The wind *whistled* among the bare branches of the trees.
Tomorrow we *can sleep* late.

When an action is indicated, the same verb becomes transitive.

> My nephew *plays* football at Michigan State.
> Peter *whistles* a tune while he cooks breakfast.
> Tonight you *can sleep* the sleep of the just.

Included with intransitive verbs are the *linking verbs:* appear, be, become, feel, grow, keep, look, remain, seem, smell, sound, stay, and taste. These verbs link the subject to a noun or pronoun (called the predicate nominative) or to an adjective (the predicate adjective).

The predicate nominative provides another name for the subject:

> Henry became a *grandfather* this year.
> The general was *emperor* for life.

The predicate adjective describes the subject:

> All your plants look *healthy*.
> This room smells *smoky*.
> The entire dinner was perfectly *delicious*.

Tense

Tense is a distinctive form of a verb that expresses the time of action. Tense is indicated by inflection, that is, a change in the form of the verb itself (sing, sang; look, looked), or by the use of auxiliary verb forms (*will* sing; *have* looked).

Present

10. The *present* tense indicates that an action is going on at the present time.

> This sale *offers* unusually low prices on all furniture.
> I *am* glad to accept your invitation.

11. The *present* tense is used to express a present fact or an unchangeable truth.

> The Rocky Mountains *are* the longest and highest mountain system in North America.
> The teacher explained that water *is* composed of two gases.

12. The *present* tense may indicate customary action.

> The committee *meets* on the first Thursday of every month.

13. The *present* tense is often used instead of the future tense, although the latter would be more precise. This usage is considered by some authorities to be colloquial, for speaking or informal writing.

   College *opens* next month.
   We *leave* for London in June.

14. The *present* tense is sometimes used to make a past event or a past statement more graphic; this usage is called the historical present.

   Dickens *is* at his best in depicting the tragedies of childhood.
   Emerson *says*, "To be great is to be misunderstood."
   The Declaration of Independence *states* that all men are created equal.

15. The *present* tense should *not* be used to express an action begun in the past that still continues; the correct tense is the *present perfect*.

   I *have lived* (not *am living*) in Boston for ten years.
   I *have known* (not *know*) this man all my life.

Past

16. The *past* tense indicates an action that occurred in past time.

   I *answered* Frost's letter yesterday.
   The commission *filed* its report several days ago.

17. The *present perfect* tense denotes an action that has been completed at some indefinite time before the present time.

   The mayor *has spent* many hours on the budget.
   We *have given* the merger careful consideration.

18. The *past perfect* tense denotes that the action of the verb was completed at some definite point in past time.

   Before I worked for Horton & Chase, I *had* never *seen* a computer.
   If he *had remained* with us, he would have been promoted.

   Note the correct use of tenses in the following sentences:

   He *didn't find* the book.
   He *hasn't found* the book yet.
   He *hadn't found* the book when the librarian asked for it.
   I *have visited* most of the capitals of Europe.
   I *have been* ten years in America.

He always *has paid* and always *will pay* his bills.
Not: He always *has* and always *will pay* his bills.

Future: Shall and Will

Until recent years, the best American usage preferred *shall* for the first person, to indicate simple futurity, willingness, and expectation.

I *shall send* my check tomorrow.
We *shall do* as you suggest.
As far as I know, I *shall attend* the Little Rock meeting.

Will was used for the second and third persons, to indicate the same simple futurity, willingness, and expectation.

The plane *will leave* at noon.
You *will find* the hotel comfortable.
He *will come* as soon as he can.
They *will know* where to find us.

However, most writers today use *will* for all three persons to show futurity, as well as determination, promise, and willingness. To emphasize intent, such adverbs as *certainly, surely,* and the like can be added.

We *will* certainly *do* our best to locate a suitable substitute.
He *will* surely *be* able to complete the repairs on time.

But: In questions and requests it seems more natural to use *shall* in the first person and *will* in the second and third persons.

Shall I call for you at nine o'clock?
How long *shall* we hold your reservation?
Will the person who took my coat by mistake please return it.
Will you please have this report on my desk by Thursday morning.

Future: Should and Would

The use of *should* and *would,* the past tenses of *shall* and *will,* is no longer so strictly observed as formerly. However, conventional usage advocates the following rules:

19. Use *should* with all persons to denote an obligation, in the sense of "ought to."

We *should* settle this problem at once.
You *should* pay the damage to the other driver's car.
The board *should* agree on the proposed bylaws.

20. Use *would* with all persons to denote habitual action or a wish.

I *would* never send out letters with erasures.
Blake *would* always report as soon as he finished the job.
Once a week the heads of departments *would* meet to discuss policies.
I wish that you *would* accept the chairmanship.

21. Use *should* in a conditional clause introduced by *if* to express contingency or simple futurity.

If I *should* decide to go, I will call you Thursday.
If he *should* accept the nomination, he will undoubtedly be appointed.

Tense of the Infinitive

22. The infinitive has two tenses, present and present perfect. Which tense to use depends upon the time expressed by the main verb.

(1) The present infinitive denotes the same time or future time in relation to the action of the main verb. Notice that in the following sentences the present infinitive is used with verbs denoting present or past time. The time denoted by the infinitive is the same as that of the principal verb or later than denoted by the principal verb.

I intend *to go* tomorrow.
I intended *to go* Thursday.
For several days I have been intending *to write* to you.
I should have liked *to do* it, but I could not (not *to have done it*).
Jim would have liked *to go* with his brother last week (not *to have gone*).
I had intended *to write* the letter before breakfast (not *to have written*).

(2) The perfect infinitive denotes action that is complete at the time of the principal verb.

The submarine was reported *to have been sighted* off Bermuda at noon.

(3) Note the difference in meaning implied by the present and perfect infinitives in the following sentences:

His men believed Washington *to be* a great general.
We believe Washington *to have been* a great general.
The Milan Cathedral is said *to be* one of the largest in the world.
The Parthenon is said *to have been* erected in the Age of Pericles.

The Subjunctive Mood

23. The subjunctive mood is little used today except in a few special cases:

(1) to express a wish

I wish I *were* in Europe.

(2) to express a contrary-to-fact condition

If I *were* you, I would take the position.

(3) Present and past conditions may be either (A) noncommittal or (B) contrary to fact.

A. A condition is noncommittal when it implies nothing as to the truth or falsity of the case supposed.

If James is angry, I am sorry. (Perhaps James is angry, perhaps not.)

B. A condition is contrary to fact when it implies that the supposed case is not or was not true.

If James were angry, I should be sorry. (James is *not* angry.)

In a noncommittal present condition, the *if* clause takes the present indicative; in a noncommittal past condition, the past, the perfect, or the pluperfect.

The conclusion may be in any form that the sense allows.

Present condition, noncommittal:

If this pebble is a diamond, it is valuable.

Past condition, noncommittal:

If that pebble was a diamond, it was valuable.
If Tom has apologized, he has done his duty.
If John had reached home before we started, he must have made a quick journey.

In each of these examples, the speaker declines to commit himself as to the truth of the supposed case. Perhaps the pebble was a diamond, perhaps not; Tom may or may not have apologized; whether or not John had reached home, we cannot tell.

Principal Parts

24. The principal parts of verbs consist of the present and the past indicative, and the past or perfect participle.

The following table shows the principal parts of many troublesome verbs, most of which are irregular. Illiterate and careless errors occur most often in the use of the past tense and the past participle; as, *has went* for *has gone*, *sunk* for *sank*.

Present	*Past*	*Past Participle*
am or be	was	been
arise	arose	arisen
awake	awoke	awaked
bear	bore	borne
beat	beat	beaten
begin	began	begun
bend	bent	bent
beseech	besought	besought
bid (card playing)	bid	bid
bid (most senses)	bade, bid	bidden, bid
bleed	bled	bled
blow	blew	blown
break	broke	broken
bring	brought	brought
broadcast	broadcast	broadcast
catch	caught	caught
choose	chose	chosen
climb	climbed	climbed
cling	clung	clung
come	came	come
dive	dived	dived
do	did	done
draw	drew	drawn
drink	drank	drunk
drive	drove	driven
fall	fell	fallen
fight	fought	fought
flee	fled	fled
flow	flowed	flowed
fly	flew	flown
forbid	forbade	forbidden
forget	forgot	forgotten

Present	Past	Past Participle
forsake	forsook	forsaken
freeze	froze	frozen
get	got	got, gotten
go	went	gone
grow	grew	grown
hang (most senses)	hung	hung
hang (punishment)	hanged	hanged
hide	hid	hidden
hurt	hurt	hurt
kneel	knelt, kneeled	knelt, kneeled
lay (to put; to place)	laid	laid
lead	led	led
leap	leaped, leapt	leaped, leapt
lie (to recline)	lay	lain
lie (to tell a falsehood)	lied	lied
loose	loosed	loosed
lose	lost	lost
pay	paid	paid
plead	pleaded	pleaded
prove	proved	proved, proven
ring	rang, rung	rung
rise	rose	risen
run	ran	run
say	said	said
see	saw	seen
seek	sought	sought
set (to place)	set	set
shake	shook	shaken
shine	shone	shone
show	showed	shown, showed
shrink	shrank, shrunk	shrunk
sing	sang, sung	sung
sink	sank	sunk
sit (to sit down)	sat	sat
slay	slew	slain
sleep	slept	slept
speak	spoke	spoken
stay	stayed	stayed
steal	stole	stolen
stick	stuck	stuck
sting	stung	stung

stop	stopped	stopped
strive	strove	striven
swear	swore	sworn
swim	swam	swum
swing	swung	swung
take	took	taken
teach	taught	taught
tear	tore	torn
throw	threw	thrown
tread	trod	trodden, trod
wake	waked, woke	waked
wear	wore	worn
weave	wove	woven
win	won	won
wring	wrung	wrung
write	wrote	written

Adjectives and Adverbs

An adjective is a word used to modify (limit, identify, or describe) a noun. An adverb is a word used to modify a verb, an adjective, or another adverb.

1. An adjective is used when the condition of the subject is described.

   The discussion was *brief.*
   A *reasonable* decision should be expected soon.

2. An adverb is used when the action of the verb is explained.

   He always speaks *clearly* over the telephone.
   The mayor answered the complaint *quietly* and *reasonably.*

3. Some words have the same form whether they are used as adjectives or adverbs: *far, fast, first.*

   The little inn was a *far* cry from our usual accommodations.
   Holt ran *far* ahead of the other contestants.
   She liked to drive *fast* sports cars.
   He typed so *fast* he made many mistakes.
   The *first* candidate spoke at length.
   First, watch your spelling.

4. Some words have two adverbial forms: *cheap, cheaply; direct, directly; loud, loudly; quick, quickly; slow, slowly; sure, surely;*

wide, widely. The choice is a matter of usage, with *ly* forms ordinarily considered more formal, the shorter forms more emphatic. The adjective is used whenever some form of the verb *to be* or *to seem* may be substituted. But when no such substitution can be made, the adverb is generally preferred.

Buy *cheap* and sell dear.
The dresses were *cheaply* made.
Mail the order *direct* to me.
The clerk went *directly* home.
Don't speak so *loud.*
The child called *loudly* to the lifeguard.
Go *slow.*
Burns drove so *slowly* that he was late.

5. The modifier should be an adjective if it denotes the condition of the subject, but an adverb if it explains the action of the verb.

We stand *firm* in our opinion.
We stand *firmly* by our decision.
They stood *silent* as the ambulance passed.
They listened *silently* to the soloist.
The house has been restored *complete* in every detail.
The house has been *completely* restored.
The patient remained *quiet.*
He walked *quietly* around the room.

6. Verbs of the senses, such as *feel, look, smell, sound,* and *taste,* as well as copulative verbs, such as *appear, be, become, seem,* take an adjective to denote the quality or the condition of the subject.

Everybody *feels* happy about John's appointment.
Fowler always *looks* cheerful.
The flowers *smell* sweet.
All the food *tasted* delicious.
The new secretary *appears* competent.
The patient *seems* better today.
George felt *bad* (or felt *badly*) about the delay.

Bad and *badly* are found with almost equal acceptance in standard English when following *feel,* although *bad* is usually preferred in formal writing. . . . When preceded by *look, sound, smell,* etc., the usual choice is *bad.*

The Random House Dictionary

7. Possessive Adjectives

The forms *my, our, your,* and *their* are possessive adjectives, as are also *his, her,* and *its,* when used to modify nouns.

His property is now worthless.
Their plans included a trip to Europe.

Possessive adjectives also modify gerunds (verb forms ending in *ing* used as nouns).

His leaving the company came as a surprise to us.
We could not think of *his* refusing our offer.
Is there any possibility of *their* buying a house in Cambridge?

Comparison

8. The comparative degree is used in comparing two persons or things. The superlative degree is used in comparing more than two persons or things.

Our expenses are *greater* than yours.
This route is *more direct* than the one through town.
Baxter & Grant's material is *less expensive* than yours.
You are the *best* swimmer on the team.

9. Adjectives of one syllable and some adjectives of two syllables form the comparative by adding *er,* and the superlative by adding *est,* to the positive.

fine	finer	finest
friendly	friendlier	friendliest

Many adjectives of two syllables and most adjectives of more than two syllables form their comparative by prefixing *more* or *less,* and their superlative by prefixing *most* or *least.*

The recent news of the expedition seemed *more hopeful.*
As a businessman he became *most successful.*
Long is the *least competent* salesman in the department.

10. Some adjectives have irregular comparative and superlative forms. If in doubt about the forms, consult a dictionary.

bad, ill	worse	worst
far	farther	farthest
	(distance)	

	further	furthest
	(in the sense of additional, and also distance)	
good, well	better	best
little	less, lesser	least
	littler	littlest
much, many	more	most

11. Strictly, some adjectives and the adverbs derived from them are incapable of comparison because they express a quality complete or perfect; as, *universal, unique, perfect, infinite, preferable.* But modern usage accepts many deviations from this rule; as, a *most complete* report, a *more perfect* example.

Such words, however, may be modified in meaning by such adverbs as *almost, hardly, nearly,* to suggest approach to the superlative.

The Articles

12. Use the indefinite article *a* before words in which the first sound is a consonant, a sounded *h,* or a long *u.*

a cabinet	a hundred pounds
a helper	a unanimous vote
a heroic rescue	a united nation
a historical novel	a union
a history	a useful machine
a hotel	

13. Use *an* before words in which the first sound is a vowel, except long *u,* and before words beginning with silent *h.*

| an envelope | an hour |
| an owner | an unnecessary word |

14. The articles *a, an,* and *the* should be repeated in referring to two separate persons or objects.

The company employs *a* typist and *a* stenographer. (two persons)
The company employs *a* typist and stenographer. (one person)
Either *a* man or *a* woman may apply.
For sale: *a* maple and *a* mahogany desk. (two desks)
For sale: *a* maple and mahogany desk. (one desk)

But when two or more nouns refer to the same person, the article should not be repeated.

Caesar was *a* general, writer, and statesman.
Mary became well known as *a* poet and novelist.

Proper Adjectives

15. A proper adjective is a descriptive adjective derived from a proper noun: *American* industry, *French* literature, *Mexican* silver.

(1) Capitalize proper adjectives unless they have lost their association with the nouns from which they were derived: *chili* sauce, *french* fry, *panama* hat, *pasteurized* milk, *platonic* love, *turkish* towels. (*See also* p. 68.)

Agreement of Adjective and Noun

16. *This* and *that* are singular and must be used to modify singular nouns. *These* and *those* are plural and must be used to modify plural nouns.

This kind (not *these* kind) of books is instructive.
These kinds (not *these* kind) of books are instructive.
That sort (not *those* sort) of answer carries little weight.

Note: I feel *kind of* sorry for him is incorrect. Say *rather* sorry.

Note that *kind of* (not *kind of a*) and *sort of* (not *sort of a*) are permissible although colloquial.

That *kind of* (not *kind of a*) boy ranks high.
That *sort of* (not *sort of a*) position is what I want.

Placement of Adverbs

17. The position of an adverb affects the meaning of the sentence.

The bookkeeper made *only* one error (not *only made*).
He *only* nominated Jones for president. (He did not vote for her.)
He nominated *only* Jones for president. (He did not nominate anyone else.)

18. An adverb should usually be placed as near as possible to the word it modifies.

> It seems *almost impossible* to finish the manuscript by June (not *almost seems*).
> Do you remember *ever signing* such an order (not *ever remember*)?

19. An adverb should be placed first in a sentence when it is meant to qualify the whole sentence or when it is used emphatically.

> *Fortunately* no one was in the shop when the fire broke out.
> *Greatly* to her surprise, she was voted chairman.

20. With a compound verb, the adverb is usually placed between the parts of the compound verb.

> The customer will *undoubtedly* find our statement correct.
> You are *probably* right.

21. Place the adverb before the participle when it modifies the participle only.

> For years the company has been *competently* managed.

Unnecessary Adverbs

22. Unnecessary adverbs should be avoided.

> Each sheet of paper should be carefully numbered (not *numbered throughout*).
> Repeat it (not *repeat it again*).
> They returned to the hotel (not *returned back*).
> Let us cooperate (not *cooperate together*).
> Finish the business (not *finish up the business*).
> They expect to divide the proceeds (not *divide up*).

For the correct use of special adjectives and adverbs, *see* p. 33.

Prepositions

1. A preposition is a connecting word that shows the relation of a noun or a pronoun to some other word in a sentence.

> The main office is *in* Boston.

The preposition *in* shows the relation of the noun *Boston* to the verb *is*.

2. Care must be taken in the use of prepositions. A dictionary should always be consulted in case of doubt as to correct usage. The following illustrations may be helpful:

among, between
(Use *among* with more than two; *between* with two.)

The candy was divided *among* (not *between*) the members of the class.
The candy was divided *between* (not *among*) the two children.

at, with
(*with* a person, *at* a thing)

Jane was angry *with* (not *at*) me.
The minority was angry *at* (not *with*) the passage of the resolution.
The lawyer was displeased *with* (not *at*) the witness.

beside, besides
(at the side of; in addition to)

George walked *beside* (not *besides*) Mary.
Besides (not *beside*) the large doors, there are several smaller ones.

back of, behind

They ran *behind* (not *back of* or *in back of*) the garage.

in, into

The boy walked *in* the room (within its walls).
The boy walked *into* (entered) the room.

of

The phrases *could of, must of,* are erroneous forms for *could have, must have.*

Idiomatic Prepositional Phrases

adapted for	The apartment is adapted for housekeeping.
adapted to	Helen soon adapted herself to her changed circumstances.
adapted from	The story is adapted from the French.
agree on	The faculty agreed on limiting the number of students.

agree to	Do you agree to this proposition?
agree with	He agrees with me on the matter.
argue about	Do not argue about the question.
argue for	They argued for the abolition of child labor.
argue with	He argued with me about Prohibition.
confide in	May I confide in you?
confide to	She confided her troubles to me.
consist in	Success does not always consist in achieving wealth.
consist of	The play consists of five acts.
denounce as	Arnold was denounced as a traitor.
denounce for	The thief was denounced for his crime.
die from	They died from exposure.
die of	She died of pneumonia.
differ about	We differ about the success of coeducation.
differ from	Mary differs from her sister in appearance.
differ in	Mother and Father differ in their opinions about our summer vacation.
differ on	They usually differ on religious questions.
differ with	I differ with you in regard to the discipline of the school.
disappointed by	We are disappointed by her mother, who failed to come.
disappointed in	Farmers are often disappointed in their yearly income.
disappointed with	The owners are disappointed with the poor prospects for sale of the property.
enter at	Enter at the front gate. He entered his daughter at Harvard.
enter for	John has entered for the championship.
enter in	She has entered the bill in her accounts.
enter into	The faculty entered into an agreement with the townspeople.
enter upon	She entered upon her new work with enthusiasm.
impatient at	The superintendent was impatient at the delay.
impatient with	Mother was impatient with the boys.

live at	He lives at the Hotel Astor.
live in	Helen lives in Florida.
live on	They live on Magnolia Avenue.
prejudice against	No one is prejudiced against you.
reconcile to	He was reconciled to his father.
reconcile with	These opinions can be reconciled with hers.

Necessary Prepositions

3. Prepositions should not be omitted when they are needed to make the meaning clear. In the following sentences note the need for the italicized prepositions:

It is *of* no use to object.
Barbara will be *at* home tomorrow.
The tree was a foot *in* diameter.
Will you refrain *from* reading aloud.
His remark is unworthy *of* your notice.
They are going either to France or *to* Italy.
On this side of the river is a group of houses.
An appointment with the dentist prevented Rose *from* going to the concert.
You will find reading a comfort in youth as well as *in* later life.
The states of the East and *of* the West stood together on the question.
I had no faith *in*, or hope *for*, the movement.

Unnecessary Prepositions

4. Prepositions should be omitted when they are not needed to make the meaning clear. In the following illustrations note the unnecessary prepositions:

The girls in the school were all *about* (not *of about*) sixteen.
No one can help observing (not *from observing*) her.
Let us examine (not *examine into*) the room.
The class entered (not *entered into*) the room.
They are going home (not *to home*).
The tree is *near* (not *near to*) the garage.
The child fell *off* (not *off of*) the chair.
They sail *about* (not *on about*) the thirteenth of June.
The club disbanded *about* (not *at about*) ten.
Where has John been (not *been at*)?

Where shall we go (not *go to*)?

She does not remember (not *remember of*) any such happening.

Conjunctions

1. Conjunctions are used to connect words, phrases, or clauses. The correct use of conjunctions can be confusing. Note the following examples of good usage:

as, as if

Do *as* (not *like*) the manager suggests.

I feel *as if* (not *like*) I need a change.

that

He doesn't see *that* (not *as*) he ought to do it.

The reason for his absence was *that* (not *because*) he felt ill.

I saw in the paper *that* (not *where*) Bankhurst became president.

She told them *that* (not *how*) she expected to go to South America.

whether

I don't know *whether* (not *as*) I can go.

I shall ask him *whether* (not *if*) he will do the work.

She didn't say *whether* (not *if*) she has seen the exhibit.

Correlative Conjunctions

2. Correlative conjunctions, that is, conjunctions used in pairs, should be placed next to the words they connect. These words or expressions should be in parallel construction.

The most common correlatives are *either-or, neither-nor, not only-but also, both-and, whereas-therefore, whether-or.*

They have read neither the book nor the magazine.

Not: They have neither read the book nor the magazine.

The work gave me both pleasure and experience.

Not: The work both gave me pleasure and experience.

We visited not only London, but also Paris, Nice, and Rome.

Not: We not only visited London, but also Paris, Nice, and Rome.

With coordinate conjunctions such as *and* and *but*, ideas must be expressed in similar construction.

He was strong in body and in mind.
Or: He was strong physically and mentally.
Not: He was strong in body and also mentally.

Subordinate Conjunctions

3. When one idea in a sentence is dependent upon another, a subordinate conjunction is used to connect the dependent with the main thought. Choose the appropriate conjunction to show the relationship between the clauses.

To show cause:	*as, because, inasmuch as, now that, since*
To indicate concession:	*although, even if, though*
To express a condition:	*but that, except that, if, if only, in case, provided that, unless*
To make a comparison:	*as, as if, more than, rather than, than*
To show manner:	*as, as if*
To explain place:	*where, wherever*
To indicate purpose:	*in order that, so that, that*
To express result:	*so that, so . . . as, so . . . that, such . . . that*
To fix a time:	*after, as, as long as, as often as, before, ever since, just as, now that, since, till, until, when, whenever, whereupon, while*

Subordinate Clauses

1. Avoid interlocking subordinate clauses. Rephrasing the sentence, even dividing a long sentence into two, will be an improvement.

Poor: The price the manager quoted me was lower than I had expected, although I had heard that the real estate market was somewhat weaker than last year.

Better: The price the manager quoted me was lower than I had expected. However, I had heard that the real estate market was somewhat weaker than last year.

Poor: When I asked for reservations, I was told the hotel would be unable to accommodate us at the time we wished to come but that we might be able to find a nearby hotel with available rooms at the price we wanted to pay.

Better: When I asked for reservations, I was told the hotel would be unable to accommodate us at the time we wished to come. The clerk did say that we might be able to find a nearby hotel with available rooms at the price we wanted to pay.

2. Subordinate clauses should be placed near the words they modify. Misplaced clauses can result in confusing or absurd statements.

Poor: The car was parked in the driveway when I arrived and appeared to have been struck from behind.

Better: When I arrived, the car was parked in the driveway and appeared to have been struck from behind.

Poor: The police have arrested the man identified by the father of the victim who saw him leaving the scene of the crime.

Better: The police have arrested a man identified by the victim's father as the man he saw leaving the scene of the crime.

Poor: While a bugler played "To the Colors," the first flag was hoisted on Grimm Park's forty-foot flagpole, followed by Martha Ferris singing the national anthem.

Better: While a bugler played "To the Colors," the first flag was hoisted on Grimm Park's forty-foot flagpole. Martha Ferris then sang the national anthem.

CHAPTER FOUR

Capitalization

1. Capitalize the first word of every sentence, whether or not it is a complete sentence.

   A secretary's greatest asset is good judgment. No doubt about it.

2. Capitalize the first word of every line of poetry.

   > To the glory that was Greece,
   > And the grandeur that was Rome.
   > EDGAR ALLAN POE

   In some modern English poetry forms, only the first word of the first line is capitalized, and sometimes even this is written lowercase.

   > Yes, light is speech. Free frank
   > impartial sunlight, moonlight,
   > starlight, lighthouse light,
   > are language.
   > MARIANNE MOORE

3. Capitalize all proper nouns that are names of individuals.

   Mary Louise DuGarm   J. Allan McIlvaine

   (1) Capitalize epithets added to proper names or applied to people or places.

the Miami Dolphins	the Empire State
William the Conqueror	the Golden Gate
Old Blue Eyes	the Windy City
the Great Communicator	the Sunbelt

(2) Capitalize *father* and *mother* when used in address, but do not capitalize such nouns when a possessive pronoun is used with them.

Yes, Mother, I am going.
My father is at home.

(3) Capitalize *uncle, aunt,* and other family terms when used with a proper noun.

I heard Aunt Lucille say that my uncle was out of town.

4. Capitalize prefixes in the names of persons as follows:

(1) In foreign names such prefixes as *d', da, della, van,* and *von* are capitalized unless preceded by a given name or title.

D'Amato; Louis d'Amato
De Paul; Cardinal de Paul
Van Kirk; A. B. van Kirk

(2) In American and British names such prefixes are usually capitalized even if preceded by a given name or title, but it is best to determine individual preference if possible.

Justice Van Dusen	Henry van Dyke
Oliver de Water	R. J. DiLeo
Laura von Schmidt	Maria De Santis

Note also that a space may or may not be left between the prefix and the rest of the name, depending on individual preference.

References for authoritative capitalization of American and British names: *Who's Who, Who's Who in America, Dictionary of National Biography, Dictionary of American Biography.*

5. Capitalize all academic degrees following the name whether abbreviated or written out.

Allan G. Buchmann, Litt. D.; Jean Davies, Ph. D.; George Schuster, J. D.; Patricia Atwater, LL. D.; Marion Holtz, Master of Arts

(1) When writing more than one degree after a name, arrange according to their importance, the most important last; when they are of the same rank, as various doctoral degrees, according to the time of their being granted. (*See* p. 147.)

Arthur J. Brookins, LL.B., M.A.
George D. Coleman, Ph.D., Litt.D., LL.D.
Saul R. Grossman, M.D., Ph.D.

6. Capitalize all academic and religious titles; as, *Doctor, Bishop, Professor, Dean,* when preceding a name.

Dr. Donald Lawlor, Bishop McAleer, Professor Louis Lowenstein, Dean Barbara Black

(1) With *Reverend,* other academic titles and abbreviations for academic degrees may be used. The following are correct forms for the use of *Reverend:*

Rev. John Blake	minister, pastor, rector, or
The Reverend John Blake	Roman Catholic priest, without
The Reverend John Blake, D.D.	doctoral degrees
The Reverend Dr. John Blake	
The Reverend President John Blake	
The Reverend Professor John Blake	
The Very Reverend Dean John Blake	
The Right Reverend John Blake (Bishop)	
The Most Reverend John Blake (Archbishop)	
The Very Reverend John Blake (Monsignor)	
The Reverend Mother Superior	

The article *the* when preceding *Reverend* in a sentence should not be capitalized. The abbreviation *Rev.* should not be used when preceded by *the.*

On Sunday *the* (not *The*) Reverend Roy Gates will preside.
We heard *the Reverend* (not *The Rev.*) Roy Gates.

(2) The title *Reverend* is an adjective, not a noun, and must, therefore, always be used with a given name or initials on the envelope or in writing the inside address.

Rev. John L. Blake   *or*   Rev. J. L. Blake   *not*   Rev. Blake

It is permissible, however, in referring to a clergyman in the body of a letter, to write

Rev. Mr. Blake   *or*   Rev. Dr. Blake

although it is considered better form to use the given name with the title in even such a reference.

(3) The titles *Reverend* and *Doctor* are usually abbreviated, but are often spelled out in formal use. *Reverend* is not used in the salutation of a letter. Where there is no other title, the salutation is *Dear Mr.* _____, *Dear Ms.* _____, *Dear Mrs.* _____, or *Dear Miss* _____.

(4) Do not capitalize the following when they stand alone (*see* Rule 9):

judge	cantor	rabbi
justice	elder	rector
principal	minister (of	attaché
professor	religion)	consul
superintendent	pastor	consul general
	priest	

The rector has engaged a new secretary.
Did the professor receive her class list from the registrar or from the clerk?
The judge asked the assistant director for all data on the case.

7. Capitalize all titles of rank, honor, or respect when preceding the name.

President _____	Speaker _____
Vice President _____	Governor _____
the Earl of _____	Mayor _____
General _____	Cardinal _____
Senator _____	Chief Justice _____
Congressman _____	Under Secretary _____

Note: *GPO Style Manual* states, "In official usage, the title Vice President of the United States is written without a hyphen." In general usage, this title may also be written in two words.

8. Capitalize all Government titles when referring to definite persons in high positions or to their positions, and all titles of honor or nobility when referring to specific persons.

the Secretary of Defense	the Senator from Florida
the Secretary of the Treasury	House Chaplain

the Assistant Secretary of the
Treasury
Acting Secretary of State
Associate Justice of the
Supreme Court
Chairman of the Committee of
the Whole
the Speaker of the House
the Congressman from Maine

Director, U.S. Coast and
Geodetic Survey
the Queen of England
the President of the French
Republic
the Archbishop of Canterbury
the Governor General of
Canada
the Duke of Norfolk

9. Capitalize a title of preeminence or distinction following the name
of a person or when used alone as a substitute for the name.

Ronald W. Reagan, fortieth President of the United States; the President;
the Chief Executive; the Commander in Chief
Jane Smith, Secretary of Agriculture; the Secretary
Susan Blank, Governor of Arkansas; the Governor of Arkansas; the Governor
Stephen Jones, President-elect

(1) Titles of city, county, or state officials (except Governor) are
usually not capitalized except as a form of courtesy in the body of
a letter, in the inside address, and after the signature.

Robert Frank, mayor of Exville
George Howell, city clerk
Laura Bradshaw, county treasurer
Horace Franklin, state superintendent of schools

(2) In reports and in correspondence, business titles referring to
positions of authority are usually capitalized as a form of courtesy
when they refer to definite individuals or when a company refers
to its own officers.

Lewis Barr, President of the Southern Cotton Association, called the
meeting to order.
The Chairman of the Board of Arnold & Cole was authorized by the
stockholders to increase the dividend.

(3) In material for publication in newspapers, magazines, or books,
the title following a name is usually not capitalized.

Dr. John D. Smith, provost of the College of Agriculture
G. E. Schuster, chairman of the Public Utility Council

10. Titles are sometimes used instead of the names of those who bear

them. In such cases, when a definite person is referred to in the singular, the title is to be capitalized.

(1) In the second person if used as synonyms of proper names

Mr. Secretary, please examine the report.
You will report, Captain, to headquarters.
Do you think, Senator, this bill will pass?

Do not capitalize *sir, madam, monsieur,* and such terms used alone in address.

What plan would you suggest, sir?
Why, madam, look what it means.

And so, my fellow citizens, the reason that I came away from Washington is that I sometimes get lonely down there.

WOODROW WILSON

(2) In the third person

When the Governor, escorted by local Democrats, appeared at the door, there was a roar from the crowd.

11. The *GPO Style Manual* presents the following on Army, Navy, and Air Force:

U.S. Army, French Army; the Army, Army Establishments, Organized Reserves, the Volunteers, 1st Regiment, VII Corps, the Corps (U.S. understood in all cases). *But:* volunteer officer, army shoe, Lee's army, Robinson's brigade, the brigade, the regiment

U.S. Navy, British Navy; the Navy, Navy (or Naval) Establishment, Navy officers, the Marine Corps, the corps, the Marines, a marine

U.S. Air Force, Royal Air Force; Andrews Air Force Base, the base; Air Materiel Command, the command

12. Capitalize the words *department, bureau, service, station, office, agency, commission,* and *board* if referring to a bureau or executive department of the U.S. Government when the name is given.

the Department of State	Newport Naval Station
the Bureau of Customs	the Foreign Service
the Federal Reserve Board	the Securities and Exchange
the Environmental Protection	Commission
Agency	

Business usage varies as to the capitalization of such words as *bureau, department,* and *office* following a name.

Adjustment Bureau *or* adjustment bureau
Savings Department *or* savings department
Department of Applied Science *or* department of applied science
Employment Office *or* employment office

Do not capitalize *department, office, bureau,* and like words when used without a name or if used as an adjective.

I am going to the office.
He was employed by one of the Government bureaus.
The department clerk filed the report.

13. Capitalize *committee* with a name or in place of the name when referring to all standing and select committees of the Senate and the House of Representatives.

House Census Committee   Committee on Ways and Means

14. Capitalize *Federal* and *State Courts* when used with a definite name. Do not capitalize *city and county courts.*

the United States Supreme   the State Court of Appeals
    Court   Court of Claims
the United States Circuit   the police court
    Court   the magistrate's court

Capitalize *Court* when meaning a judge or judicial tribunal in direct personal reference to such a judge or tribunal.

15. Capitalize the word *Cabinet* when referring to the Cabinet of the President of the United States.

Cabinet officer
the President's Cabinet
the chief post of the Cabinet

16. Capitalize *Federal* when referring to the U.S. Government.

He was in the service of the Federal Government.

17. Usage varies as to the capitalization of *administration.* When referring to the political party in power or when used with a name to designate a Government board, *administration* is usually capitalized.

the Republican Administration
the Administration
the Reagan Administration

a former administration
Veterans Administration

18. Capitalize *Government* when used synonymously with the U.S.
Government or when referring to that of any foreign nation.

a Government official	the Italian Government
Federal Government	Imperial Government
National Government	Her Majesty's Government
Government ownership	a Government bureau

Do not capitalize *government* when referring to that of a state
in the United States or to that of any possession of the United
States.

19. Capitalize *commonwealth, confederation, powers, union,* and so
forth, if used with proper names or as proper names or as proper
adjectives.

Commonwealth of Massachusetts
Swiss Confederation
United Nations
Union of Soviet Socialist Republics

20. Capitalize *Constitution* when referring to that of the United States
or to a specific national constitution.

James Madison was called the Father of the Constitution.
The Constitution of the United States of America was adopted in 1789.
The Constitutional Convention of Philadelphia set up the Federal Gov-
ernment of the United States.
Constitutional Committee, Constitutional Amendment

But: New York constitution

Act, bill, code, law, report, and *treaty* with a name or number
to designate a particular document are capitalized.

Smith Act	Annual Report of the
Bill of Rights	Secretary of Defense
Internal Revenue Code	Jay Treaty
Public Law 9	

21. Capitalize any U.S. Government *commission* when it is designated
by its name.

Atomic Energy Commission
Commission of Fine Arts

Federal Communications Commission
Interstate Commerce Commission
Securities and Exchange Commission
U.S. Tariff Commission

Also capitalize *commission* when it stands alone if it refers to a national or international commission already named.

22. Capitalize all names of state legislatures when used with the name of the state and all names of national legislatures and their branches.

Florida Legislature
the Assembly of New York
the Ohio House of Representatives
the General Court of Massachusetts
the Eighty-ninth Congress
House of Commons
Chamber of Deputies
Rigsdag

But do not capitalize *assembly, general court, legislature* if they stand alone without the name of the state to which they belong. Do not capitalize *national legislature,* meaning the United States Congress; or *city legislature,* meaning City Council or Board of Aldermen; or *executive session, special session.*

23. Capitalize *nation* and *republic* when used as a synonym for the United States or when used with a name to designate a definite nation.

These defense measures are essential to the safety of the Nation.
"With the election of this great statesman, the future of the Republic is assured," declared the chairman of the winning party.

But: Every nation in this hemisphere is invited to participate in the forthcoming conference.

Capitalize *national* when it precedes a capitalized word.

National Capital
National Academy of Sciences
The National Government

But: national ideas, national pride, national anthem, a national monument
The national defense demands not merely force but intelligence.

24. Capitalize *state* when used with a name or when used in place of the name, but lowercase when used as a general term.

New York State
the State of Ohio
the State leaders
State ticket

State government
State Democratic
    headquarters

This State must cope with its own problems.

Note the usage of capitalization in the following examples:

state prison
states' rights
State's attorney
state's evidence

Mountain States
Southern States
Thirteen Original States
a foreign state

25. Capitalize the names of organized bodies and their adherents.

Republicans
Shriners

Socialists
Elks

Usage differs as to the capitalization of the word *party.*

the Communist Party *or* the Communist party

26. Capitalize names of clubs, associations, institutes, orders, companies, foundations, funds, groups, and so forth.

the Moravian Club
Macmillan Publishing
    Company
Order of the Sacred Heart
American Academy of Arts
    and Letters

Knights of Columbus
National Institutes of Health
the Cambridge Group
American Association of
    University Women

Do not capitalize clubs, associations, institutes, orders, colleges, and the like when used alone unless they have the value of a proper noun.

He belonged to a carpenters' union.
The clubs and associations of this city are numerous.
The Association voted on the question of dues.
The Board will meet on June 15.

27. Capitalize names of squares, parks, towers, monuments, statues, buildings, thoroughfares, churches.

Union Square
the Tower of London
Park Row
Gramercy Park

Trinity Church
the Washington Monument *or*
    the Monument
the House (National)

the Mall	Halls of Congress
Eiffel Tower	the Capitol Grounds
the Capitol (Washington)	the Lincoln Memorial
Metropolitan Museum of Art	the Mormon Temple
the Library of Congress	the Golden Gate Bridge
Temple Emanu-el	Capitol Halls of Congress
Avery Library	Governor's Mansion
the Hall of Fame	Kingsway
the Executive Mansion	the Pennsylvania Turnpike
Mansion House (London)	Capitol Chamber
the Guild Theater	Westminster Abbey
the White House	Champs Elysées
Statue of Liberty	Rock Creek Park

But: the statue of Lincoln, the tomb of Washington

In some telephone and city directories, and in many newspapers, the words *avenue, street, boulevard, square, place,* and *court* are not written with initial capitals, even when used to indicate particular places. This style, however, is not recommended for use in correspondence and business writing.

The plural form of a common noun written as part of a proper noun is capitalized according to Government usage, but many publications advocate writing the plural form of the common noun without initial capital.

Capitalize a common noun when it is used as a well-known short form of a specific proper name.

the Canal (Panama Canal)   the Lakes (Great Lakes)

Place references when merely descriptive and preceded by *the* are not capitalized.

the mountains of North   the valley of the Susquehanna
Carolina

28. Capitalization of a geographical term follows various usages. The following rules and lists of terms have been adapted from *GPO Style Manual.*

(1) In business writing the following geographical terms are usually capitalized in the singular or plural, immediately following the name:

archipelago	gap	park
basin	glacier	passage

bend	gulch	peninsula
branch (stream)	harbor	plateau
butte	hill	point
canal	hollow	pond
channel	inlet	range (mountains)
cove	island	reef
crater	mesa	ridge
creek	mountain	run (stream)
current	narrows	shoal
flat(s)	ocean	sound

(2) In business writing the following words are usually capitalized, singular or plural, when they stand before a name or after it, or when they are used as a part of a name:

bay	lake
bayou	mount
camp (military)	oasis
cape	pass
desert	port (*but* port of New York)
falls	river
fort	sea
head	strait
isle	valley

(3) Capitalize the following words if part of a name. Do not capitalize them when they are used in a general sense; as, the *rivers* of Maine, the *valleys* of California and North Carolina:

airport	gulf	rapids
beach	lagoon	reservation
borough	landing	reservoir
cavern	lighthouse	spring
ferry	plain	tunnel
forest	prairie	volcano
gorge	province	woods

(4) Do not capitalize the following terms, even when they are used with a name or a number:

breakwater	drydock	spillway
buoy	levee	watershed
chute	lock	weir
dike	pier	wharf
dock	slip	

29. Capitalize special names of countries or regions of countries, cities or sections of cities, rivers, bays, oceans, mountains, islands, and other geographical names.

Old World	the Tropics
New World	the Eternal City
Orient	the Left Bank (Paris)
Occident	the Hill (Capitol Hill,
Far East	Congress)
the Levant	the Southland
the Continent (*but* the	Greater Seattle
continent of Europe)	the Loop
the Empire State	the North End (Boston)
the Middle West	the Sunbelt
the Northern Pacific States	the Lower East Side (New
the South Pole	York)
the Great Plains	the Delta

If a common noun or adjective forming an essential part of a name becomes removed from the rest of the name by an intervening common noun or adjective, the entire expression is no longer a proper noun and is therefore not capitalized.

Union Station, union passenger station
Eastern States, eastern farming states

30. Capitalize points of the compass when they designate geographical parts of the country.

Southern States	the Northwest
out West	Midwestern States

The South has increased its manufactures.
Election returns from the East are eagerly awaited.
The North took a decided stand on the question.
Big buying orders credited to Eastern sources were in evidence.

Do not capitalize such words when used merely to indicate direction.

in Virginia and the colonies to the north and south of it

facing south	north of Boston
driving east	west of the Rockies

(1) Do not capitalize adjectives derived from regional names when they are merely descriptive in character.

continental customs	oriental life
western hospitality	southern cooking
eastern fashions	northern climate
tropical fruits	an east wind

(2) Capitalize *northern, southern, western, eastern,* and so forth, when used as part of proper names to designate a world division; do not capitalize such words when used to indicate parts of states.

Central and Southwestern	western New York
Europe	eastern Pennsylvania
Eastern Asia	southern California
West South Africa	northern Ohio
Eastern Hemisphere	eastern Texas

(3) Nouns referring to the inhabitants of different sections of the United States may or may not be capitalized.

Northerner *or* northerner
Easterner *or* easterner

31. Capitalize all proper names denoting political divisions.

United Kingdom	Ward Ten
French Republic	Nineteenth District
the Dominion of Canada	Fourth Precinct
the Commonwealth of	Thirteenth Congressional
Massachusetts	District
the Republic (United States)	Orange County
the South American Republics	City of New York
the Papal States	

32. Capitalize *college, university, seminary, school, high school,* and so forth, when used with a proper name. When such words are used alone, do not capitalize unless the word stands for a definite college or university and has the value of a proper name.

Elmira College	Oak Park High School
the College of Fine Arts	Bacon Academy
the School of Engineering	Students Hall
the Graduate School	Columbia University

33. Capitalize *church* when used with a name to designate a body of religious belief or a building and also when it designates the Church Universal; capitalize *cathedral, synagogue, temple,* and *chapel* when used with a name.

the Roman Catholic
  Church
the Church of England
High Church
Protestant Episcopal
  Church
the Presbyterian Church
the dignitaries of the
  Church
Church and State

the Cathedral of St. John the
  Divine
St. Patrick's Cathedral
the National Cathedral
Temple Emanu-el
Free Synagogue
Riverside Church
Harkness Chapel
the Unitarian Church

When *church, cathedral, synagogue, temple,* and *chapel* are used without a name or in a general sense, do not capitalize them.

church history
cathedrals of France
chapel exercises

synagogue services
the temple driveway

34. Capitalize all names for the Bible, for parts and versions of the Bible, and all names of other sacred books.

Bible
Scriptures
Holy Writ
Word of God
Holy Bible
Old Testament
New Testament
Pentateuch
the Ten Commandments
Gospels (*but* gospel teachings)

Lord's Prayer
Twenty-third Psalm
Gospel of Mark
King James Version
Authorized Version
Vulgate
Revised Standard Version
Apocrypha
Koran
Talmud

Authorities differ regarding the capitalization of some adjectives derived from such nouns. The following examples are given in *The Random House Dictionary of the English Language:*

apocryphal
biblical
rabbinical

scriptural
Talmudic
Vedic

35. Capitalize all names for the Deity.

Father
Almighty
Judge of Nations
Jehovah

Supreme Being
First Cause
Divine Providence
Lord of Hosts

Messiah the Comforter	Holy Spirit
Son of Man	Holy Trinity
King of the Jews	Redeemer
Holy Ghost	Savior

Do not capitalize *fatherhood, sonship, messiahship, messianic.*

36. Capitalize the *Virgin Mary,* the *Virgin,* the *Blessed Virgin, Madonna,* the *Holy Mother, Our Lady.*

37. In the Bible and in the Book of Common Prayer, pronouns relating to the Deity are not capitalized.

O Lord, thou hast been our dwelling-place in all generations.
And he looked up and saw the rich men that were casting their gifts into the treasury.

Opinions of publishers of other books differ in regard to the capitalization of pronouns relating to the Deity.

The nominative and the accusative of the personal pronouns—He and Him, Thou and Thee—are capitalized in this connection, but not the possessives, his and thine.

All pronouns referring to the Supreme Being, or any member of the Christian Trinity when closely preceded or followed by a distinct reference to the Deity, should be capitalized.

"Trust Him who rules all things" (*but* "When God worked six days he rested the seventh").

38. Capitalize *Heaven* when referring to the Deity, and *Paradise* and *Heaven* only when referring to the hereafter; also *Hades,* but not *hell.*

Her prayers, whom Heaven delights to hear.

WILLIAM SHAKESPEARE

New thoughts of God, new hopes of Heaven.

JOHN KEBLE

But: Sharecropping, no heaven for the tenant, was no paradise for the farmer.

He descended into hell.

BOOK OF COMMON PRAYER

And in Hades, he lifted up his eyes, being in torment.

GOSPEL OF LUKE (REVISED STANDARD VERSION)

39. Capitalize the *Pope*, or the *Popes*, always; also *Holy Father, Pontiff*, and *Holiness*, meaning the Pope; *Cardinal, Apostolic Delegate, Archbishop, Bishop, Moderator*, and *Presiding Elder* before personal names; also when used separately after the person has been mentioned or when used in direct reference to persons holding office.

The New York Times Manual of Style and Usage

Every heart that has not been blinded and hardened by this terrible war must be touched by this moving appeal of his Holiness, the Pope.

WOODROW WILSON

40. Capitalize all names of creeds and confessions of faith and general biblical terms.

the Apostles' Creed
Nicene Creed
Canon Law
Westminster Confession of
   Faith
The New Testament

the Westminster Catechism
Thirty-nine Articles
Lord's Supper
Creed of Pius IV
the Ten Commandments

41. Capitalize *Devil*, the *Evil One*, the *Adversary*, the *Father of Lies*, and *Beelzebub* meaning Satan.

And the great dragon was thrown down, that ancient serpent, who is called the Devil and Satan . . .

REVELATION 12:9 (REVISED STANDARD VERSION)

Do not capitalize when used in a general sense or as an expletive.

42. Capitalize all names of holy days and holidays.

Christmas
Easter
Good Friday
Labor Day
Yom Kippur
Fourth of July
Columbus Day
Passover

Feast of Tabernacles
Whitsuntide
Memorial Day
New Year's Day
Thanksgiving Day
All Saints' Day
Michaelmas
Lincoln's Birthday

43. Capitalize the first word following a colon when it introduces an independent passage or sentence. (*See* p. 84.)

A claim letter that makes unreasonable demands does one of two things: It antagonizes the recipient, or it convinces him that the grounds of complaint are unwarranted.

But do not capitalize a short list of words or phrases following the colon directly.

There are three steps of a century of educational development in America: industrialism, urbanization, mass schooling.

44. Capitalize the first word of each item in an outline:

1. Attracting attention
2. Creating desire
3. Convincing the mind
4. Stimulating action

45. Capitalize the first word of every complete quotation.

The child cried, "Where is my new ball?"

(1) Do not capitalize the first word of a direct quotation when the quotation is introduced indirectly in the text.

The governor called the explosion "a medical disaster and a legal quagmire."

(2) Do not capitalize that part of a quotation resumed within the same sentence.

"Nature," said Lowell, "abhors the credit system."

(3) Capitalize the first word of a question made in direct form but not quoted.

The eighteenth century asked of a thing, Is it rational? The seventeenth century asked of a thing, Is it legal? or, when it went further, Is it according to conscience?

(4) Do not capitalize the first word of an indirect question or statement.

He asked what was the meaning of the party's steady growth in power. Stevenson says that it is charm which is the basis of enduring art.

(5) Do not capitalize a partial quotation when this quotation is used as a motto on a title page or as a heading of a chapter.

... the cherished companion of my life, in whose affections, unabated on both sides, I had lived the last ten years in unchequered happiness.

THOMAS JEFFERSON

(6) Do not capitalize a parenthetical statement that occurs in the middle of a sentence.

The planes (all of them now out-of-date) were grounded.
The model she chose (he arrived as we were speaking) assumed a languid pose.

46. Capitalize the first word of exclamatory or of interrogative sentences used in a series.

O Rome! My country! City of the soul!

BYRON

Have you any idea what the habit of being loyal is worth?
Do you know what it means to your happiness? To your success?

47. Capitalize *Whereas* and *Resolved* in resolutions and the first word following *Resolved*. A comma follows *Resolved*.

Whereas the United States Tariff Commission . . .
Resolved, That the Unitarian Universalist Association urges its member churches and fellowships to work for . . .

But: When *whereas* is written in full capitals, a comma follows:

WHEREAS, in order to preserve open space for the enjoyment of present and future generations . . .

48. Capitalize the article *the*, or its equivalent in a foreign language, when it is the authorized part of a geographical name, of a title of a book or of a work of art, or when incorporated as part of the legal name of a company or of an institution.

Geographical names: The Dalles, The Hague, The Netherlands, The Weirs, El Salvador, La Paz, Le Havre; *but* the Gulf States, the Midwest, the Orient, the Western Hemisphere.

Titles: *The Nine Tailors, The Bartered Bride, My Life in Art.*

Names of companies or institutions: The Federal Sugar Refining Company, The English-Speaking Union.

This rule is usually disregarded in newspapers and in informal writing when mentioning periodicals, ships, firm names, and so forth; as, the *Atlantic Monthly,* the *Olympia,* the Carborundum Company.

When used with personal titles if it is not the first word in a sentence, *the* should not be capitalized.

Two new ex officio members of the Board were the Reverend Joseph O'Donnell and the Honorable James Ryan.

49. Capitalize references to divisions of a work when referred to in the same work.

See Chapter 4 in Part II.
Definitions will be found in the Glossary.

Do not capitalize these when used in a general sense.

We learned how to make an index.

50. Capitalize the names of the seasons only when they are personified.

If Winter comes, can Spring be far behind?
Percy Bysshe Shelley

We are going in the spring.

51. Personifications of abstract ideas or objects are sometimes capitalized.

In the name of Reason, will you please consider the results of such actions. It has been said that Man proposes, God disposes.

But: It is not reason but habit that usually prevails.

52. Capitalize the names and synonyms for flags of nations: the Star-Spangled Banner, Old Glory, the National Emblem, the Union Jack.

53. In typewritten work, such as business letters and reports, when a noun is followed by a code reference or by a number, the word is ordinarily capitalized. When used generally, such words are not capitalized. The word *number* and its abbreviation *No.* are always omitted after *Form.*

Bulletin CL-50, a new bulletin
Catalogue B-4, our recent catalogue
Form 1040A, a shortened form
Contract No. 65, a long-term contract

54. Capitalize nouns followed by a capitalized Roman numeral.

Act I, Vol. V, Book II

Often *in references* such nouns and Roman numerals are not capitalized.

Subdivisions and their abbreviations in literary references are not capitalized.

article—art.	line—l.	page—p.	verse—vs.
chapter— chap.	note—n.	section—sec.	volume—vol.

55. Capitalize all principal words (that is, nouns, pronouns, adjectives, adverbs, verbs, and first words) in titles of books, pictures, plays, radio programs, television shows, musical compositions, documents, reports, papers, proceedings, captions, display lines, headings. (*See* p. 109 for use of italics with various kinds of titles.)

Books:	*Lake Wobegon Days*
	Handling Executive Stress
Pictures:	a print of "American Gothic"
	Leonardo's "Last Supper"
Radio programs:	*Sportsnight with Jack Spector*
	All Things Considered
Television shows:	*Hill Street Blues*
	Masterpiece Theatre
Musical compositions:	Stravinsky's *Firebird*
	The Grand Canyon Suite
	Chopin's Nocturne, Opus 37, No. 2
	"The Star-Spangled Banner"
Documents, reports, and proceedings:	U.S. Constitution
	Report of the Special Committee on Immigration
	Proceedings of the Fifth Annual Conference on Learning Disabilities
Captions:	Sampling Fine Wines of the Valley
	Foreign Equities Gain Favor

In informal usage in letters and advertisements book titles may be given in full caps.

I have enjoyed reading THE GREENER GRASS.

56. Capitalize scientific names of the world's eras, common names for historical epochs, periods in the history of literature or language, and important events.

the Neolithic age	the Wars of the Roses
the Paleozoic period	Colonial days
the Fourth Glacial age	Revolutionary period
the Christian Era	the days of the Second
the Crusades	Empire
the Middle Ages	the Louisiana Purchase
the Renaissance	the Battle of Bull Run

57. Capitalize all names of the bodies of the solar system except *earth*, *moon*, *stars*, and *sun* (unless they are personified or used in an astronomical context).

the Milky Way	Orion
the Great Bear	Cassiopeia's Chair
the Big Dipper	the North Star
Venus	the Southern Cross

58. Capitalize in botanical, geological, zoological, and paleontological matter the scientific (Latin) names of divisions, orders, families, and genera, but not their English derivatives.

Cotylosauria, *but* cotylosaurs
Cruciferae, *but* crucifers

59. In botanical, geological, zoological, paleontological, and medical matter the names of species are never capitalized.

Cedrus libani	*Styrax californica*
Felis leo	*Conodectes favosus*
Cocos nucifera	*Epigaea repens*

60. Do not capitalize abbreviations unless the words they represent are usually capitalized, as, *F.* or *Fahr.* (*Fahrenheit*) or *C.* (*Celsius*); or unless the abbreviation has been capitalized by custom, as *ETA* (*estimated time of arrival*) or *No.* (*number*).

61. Abbreviations for forenoon and afternoon may be written as follows:

a.m. *or* A.M.
p.m. *or* P.M.

62. Do not capitalize units of measurement such as *6 ft.*, *4 lbs.*, *3 qts.*

63. Capitalize the trade names of manufactured products, but lower-case the words following a trade name that are not part of the name.

Bon Ami	Celotex	Pet milk	Goodyear tires

64. Capitalize most adjectives formed from proper nouns. Do not capitalize such adjectives in French, Italian, Norwegian, Spanish, and Swedish text.

Arabic	Nipponese
British	Olympian
Canadian	Pan-American
Chesterfieldian	Papal
Elizabethan	Parisian
Gregorian	Rooseveltian
Hellenic	Semitic
Latin	Swiss
Napoleonic	Victorian

65. In advertising and in journalistic writing, capitals are often used for emphasis. This should be done sparingly, as excessive capitalization tends to weaken rather than to emphasize.

66. Capitalize both parts of a hyphenated word if each part is ordinarily capitalized: *Anglo-American* attitude, *Scotch-Irish* ancestry. When a prefix that is part of a hyphenated word is ordinarily written without a capital, it is not capitalized when combined with a proper noun except when used as the name of an organization or in a title that would require capitalization.

anti-American	non-Swedish
intra-European	trans-Canadian
but	
Inter-American Artists	Trans-Siberian Railway

While authorities differ on the capitalization of hyphenated words in titles and headings, the following rule is generally accepted:

In titles and headings, capitalize words that form parts of hyphenated compounds without regard for hyphens.

New Do-It-Yourself Landscaping Guide
Test-Tube Plants Assure Virus-Free Strawberries
How to Make an Ice-Cream Drive-In Pay

67. A list of words and expressions showing their generally accepted capitalization follows. Note that some words derived from proper nouns have developed a special meaning; these words are no longer capitalized.

afghan (lap robe)
Afghan hound
Allies (World Wars I & II)
American history
Americanization
anglicize
Anglo-French entente
artesian well
bologna sausage
boycott
braille
brussels sprouts
cesarean section
Cheshire cheese
chinaware
delftware
English literature
French château
french dressing
Georgian architecture
Gothic architecture
gothic novel
Grades I–XII
Icelandic legends
india ink
Indian corn
lyonnaise potatoes
macadamized road
madras cloth

melba toast
mercurial
mid-Atlantic
morocco leather
oxford shoe
plaster of paris
Pompeian red
poor whites
portland cement
pro-British
Province of Quebec
Puritan colony
puritanical ethics
Roman citizens
roman type
Room 224
russian dressing
Russian olive
spanish omelet
Statement No. 2
Table No. 5
transatlantic
transoceanic
tropical fruits
the tropics
un-American
Wedgwood ware
x-ray (verb)
X ray (noun)

CHAPTER FIVE

Punctuation

The Period

1. Place a period at the end of a declarative sentence, at the end of an indirect question, and at the end of an imperative sentence that does not express strong emotion.

   Green belts around cities are attractive and provide oxygen.
   He could not determine why the changes had not been made.
   Leave two lines blank below your name and address.

2. Place a period after a request. A question mark is not used when a request or order is implied.

   Will you please sign and return the application.
   May I have your opinion of this proposal.

3. Place a period after an abbreviation that stands for a single word. (*See also* Rules 5 and 6.)

   | John Smith and Co., Inc. | Mrs. Susan Richards |
   | the first century A.D. | Jan. 6 |

   However, the trend is to eliminate periods in abbreviations, especially in units of all kinds.

lb *or* lb.	mph *or* m.p.h.
hr *or* hr.	mpg *or* m.p.g.
oz *or* oz.	yd *or* yd.

Note the uses of the period after an abbreviation in connection with other punctuation marks.

(1) When the last word in a sentence is abbreviated, one period will suffice.

We plan to meet at 9 A.M.

(2) Before a colon

These instructions came from Cox & Box Ltd.: Never use chemicals on the lens; use only mild soap and water.

(3) Before a semicolon

The gardens are open from 9 A.M. to dusk daily, May–Sept.; 10 A.M. to 5 P.M., Oct.–April.

4. Do not place a period after *Mme* and *Mlle* in French (American usage, *Mme.* and *Mlle.*); after abbreviations of well-known publications, as *PMLA* (Publications of the Modern Language Association); or after abbreviations for linguistic epochs, as *OE* (Old English), *MHG* (Middle High German).

5. Ordinarily do not place a period between letters indicating the names of government boards, commissions, and services; as, *AEC*, *FBI*, *TVA*; or after the call letters of broadcasting stations: *WCBS*, *WNBC*, *WTOP*.

6. According to individual preference, periods may or may not be placed after initials representing full personal names; as, *R. L. S.*, *T. R.*, *F. D. R.* or *RLS*, *TR*, *FDR*.
    In monograms periods are always omitted.

OWR   BI

In indicating the initials of a person dictating a letter and those of the typist, periods are always omitted.

AJ:STM   LPD:jb   lpd:jb

7. Do not place a period after Roman numerals except in a table of contents or in lists.

Vol. X   Elizabeth II   John Delano III

   I. Preparation of Content of Report
   II. Arrangement of Content

III. Typing the Report

8. Do not place a period after letters when they refer to a person; as, *Mr.* A has paid his monthly common charges.

9. Place periods after letters or figures in an outline when they mark the chief division of a subject. Omit the periods when the letters or figures are enclosed in parentheses.

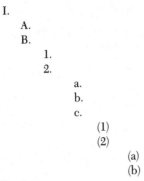

I.
  A.
  B.
    1.
    2.
      a.
      b.
      c.
        (1)
        (2)
          (a)
          (b)
II. etc.

10. Place a period before a decimal fraction.

$20.38   .05   12.6   0.31416

11. A period may be used between figures denoting hours and minutes; as, 10.15. However, the colon is generally used; as, 10:15. (*See* p. 85.)

12. Place the period inside the parentheses when they enclose an independent sentence. (*See* pp. 95–97.)

The firm was incorporated a few years ago. (I am not sure just when.)

13. Place the period outside the parentheses when the enclosed matter forms part of the preceding statement and is not an independent statement.

These campaign techniques proved effective (so the experts decreed, though they could offer no proof).
Orders were placed for F-14 and F-15 aircraft (then still in development).

14. Place a period inside quotation marks. (*See* p. 92.)

I am going to read Tomlinson's "Gifts of Fortune."
Do not use such expressions as "Best on the market."

15. Omit the period after all display lines; after running heads; after centered headlines; after side heads set in separate lines; after cut-in heads; after box heads in tables; after superscriptions and legends that do not make more than a single line of type; after items in enumerated lists; after date lines heading communications; and after signatures.

   However, if one item in a list is a complete sentence, a period is used. In that case, all items are followed by a period.

16. Do not place a period after chemical symbols, the words indicating size of books, or the word *percent*.

   H_2O 16mo   10 percent

17. Omit the period after a signature and after a title following a signature in a letter.

   Yours very truly,
   Martha Alexander
   Personnel Director

18. Use three periods separated by spaces to denote an omission in quoted matter. When the omission occurs at the end of a sentence, the sentence period is retained as well. Use seven periods spaced across the page to denote the omission of one or more paragraphs of quoted matter.

   Henry Clay declared that the veto is totally irreconcilable with the genius of representative government if it is . . . employed with respect to the expediency of measures, as well as their constitutionality.

The Comma

1. Use a comma to separate words and phrases in a series.

   When the electricity fails, there's no elevator, no light, no television, none of the amenities.

   The comma causes trouble equally by its absence, by its presence, and by wrong placement.

   WILSON FOLLETT, *Modern American Usage*

   Business positions differ greatly in the training required, in the opportunities for advancement, and in the financial rewards.

From the campuses has come the expertise to travel to the moon, to crack the genetic code, and to develop computers that calculate as fast as the speed of light.

Sharing in the indicated larger yields were corn, potatoes, apples, tobacco, and peanuts.

Present usage advocates the use of the comma before *and* connecting the last two words of a series; some writers, however, prefer to omit the comma before *and*.

(1) Do not use a comma when the conjunction connects all the words in a series.

Reading and writing and 'rithmetic are still basic.

(2) When *etc.* ends a series, it should be preceded and followed by a comma. (*Etc.* is, of course, the abbreviation of *et cetera*, and since *et* means *and*, the word *and* should not precede *etc.*)

Last week a sale of chairs, beds, desks, etc., was advertised by Law & Dutton.

(3) In company names consisting of a series of surnames, most organizations omit the comma between the last two members: *Hudson, Blair & Grant; Lawrence, Stevenson and Kane.* When the word *company* completes the series, the comma is omitted: *Green, Lake and Company.*

2. Use a comma between adjectives preceding a noun when they are coordinate qualifying words.

The managers agreed on a form for a shortened, simplified, uniform report.

Do not use a comma between two adjectives preceding a noun if using the comma destroys the intended relationship, since the adjectives are too closely related to be separated.

additional reasonable cost   huge boxlike building
quaint old mining town   outstanding military service

3. Use a comma to separate pairs of words in a series.

Official and nonofficial, national and state agencies attended the convention in Boston.

4. Use a comma or commas to separate the name of the person addressed or his or her title from the rest of the sentence.

I suppose, Mrs. Harrison, that this is your final offer.
We are glad to welcome you, Captain Bligh.
Well, Professor, this is the first I have heard of the idea.

5. Use a comma to set off words in apposition.

   Martha L. Ferris, chairman of Consolidated Amalgams, has announced
   the merger.
   The minimum daily requirement of minerals, such as iron, zinc, calcium,
   and manganese, differs among species.

6. Do not separate compound personal pronouns from the words they
   emphasize.

   Bruce himself sent the telegram.
   The members themselves will make up the deficit.

7. Do not use commas when a word or phrase is in italics or enclosed
   in quotation marks.

   The word *caprice* is derived from the Latin word *caper*.
   A little south of the "northern tier" barrier reef . . .

8. Omit the comma when an appositive has become part of a proper
   name.

   Eric the Red   William the Conqueror

9. Omit the comma when the connection is unusually close between
   an appositive and the word it modifies.

   Our salesman Brown covers the New England territory.

10. Use a comma to set off inverted names in bibliographies, in in-
    dexes, in directories, or in other reference lists.

    Cleveland, Orford B.   Babineau, Celeau
    Rabinowitz, Melvin, D.C.   Laszlo, Sandra, M.D.

11. Use a comma to separate a name from a title or degree that fol-
    lows it.

    Arthur Brookins Cudworth, dean of McGrath Law School
    Nijland S. Andersen, Ph.D.

    A comma may or may not be used before and after *Jr.* and *Sr.*
    following a name.

John Lyons, Jr., presided.
John Lyons Jr. presided.

Omit periods and commas before and after II, III, and IV with names.

Henry Lord III conducted the meeting.

12. Use a comma to set off a contrasted word, phrase, or clause.

Saving, not spending, is the way of security.
It is important for drivers to be vigilant, not heedless.
The effective writer aims not at broad target areas, but at bull's-eyes.

13. Use a comma to set off a transitional word or expression; as, *then, indeed, nevertheless, moreover, of course,* when a pause is needed for clearness or for emphasis.

Indeed, we all considered the matter closed.
On the contrary, a college degree does not guarantee employability.
Nevertheless, he found himself at a loss for words.
She intended, as a matter of fact, to double the plant's output in six months' time.
The more you travel, obviously, the easier you should find it to adjust to other people's customs.
Knowing one's limitations may, it is true, discourage one from trying new ways.

When such parenthetical words, phrases, and clauses do not interrupt the thought or require punctuation for clearness, the commas should be omitted.

The jury therefore gave a unanimous decision.
We are accordingly signing the contract.
It is indeed strange that so few children read well today.
The decision in this case is probably not significant.

14. Use a comma to indicate the omission of a word, usually a word that has been used before in the sentence.

Common stocks are preferred by some investors; bonds, by others; and mortgages, by still others.

Often, however, commas are omitted if the meaning is clear without them.

The Englishman's virtue is wisdom; the Frenchman's is reason; the Spaniard's serenity.

15. A comma should follow *yes, no, why, well* when one of these words is used at the beginning of a sentence.

   Why, we expected him to be appointed district manager this year.
   Well, the decision has been made and we have to live with it.

   But: When *well* or *why* is used as an adverb, no comma is needed.

   However well she played, her teacher failed to encourage her.
   We could not determine why the machine stopped suddenly.

16. Use a comma to set off light exclamations.

   Oh, a change would be nice, but I can't afford a vacation just now.
   Heavens, I never expected to be taken so seriously.

17. Use a comma to set off a phrase denoting residence or position but not before ZIP Codes.

   Alexander Vanderpoll, a resident of Larchmont, N.Y., addressed the meeting.
   Address the letter to Mr. Alexander Vanderpoll, President of the Dandy Popcorn Company, 5 Cliff Way, Larchmont, NY 10538.

18. Use a comma in dates.

   The University of Southern North Dakota was founded at Hoople on April 1, 1958.

   A comma may be used to separate the month from the year when the date is omitted; as, *June, 1982;* current usage, however, permits *June 1982.*

   Record temperatures were set in June 1982 in New York.

19. Use a comma to set off figures in groups of more than four digits; as, 1,000,000. (*See* p. 112.)

20. Use a comma to separate two figures or words indicating figures in order to make their meaning clear.

   On November 14, 379 stocks closed at the highest for the year.
   Instead of thousands, millions were spent.

21. If such introductory words as *as, for example, for instance, namely, viz., that is* and the terms following form parenthetical expressions

and do not introduce enumerations, a comma precedes and follows the introductory word. (*See* pp. 80–83 for use of semicolon and pp. 83–85 for use of colon.)

Many smaller universities, for example, Pace and Sacred Heart, have instituted courses in business administration.

You know that our November holiday, that is, Thanksgiving, was a New England institution.

Perhaps the most important factor of all is the psychological one, namely, the glamour of aviation, for the Armed Forces never lack for volunteers in this branch.

The use of the comma after *e.g.* (*exempli gratia*, for example) and *i.e.* (*id est*, that is) is optional. The present tendency is to omit the comma.

22. The use of the comma after phrases and clauses at the beginning of a sentence is not an arbitrary requirement.

(1) Use a comma after a long introductory prepositional phrase out of its natural order or when punctuation is needed for clearness.

In regard to the cost of remodeling your home, it is likely to be more economical than buying another house at present interest rates.

Besides having to buy a car, he needed to find a place to live.

For the billing department, new procedures were to be implemented as quickly as possible.

But usually short introductory prepositional phrases need not be followed by a comma, except when they are distinctly parenthetical; as, *for example, in fact, on the other hand.*

In recent months many changes have taken place in the city.

During the last twenty years the company's profits have tripled.

On Saturday the offices are closed.

(2) Use a comma after introductory participial and absolute phrases.

The matter being decided, the President continued his report.

Realizing the need for more storage room, we built a new wing.

Generally speaking, her successes go unnoticed.

All things considered, the decision was just.

(3) Use commas to set off nonrestrictive participial phrases. A nonrestrictive participial phrase adds an additional thought and might be omitted without interfering with the meaning.

The letter from the Brooks Company, just received by Collins, clarifies
the problem.
The stock, having reached 175, remained there for three weeks.

(4) Do not use a comma to set off restrictive participial phrases.
A restrictive participial phrase is essential to the meaning of the
sentence.

All persons known to have seen the accident will be questioned.

(5) Use commas to set off descriptive phrases following the noun
they modify.

The child, pale with fatigue, waited for her mother.

23. When a dependent adverbial clause precedes a main clause, a
comma is generally used.

While the general trend has been upward, decreases in the tax rates are
not unknown.
Before the sale is advertised, we must take an inventory of our present
stock.

But a short introductory adverbial clause may need no comma after
it if there is no uncertainty where the main clause begins; this is
likely to be the case when the subject of both clauses is the same.

If we go back in American history we find this country has never kept
silence as to what it stands for.
Before I began to write novels I had forgotten all I learned at school and
college.

Note that when the dependent clause follows the main clause, the
comma is usually omitted, except when the clause is plainly nonrestrictive, that is, adds a reason or concession introduced by *because, since, as, though.*

She was always at hand when there was difficult work to do.
He saw that some causes of international jealousy and of war would be
removed if the grosser forms of exploitation of labor and the more
distressing kinds of competition in this field . . . were eliminated.
Loyalty is one of the cardinal virtues of a secretary, because of the confidential nature of the position.

24. Use a comma between the parts of a short compound sentence
when punctuation is needed for clearness or to give an additional
idea. (*See* p. 80–83 for use of semicolon.)

We have been planning this expansion for years, and I am glad the time has come to make a start.

But: Do not use commas to separate the members of a compound sentence when the clauses are short and closely related.

Fill in the enclosed blank and mail it today.

Distinguish between a compound sentence (two or more independent clauses) and a simple sentence with a compound predicate (two or more verbs with the same subject). Do not use a comma between the verbs of a compound predicate.

She joined the firm as an accountant and in time became manager.
They changed their plans and set up a dummy corporation.

25. Use a comma to separate similar or identical words standing next to each other, even when the sense or continuity does not seem to require it.

Whatever is, is right.   Whenever you go, go quickly.

26. Use a comma to set off a nonrestrictive adjective clause. Such a clause is one that is not needed to make the meaning clear.

Engraved stationery, which conveys the impression of dignity and reliability, adds to the attractiveness of correspondence.
Dr. Paula Grossman, who is regarded as one of the leading theorists in the study of anorexia, will address the meeting.

27. Do not use a comma to set off a restrictive adjective clause. Such a clause is one that is needed to make the meaning clear.

Many of the sales are made to people who are footloose or retired and who see in the mobile home a means of dispensing with the problems of ordinary home ownership.
Anyone who has not learned to appreciate classical music is unfortunate.

Present usage generally favors *which* when the relative clause conveys a qualification or statement simply additional or parenthetic, and *that* when it is definitely restrictive.

Our advertisements, *which* we strive to make truthful and convincing, have increased our business enormously this year.
We keep books *that* are valuable in locked cases.
All material *that* is on sale has been reduced in price.

28. Use a comma to set off informal direct quotations.

"Wherever I am needed," declared the volunteer, "there I will gladly go."

The doctor remarked, "I haven't seen many cases like yours as yet this season."

"Let us reason together," I urged.

Note that no comma is needed in an indirect quotation.

The supervisor told us all that chronic absenteeism would not be tolerated.

We asked what the price for the larger refrigerator would be during Saturday's sale.

Experience has shown how best to manage exit interviews.

29. Use a comma to set off words, phrases, and clauses that would otherwise be unclear.

Wrong: This ticket is good for dinner or bed and breakfast.
Right: This ticket is good for dinner, or bed and breakfast.
Wrong: When I was about to begin the speech ended.
Right: When I was about to begin, the speech ended.

30. For use of the comma with parentheses, *see* pp. 96–97.

31. Omit the comma before the ZIP Code in an address on an envelope; place the number two spaces after the two-letter state abbreviation.

The Semicolon

While the comma is frequently used in place of the semicolon in business letters, newspapers, and magazines, the semicolon has a place in modern writing. The following are the generally accepted rules for the use of the semicolon.

1. Use a semicolon between the clauses of a compound sentence when the conjunction is omitted or when the connection is not close.

The Working Girl, long harassed and patronized, has earned her way to linguistic equality; a sign of the changing times is that it is not possible to say that Heaven protects the Career Woman.

WILLIAM SAFIRE, *On Language*

The statistical evidence is there; it cannot be denied.

I had no flair for politics as an art form; my interest was solely in the content of the candidate's message.

GEORGE BALL

2. Use a semicolon to separate coordinate clauses when they are long or when they contain commas.

> The good modern letterwriter does not employ hackneyed expressions, for they make letters sound boring, lacking in individuality; they deprive letters of personal flavor; they clog the message, blur the meaning, confuse the construction.

> We are not happy simply being useful; we want to identify with something, and thus we have courses on creative writing, creative advertising, and creative salesmanship.
>
> J. S. Bruner

3. Use the semicolon in lists of names with titles or addresses and in other lists that would not be clear if separated by commas.

> Other speakers on the program were L. R. Alderman, Specialist in Adult Education in the U.S. Bureau of Education; Ms. Willie Lawson, Deputy State Superintendent of Public Schools, Little Rock, Arkansas; and Reed Lewis, Director of Foreign Language Information Service, New York City.

> Officers elected for the coming year are as follows: president, Jane Thomas; secretary, Raymond Colt; treasurer, Kenneth Graham.

> The survey was made in Hartford, Torrington, and Winsted in Connecticut; and in Springfield, Worcester, and Boston in Massachusetts.

> Invitations to the dedication should be sent to Mrs. Burton Allen, 11 Lake Road, Newton Centre, Massachusetts; Ms. Helen Wollaston, 26 Adelaide Avenue, Barrington, Rhode Island; and Dr. Luke Randall, Pleasant Valley, Connecticut.

> Horton's experience, according to his letter, has been two years as salesman for Bradford & Crane, Orlando, Florida; four years as sales manager for The Norton Company, Kansas City, Missouri; and five years as buyer for Hall Brothers, Richmond, Virginia.

Where there would be no confusion, the comma may be used instead of the semicolon.

> Regional offices are located in New York, New York, Chicago, Illinois, and Dallas, Texas.

In lists of books with specific references to volume number, chapter number, pages, and so forth (often given in footnotes to speeches, reports, or articles), each complete item should be separated by a semicolon.

Political Conditions in the South in 1868: Dunning, *Reconstruction, Political and Economic* (American Nation Series), pp. 109–123; Hart, *American History Told by Contemporaries*, Vol. IV, pp. 445–458, 497–500; Elson, *History of the United States*, pp. 790–805.

Psalms 23:1–4; 37:2–5; 91:1–10.

4. Use a semicolon to separate groups of words, whether phrases or clauses, dependent on a general term or statement.

He declared that physical exercise has many benefits: it strengthens the muscles of the legs; it increases the flow of blood throughout the body; it improves the appetite; and it helps to prevent osteoporosis.

We hold these truths to be self-evident—that all men are created equal; that they are endowed by their Creator with certain inalienable rights; that among these are life, liberty, and the pursuit of happiness.

THOMAS JEFFERSON

5. Use a semicolon to precede *for example, namely, for instance, viz., to wit, as, i.e.* when they introduce an enumeration of examples not felt to be parenthetical or when they precede a principal statement or a sentence. (*See* pp. 72–80 for use of comma, and pp. 83–85 for use of colon.)

The examinations will include practical demonstrations of professional skills in actual life situations; for example, a secretary in an actual office situation, a teacher in an actual classroom, and a nurse with an actual patient.

Before purchasing a condominium, a buyer should consider a number of aspects; namely, location, construction quality, and financing.

[A stampede of cattle] could not be foretold; anything might start it; for instance, the sudden bark of a coyote, a rumble of a summer storm, lightning, the rearing of a horse, or the scream of a panther could all set off a disastrous stampede.

HORAN and SANN, *Pictorial History of the Wild West*

6. Use a semicolon to separate clauses joined by such transitional words as *hence, moreover, however, also, therefore, consequently.* Follow these words by commas when they themselves should be emphasized.

The principles are almost universally accepted; hence you should learn them.

The speaker saw no objection to the suggestion; therefore, she accepted it.

7. Use a semicolon to separate lengthy statements following a colon.

Amos Rapoport in *House Form and Culture* supports this view when he carefully lists three categories of architecture: 1. primitive—built with few modifications by all people on a common model; 2. vernacular—divided into preindustrial, which is built by tradesmen on a model that comes from the people (folk art), and post-industrial, built by specialists, from a model for the people (mass-culture art); and 3. high-style—built by specialists (architects) for an elite cultural group.

ROBERT L. VICKERY, JR., *Sharing Architecture*

8. Place a semicolon outside quotation marks. (*See also* pp. 92–93.)

We called him "Lucky"; he preferred "Lawrence."
"Infer" means "conclude"; "imply" means "suggest."

9. Place a semicolon after the parentheses when the parenthetical matter explains something that precedes.

What we are actually discussing here is the Planned Unit Development (PUD as it is called within the development profession), which is a large assemblage of land, usually 100 acres or more, in which single-family houses are mixed with higher density apartments and are clustered around culs-de-sac.

ROBERT L. VICKERY, JR., *Sharing Architecture*

The Colon

1. Use a colon to introduce a list, or to introduce formally a statement, an enumeration, or an illustration.

By mid-1942 various modifications [of the Selective Service Act] were introduced: All males between eighteen and sixty-five were required to be registered; the lottery was discarded and registrants were called by order of date of birth; voluntary enlistments were severely restricted . . .

CALABRESI AND BOBBITT, *Tragic Choices*

Suggested accompaniments for sweet breads and rolls are:
1. Flavored sugars
2. Flavored butters
3. Glazes (frostings)

When such introductory expressions as *namely, for example, for instance* are omitted before a list, a colon is used.

There were three reasons for his failure: laziness, ill health, and lack of training.

When the enumeration is informal or closely connected with the verb, the colon should be omitted.

Children need food, shelter, love, and education.
The early settlers were forced to clear land, plant crops, fish, and hunt game in order to survive.

2. Use a colon to introduce a formal or long quotation.

The director gave the requirements for residence:
Each resident must be able to care for herself or himself.
The cost of two meals per day and maid service every other week is included in the rent.
Rent is payable on the first day of the month.
Each resident must have a relative or other responsible person who will be called upon to make important decisions in the event the resident is unable to do so.

3. Use a colon after a formal salutation in a letter.

Dear Sir: Gentlemen: Dear Madam:

4. A colon is sometimes used instead of a comma after the place of publication in bibliographical matter.

Stassinopoulos, Arianna. *Maria Callas: The Woman Behind the Legend.* New York: Simon and Schuster, 1981.

5. A colon is often used in the title of a magazine article or book, as in the previous example.

Jazz Lives: Portraits in Words and Pictures

6. Use a colon preceding a restatement of an idea.

The sentence was poorly constructed: it lacked both unity and coherence.

7. A colon is often used to precede an extended explanation.

True democracy presupposes two conditions: first, that the vast majority of the people have a genuine opinion upon public affairs; secondly, that electors will use their power as a public benefit.

ANDRÉ SIEGFRIED

8. Capitalize the first word following a colon when it introduces an independent passage or sentence. Do not capitalize the first word following a colon when it introduces an explanatory element or one logically dependent on what precedes.

The director gave these instructions: "Arrive on time, come regularly, telephone if you are too ill to come in, and take only one hour for lunch."

[Sourdough breads] rightly belong to the Far West: the old-time mountain men, sheepherders, prospectors, and miners.

DOLORES CASELLA, A World of Breads

9. A colon may be placed between figures denoting hours and minutes; as, 2:30. (*See* pp. 71 and 114.)

10. When a colon follows an abbreviation of two words (such as *i.e.* or *A.M.*), do not place a period after the abbreviation.

Our morning routine may vary, i.e: some days we hike two miles before breakfast, and other days we work out at the gym after we leave the office.

We expect delivery of the merchandise by 5 P.M: no later, earlier if possible.

The Question Mark

1. Use a question mark at the end of a direct question.

One must always ask, Does this open space lead to a school or playground? To shopping or to community activity?

ROBERT L. VICKERY, JR., Sharing Architecture

"Where can one find someone with the qualifications we need on our board?" asked the chairman.

An indirect question is followed by a period.

The chairman asked where one could find someone with the qualifications we need on our board.

A request is usually followed by a period, rather than by a question mark. (*See* p. 69.)

May I ask you to come early on Friday morning.
Would you mind letting me know whether or not he is still with the company.
Will you please look into this matter and let us have your comments.

2. When an emphatic question occurs within a sentence and is not a direct quotation, use a question mark.

Will advertising to such an extent pay? is a question.
But the real question is: How can our community afford to permit maintenance of school buildings to be delayed or overlooked?

When the question is not emphatic, a comma is generally used instead of a question mark.

How can such heavy expenditures be met, is a question that the administration must consider.
Her main test for a salesman is, Will he create goodwill for the company, What kind of impression will he make?

3. Use a question mark after a quoted question at the end of a sentence.

The subject he will discuss is "How can credit be controlled?"

4. Use a question mark to indicate the end of a parenthetical question.

They wanted to know (would you believe it?) if the plane went nonstop from San Francisco to Honolulu.
The employees were pleased (who would not have been?) to be given an extra day off each month when the plant's quota had been filled.

5. A question mark in parentheses is sometimes used to indicate doubt or irony.

The present City Hall dates from 1758 (?).
The high point (?) of the evening came when the door prizes were awarded.
He provided documentation (?) of an earlier discovery by Norsemen.

6. Place the question mark inside the quotation marks when it belongs to the quoted matter.

The treasurer asked, "What will be the departmental budget for travel next year?"

But place the question mark outside the quotation marks when it is not a part of the quoted matter.

Do you agree to "Out of sight, out of mind"?
Who was it that said, "It ain't over till it's over"?

7. Use a question mark to express more than one question in the same sentence.

To judge a story or a motion picture, ask yourself the following questions: Is it realistic? romantic? whimsical? possible but not probable? Does the action get off to a fast start? How is suspense maintained?

The Exclamation Point

1. Use an exclamation point to mark an exclamatory word, phrase, or sentence.

    "The very thought of such a catastrophe is appalling!" declared the manager.
    Where in the world have you been! Just look at your clothes!
    What a magnificent achievement!

2. If the whole sentence is exclamatory in form, place an exclamation point at the end.

    How complicated these registration forms are!

3. Use an exclamation point at the end of sentences that are interrogatory in form but exclamatory in meaning.

    Is this the best that you can do after years of lessons!
    Now, I ask you, is that fair!
    Wouldn't you think he could hang up his own coat!

4. When an exclamation is not emphatic, place a comma instead of an exclamation point after it.

    "So this is all you have to offer, is it," said Joe, "and I'm expected to make the best of it."

5. Use an exclamation point to express irony, surprise, and dissension.

    Imagine a city without garbage!
    The doctor said my anxiety about being left alone is really a childish fear!

6. An exclamation point is used after a command.

    Ready, set, *go!*
    This is what I want done, and *now!*
    Call the fire department!

The Apostrophe

1. To form the possessive singular of nouns, add an apostrophe and *s*: the *woman's* child, the *secretary's* report, the *professor's* book, the *witness's* testimony.

2. To form the possessive singular of compound nouns, add an apostrophe and *s* at the end of the word: his *daughter-in-law's* manners, the *vice-consul's* arrival, a *letter carrier's* appointment.

3. To form the possessive singular of expressions used as compound nouns, add an apostrophe and *s* to the last word of an expression: *Charles the First's* failure, *Peter Miller Jr.'s* education, the *Duke of York's* palace.

4. To denote the possessive when a phrase is regarded as a compound noun and means a person or persons, the apostrophe and *s* are added to the last word of the phrase: the *University of Chicago's* second revolution in education, the *Bank of the Republic's* gold reserve.

5. To form the possessive plural of nouns, add an apostrophe if the plural ends in *s:* the *girls'* coats, *bankers'* hours.

6. If the plural does not end in *s*, add an apostrophe and *s: children's* games, *women's* clubs.

7. To form the possessive plural of compound nouns, add an apostrophe and *s* at the end of the word: his *sons-in-law's* taxes.

8. In expressions like *someone else, everyone else, nobody else,* and *no one else,* add an apostrophe and *s* to *else: someone else's* car, *everyone else's* wishes, *no one else's* business, *nobody else's* responsibility.

9. To form the possessive of two or more words in a series connected by conjunctions and denoting joint possession, use the apostrophe and *s* after the last noun only: *Lord & Taylor's, Park and Tilford's.*

10. When joint possession is not denoted, use the apostrophe and *s* after each noun: *Macy's and Gimbel's, Altman's and Bonwit Teller's, Wordsworth's and Shelley's* poetry, *Kennedy's and Reagan's* policies, *ladies' and children's* apparel.

11. In proper nouns ending in *s*, add an apostrophe and *s* to indicate the possessive: *Adams's* chronicle, *Dawes's* bank, *Cross's* theory, *Ayres's* references, *Ellis's* psychology, Sinclair *Lewis's* last novel, *Watkins's* lectures, Lily *Pons's* song recital, *Keats's* poems, *Dickens's* stories, *Brooks's* composition, Mrs. *Gates's* estate, *Wells's History of the World, Schultz's* case.

    (1) Some authorities prefer to add only the apostrophe to nouns ending in *s* or an *s* sound; as, *Jones', princess'.*

    (2) Notice the omission of apostrophes in some titles: *Teachers* College, *Governors* Island, *Citizens* Bank, American *Bankers* As-

sociation, *Veterans* Administration. But many organizations follow the general rule: The *Actors'* Dinner Club, Southern *Women's* Educational Alliance.

12. The object of an action should be expressed by an *of*-phrase rather than by the possessive case: the assassination *of President Kennedy*, the retirement *of the Blakes.*

13. Note that the possessive case and the *of*-phrase may sometimes be used interchangeably, the choice often depending upon the sound of the expression in the sentence: the *secretary's* work or the work *of the secretary, Roosevelt's* Administration or the Administration *of Roosevelt.* The possessive, however, does not always mean the same as the objective with the *of*-phrase. Compare *Mary's* picture, a picture *of Mary.*

14. In certain idiomatic expressions both the apostrophe and *s* and the *of*-phrase (sometimes called the double possessive) are used: This is a favorite pen *of John's;* I have examined that report *of the bookkeeper's.*

15. To denote the possessive of inanimate objects, an *of*-phrase is used instead of the possessive form: the success *of that store*, the routine *of the office*, the chapters *of the book*, the thunder *of the surf.*

    (1) When an inanimate object is personified, the apostrophe and *s* may be used: *Death's* approaching stride, *Love's* old sweet song.

    (2) Certain idiomatic expressions referring particularly to time are written with the apostrophe and *s*: *a day's vacation, a day's work, a day's journey, a week's work, a month's notice, four months' wages, a year's interest, three years' salary,* but *a two-year lease.* Notice also *a stone's throw, my heart's desire, the world's work, a dollar's worth, ten dollars' worth, thirty days' grace, the week's development.*

16. The *'s* may be added to figures, signs, symbols, and letters of the alphabet to form the plural. There is, however, a growing tendency to omit the apostrophe in such cases when there is no possibility of mistaking the meaning: *ABC's* or *ABCs, YMCA's* or *YMCAs.*

    Your *a's* look very much like your *o's.*

    In our great-grandmothers' day the three *Rs* (or *R's*) formed the basis of education.

    In the *1900s* (or *1900's*) technology spread through every aspect of human life, from transportation and cooking to *in vitro* fertilization.

17. Do not use an apostrophe to denote the omission of a letter or letters in an abbreviation.

Agcy.	chg.	pkg.	Supt.
Dept.	Comdt.	shpt.	Wm.
Chas.	pfd.	sgd.	mdse.

18. Sometimes the apostrophe is used in place of the first two figures for the year: the Class of '85, late in '79.

19. A noun modifying a gerund is usually in the possessive case.

I had not heard of *John's* leaving.
Perlman's playing of the *Kreutzer* Sonata delighted his audience.

20. For the use of the apostrophe in words referred to as nouns, *see* p. 14.

Quotation Marks

1. Use double quotation marks to enclose a direct quotation.

"The force of a sentence may be measured to a great extent by the vigor of its verb," says Morton S. Freeman in *The Grammatical Lawyer*. "Verbs ignite the sparks that give life and movement to the sentence. And the power they generate far exceeds that of the most carefully selected noun or adjective."

"For the life of me, I can't understand why you want to learn to play the drums," declared her mother.

Do not use quotation marks to set off indirect questions.

Wrong: He remarked "that he was tired."
Right: He remarked that he was tired.
Right: He remarked, "I am tired."

Do not capitalize the first word of a quotation introduced indirectly in the text.

All my broker will say is that "it's just too early to spot a trend."

The Russian leader also cited what he called "the policy of boycotts, embargoes, 'punishments' and broken trade contracts that has become a habit with the United States."

Time

2. When two or more paragraphs are quoted, quotation marks should be placed at the beginning of each paragraph, but only at the end of the last.

"It is summer of the year I have spent at home in Oslo.

"I am sitting on a bench outside my house, eating homemade waffles and jam, forgetting that I want to lose weight. The heat is buzzing in my head.

"In Los Angeles no one would understand what it is like to have a feast of waffles in the sun after a long, dark winter. Life there is so remote from this."

LIV ULLMANN, *Changing*

Modern usage omits quotation marks around single extracts quoted in smaller type or placed in paragraphs indented on the left. Double spacing above and below the excerpt should be allowed to set it off from the rest of the text.

Robin Winks writes in *An American's Guide to Britain:*

One of the most common symbols on a highway map of Britain (and especially of England) is a tiny red mark that appears to have been lifted from the chess set; it indicates one of the several hundred castles, mostly in ruins, which dot the countryside. There may be other countries in which crenellated towers thrust from the landscape as often, but there can be no others in which so wide a variety of castle architecture is compressed in so small a space.

3. Use single quotation marks to enclose a quotation within a quotation. When it is necessary to use quotation marks within these, use double marks again.

We received the following instruction: "Proceed cautiously until you hear 'All clear' from the guard."

"When you learn to 'ankle' efficiently," said the cyclist, "you can ride for hours without tiring. 'Ankling' simply means efficient pedaling."

4. Use quotation marks or italics to set off from the context any quoted or emphasized word or short phrase.

With a "now-or-never" expression on his face, Bill marched into the manager's office.

One witness said the explosion lit up the predawn sky "like a doggone sunset."

The reporter asks "Who," "What," "Where," and "When." The interviewer also asks "Why."

5. Use quotation marks to enclose text following such terms as *entitled, the word, marked, designated, referred to as.*

Following the word "can," insert "not."
All items marked "out" should be deleted.

But: Omit quotation marks after *so-called, known as,* and *called.*

Your so-called vacation home is actually rental property.
His son John, also known as Jack, is quite a golfer.

6. Quotation marks sometimes indicate the ironical use of words.

Women may not have won equal rights yet, but they have "won" equal responsibilities.

ELLEN GOODMAN, *At Large*

Everyone in the dormitory "borrowed" my soap until it was all used up.

7. Quotation marks are used to enclose the titles of articles, poems, stories, speeches, and parts of whole printed works. The titles of periodicals, books, plays, operas, motion pictures, radio and television series, and other complete works are italicized.

"Ruth Waltuch Jonas Opens Office in Norwalk"
"Major Art Show in Washington"
"Fighting to Cure the 'Incurable' "
The Nobel Prize Treasury includes works by many famous authors.
Dallas is seen weekly by millions of television fans.
A Prairie Home Companion originates in Minneapolis.
His first story appeared in *The New Yorker.*

Too many quotation marks on a page are unattractive. The titles of lectures, sermons, and the like on programs may be set in italic, small caps, or roman.

8. Following are rules for using quotation marks with other marks of punctuation.

With the comma and the period, place quotation marks outside:

"We shall always remember you," said the speaker, "as a dedicated leader, a cheerful giver, and a hopeless tennis player."

With the semicolon and the colon, quotation marks are placed inside:

The evidence looked, as Representative ——— would declare when it became public, "like a smoking gun"; it tied the President directly to a criminal obstruction of justice.

The New York Times

He gave up acting in westerns after many years of "tall in the saddle": he felt he had earned a change of scene.

With the exclamation point and the question mark, the quotation marks are placed outside when the quoted matter is an exclamation or a question:

"Look, Mommy, I'm flying!" cried the little boy.
"Can't you understand what I am saying?" she asked.

But: When the exclamation or question is not included, place the quotation marks inside:

Didn't you mean to say "deprecate" rather than "depreciate"?
I doubt that any mayor likes to be referred to in print as "hizzoner"!

With the dash, quotation marks are placed inside or outside the dash, depending on the context.

Suddenly—"Fire in the engine room!"—sounded through the dark.
She answered, "I suppose so, but—"

9. Use quotation marks around an unfamiliar word for the first use only.

A "bight" is formed by turning the rope end so that the end and the standing part (the rest of the rope) lie alongside each other. A square knot consists of two interwoven bights.

Fieldbook for Boys and Men (Boy Scouts of America)

10. Quotation marks should be omitted with such statements as:

I am writing to say thank you for all you have done.
We wish you all the best in the days ahead.

The Dash

1. Use a dash to indicate an abrupt change in a sentence.

We see words that blow like leaves in the winds of autumn—golden words, bronze words, words that catch the light like opals.

JAMES J. KILPATRICK, *The Writer's Art*

2. Sometimes a dash is used to set off interpolated explanatory matter.

> There are many differences—aside from the physical ones—between men and women.

> All through history young women have been to culture rather what wind is to thistledown—great carriers of it to new places.
>
> JOHN FOWLES, *The Enigma of Stonehenge*

3. Use a dash to indicate a sudden break in a sentence. (When a sentence ends in a dash, no period is needed.)

> "Let me know if you ever need—" She broke off in tears.
> I wouldn't—I couldn't permit you to say such a thing without a word of protest from me.

4. A dash may be used to set off a long phrase in apposition, particularly when the phrase is punctuated with commas.

> The male rampant—killing animals for food and clothing, digging out caves, and putting up huts, driving off enemies—early came to be associated in the mind of the elemental female with warmth, well-being, safety, and the kindred creature comforts.
>
> JAMES THURBER, "Listen to This, Dear"

> We also increase value by providing more options—a wider range of choice.

5. A pair of dashes may be used instead of parentheses.

> All branches of the family produced their individual eccentrics—there was even an uncle who believed in the Single Tax—but they were united in their solid understanding of the value of money as the basis of a firm stance in this world.
>
> KATHARINE ANNE PORTER, "Gertrude Stein: A Self-Portrait"

> It is obvious that practitioners of opera—especially in our age when the trend toward cultivation of the languages in which operas were originally written is strong—must know other languages in addition to their own mother tongue.
>
> ERICH LEINSDORF, *The Composer's Advocate*

6. Use a dash instead of the word *to* in reference to dates, pages, paragraphs, verses, and cantos.

1910–1940	Genesis 2:10–14
pages 10–49	verses 5–10
paragraphs 1–14	Cantos I–IV

7. Use a series of dashes under names in a catalogue to indicate repetition.

> Crow, John A. *Italy: A Journey Through Time.*
> ————. *Mexico Today.*
> ————. *Spain: The Root and the Flower.*

But note that the dash for this purpose must never be used at the top of a page.

Parentheses

1. Use parentheses to set off parenthetical matter not necessary to the grammatical structure of the sentence but too important to omit. (Shorter expressions of this kind may be set off by commas or dashes.)

> People who are constantly expecting disaster (and I count myself among them) can always produce examples of such events to prove their point.

> The due date of the monthly payment (once the loan has been approved) can be the day most convenient for you.

> [Evelyn Waugh] too took great quantities of Latin (and Greek as well), and recalled in his autobiography that he forgot all of it as he grew older.
> JAMES J. KILPATRICK, *The Writer's Art*

2. Parentheses may be used to enclose figures or letters marking the divisions of a subject.

> The search for a new executive director involved:
> (a) Placing advertisements in professional journals and newspapers in the area
> (b) Evaluating the résumés received and choosing the ten most promising for interviews
> (c) Interviewing the ten finalists

> We set our priorities as follows:
> (1) To raise funds to meet our present budget
> (2) To provide an endowment for future funding
> (3) To seek a larger building for the agency

Parentheses are omitted when using Roman numerals.

3. Use parentheses to enclose explanations inserted in the text.

The Oyster Festival (a recently established event) has become a popular celebration in Norwalk.

The figure of a knight in armor (see plate 4) shows the style worn by King Richard I.

Use spring water only. (Chlorinated water will darken the color in the final stages.)

4. In legal documents or whenever double form is required, use parentheses to enclose a figure inserted to confirm a statement given in words: thirty (30) days; sixty (60) dollars, *not* sixty dollars (60); twenty dollars ($20), *not* twenty ($20) dollars.

5. The use of parentheses with other marks of punctuation requires careful consideration. No additional punctuation is needed with parentheses unless it is needed to clarify the meaning of the sentence.

With the period outside:

Among those mentioned in the article on pianists was Willie "The Lion" Smith (1897–1973).

Take the blue-blazed trail down a moderately steep slope to the inlet of Riga Lake (3.5 miles).

With the period inside:

The value of the stolen jewelry was not mentioned. (It later developed that the jewelry had not been appraised for many years.)

If copy reads 3½ million dollars, change to read $3.5 million. (To be used only in amounts of a million or more.)

With the question mark and the exclamation point:

Mr. McLean (or was it Mr. McLune?) asked to be remembered to you.

Walking is a highly recommended exercise (and I don't mean strolling!).

Thomas Jefferson sold his library of 6,000 volumes for $23,950 (less than half its auction value)!

Note: The exclamation point or question mark, enclosed in parentheses, is sometimes used to express irony or sarcasm.

The effect of his oration (?) was to induce sleep in his audience rather than to arouse us to action.

A recent graduate of a leading college wrote that he was *elegeble* (!) and interested in obtaining a *franchize* (!).

Do not use a comma, semicolon, or colon in front of an opening parenthesis.

Right: He lives in Minot (N.D.) and attends college in Chicago.
Wrong: He lives in Minot, (N.D.) and attends college in Chicago.
Right: This case (124 U.S. 329) is not relevant.
Wrong: This case, (124 U.S. 329) is not relevant.

Do not place a comma, semicolon, or colon after the closing parenthesis unless such punctuation would be needed if there were no parentheses.

When we arrived, we found a young man (presumably the fiancé) talking to Jenny's mother.

Interviews will be held next week for freshmen (Tues., 10–12 A.M.); sophomores (Wed., 2–4 P.M.); juniors (Thurs., 10–12 A.M.); and seniors (Thurs., 2–4 P.M.).

Brackets

1. Use brackets to enclose words and phrases independent of the sentence, such as explanatory notes, omissions, and comments that are not written by the author of the text.

The following year [1620] the Pilgrims landed at Plymouth.

[Marshall] still retains that vigor of intellect which has for so many years rendered him the ornament of the bench.
HUGH GRIGSBY, quoted in John Marshall by LEONARD BAKER

2. Use brackets to enclose *sic* following an error in spelling or usage in copied matter.

The Rosevelt [*sic*] family contributed two presidents.
Be sure to buy Hawaiin [*sic*] pineapples.

3. No punctuation is used with brackets unless required by the matter bracketed and the sense of the rest of the sentence.

Between human beings [Galbraith wrote] there is a type of intercourse which proceeds not from knowledge, or even from lack of knowledge, but from failure to know what isn't known.
JOHN KENNETH GALBRAITH, The Great Crash 1929

No punctuation is used before or after bracketed matter inserted in a quotation.

Ellipses

Ellipsis is the term for omission of words or paragraphs from a quotation. It is indicated by the use of periods. Within a sentence, the dots follow any punctuation in the quotation. A space is left before each dot and also after the last if a word follows.

Cézanne's world is still to the point of being timeless. The landscapes, while they often give a vivid sense of reality, are rarely seen at a particular time of day or in particular light conditions, . . . but rather in a situation as permanent as if they had been represented by a sense of touch rather than by sight.

JAMES S. ACKERMAN, *Brief Lives*

There are other countries, as well as Greece as it now is, where it is possible to learn important elements of the ancient world. . . . One can study the permutations of Greek architecture all over Europe, and see the most thrilling Greek museum material all over America. But the country itself, with its special climate, its own sea, its unique limestone and marble geography, and above all its language and its ruins, still has something special to say, something genuine, something not said elsewhere.

PETER LEVI in *The Greek World* by Eliot Porter

When a paragraph or more of text is omitted within a quotation, a line of spaced periods is used to indicate the ellipsis. The periods are spaced apart; three, five, or seven are used, depending on the width of the page.

Hyphenation and Compounds

The Hyphen: General Uses

A hyphen is used to indicate the following:

(1) Words compounded of two or more words to represent a single idea.

(2) The division of a word into syllables.

(3) The division of a word at the end of a line.

Since usage varies, it is impossible to make inflexible rules for hyphenating phrases. Two or more words that represent a single idea may stand as separate words or become hyphenated or be written as one word. The usual sequence is for the words to be written separate at first, then to become hyphenated, and finally to be written solid. The overall rule is to avoid ambiguity.

When there is doubt whether a phrase should be written solid, as two words, or hyphenated, it is advisable to consult an authoritative source, such as an up-to-date dictionary.

The following rules may be regarded as a guide to current practice.

1. Use a hyphen as follows between units forming a compound adjective before the noun modified:

first-class bond	one-man job
deep-blue color	up-to-date fashion
four-year-old girl	high-minded attitude
house-to-house search	hard-hitting policy
one- and two-story houses	teacher-pupil relationship
a medium-sized commercial	Three-State Bus Line
town	long-distance telephone

Note that the hyphen should be inserted after a series of hyphenated adjectives modifying the same noun when the noun occurs after the last adjective only: *four-, five-, and six-story buildings; 7- to 10-day trips; 29-year-old bird.*

2. When a compound adjective follows the noun or the predicate, ordinarily it is not hyphenated.

    Her fame, well deserved and worldwide, rests on her scientific achievements.

3. An adverb ending in *ly* is not joined with a hyphen to the adjective that it qualifies; as, a *highly* developed intelligence, a *fully* balanced ration, a *beautifully* told story.

4. Surnames written with a hyphen are in most cases considered as one name; as, Harley *Granville-Barker,* Sheila *Kaye-Smith,* and Madame *Schumann-Heink.*

5. Proper names used adjectively are not joined by a hyphen; as, *New England* winters, *Fifth Avenue* shoppers, *South American* Indians.

    But notice such forms as *German-American, Anglo-Indian, Indo-European,* which are purely adjective in nature and always hyphenated.

6. Use a hyphen in compound numerals; as, *forty-six, twenty-one* hundredths, *twenty-first.*

7. Use a hyphen when compounding numerals with other words; as, *five-o'clock* tea, *twenty-foot* pole, *150-yard* dash.

8. Fractions are hyphenated when the word is used as an adjective; as, They are entitled to *ten and one-half* shares of stock. When the fraction is used as a noun no hyphen is necessary; as, He invested *one third* of his money in real estate. But there is a growing tendency in business writing to use the hyphen in both the adjective and the noun.

9. Use a hyphen in certain compounds made up of nouns and prepositional phrases.

sons-in-law   hand-to-hand   fleur-de-lis
man-of-war   vis-à-vis

However, there are many exceptions to this rule: *commander in chief, editor in chief, maître d'hôtel,* and many others.

10. Use a hyphen in titles compounded with *ex* and *elect.*

ex-Governor   Governor-elect
ex-Senator   President-elect
ex-President

11. Civil and military titles (single) are not hyphenated.

GPO Style Manual

Civil Titles

Ambassador at Large
Ambassador Extraordinary and
  Plenipotentiary
Assistant Secretary
Associate Justice
Attorney at Law
Attorney General
Chargé d'Affaires
Chief Clerk
Chief Executive
Chief Justice
Chief Magistrate
Chief of Police
Chief of Protocol
Congressman at Large
Consul General
Counselor of Embassy
Deputy Commissioner
Director General

Editor in Chief
Envoy Extraordinary and
  Minister Plenipotentiary
First Secretary
Second Secretary
Third Secretary
Governor General
Lieutenant Governor
Military Attaché
Naval Attaché
Postmaster General
Public Printer
Secretary of Labor
Secretary General of the
  United Nations
Sergeant at Arms
Under Secretary
Vice Consul
Vice President

Words denoting the office itself are hyphenated; as, *under-secretaryship, vice-presidency*.

Military and Naval Titles

Adjutant General	Lieutenant General
Brigadier General	Major General
Brigadier General	Quartermaster General
Commandant	Rear Admiral
Commander in Chief	Surgeon General
Lieutenant Colonel	Vice Admiral
Lieutenant Commander	

In British usage the following titles are hyphenated:

Field-Marshal	Major-General
Lieutenant-Colonel	Rear-Admiral
Lieutenant-Commander	Vice-Admiral
Lieutenant-General	

12. Use the hyphen in compounds made up of prefixes joined to proper names.

anti-American	pseudo-Gothic
mid-Atlantic	un-American
mid-August	anti-Suffragist
neo-Platonism	non-European
pan-Hellenic	Pan-American

For capitalizing words in titles and headings that form parts of hyphenated compounds, *see* pp. 67–68.

13. Do not ordinarily use the hyphen between a prefix and the stem when the added word is not a proper noun.

antisocial	intramural
biannual	nonconformist
bicentennial	nonessential
biennial	nonofficial
coauthor	preview
extracurricular	retroactive
foreclose	semiyearly
intercollegiate	supermarket

Compounds are hyphenated when otherwise a vowel would be confusingly doubled in combination: *anti-imperialist, co-owner, intra-atomic, semi-independent*.

Exceptions: *Cooperate* and *coordinate* and their derivatives are usually written thus as solid forms, because of their great frequency and familiarity.

14. Use the hyphen in the following examples to distinguish words spelled alike but differing in meaning:

re-cover, to cover again	re-count, to count again
recover, to regain	recount, to relate in detail

15. Use the hyphen to form adjectives compounded with *well* preceding the noun; as, *well-bred, well-born, well-to-do, well-earned, well-expressed, well-known.*

    His *well-known* courtesy made him a favorite.

    Do not use the hyphen with such expressions when they follow the word modified.

    She showed herself a woman *well versed* in the ways of the world.

16. Use the hyphen generally in words compounded with *self* as a prefix; as, *self-conceit, self-confidence, self-control, self-reliance, self-respect, self-starter, self-assured, self-explaining, self-governing, self-made, self-taught, self-willed.*

    Do not use the hyphen in *selfsame* and *selfless* or in pronouns compounded with *self*; as, *myself, himself, herself, itself, oneself, ourselves, themselves.*

17. Foreign phrases used adjectively should not be hyphenated; as, an *a priori* argument, a *noblesse oblige* attitude, an *ex cathedra* pronouncement.

Guide to Compounding

In the following list, forms marked (G) are written in accordance with the *GPO Style Manual,* those marked (W) are in accordance with *Webster's Ninth New Collegiate Dictionary,* those not marked are in accordance with both books.

aforementioned	airbrake (G)
afterthought	air brake (W)
airbase (G)	airfield
air base (W)	airline

airmail
airplane
airport
all right
anybody
anyhow
any one (of them)
anyone (anybody)
anything
audiofrequency
audiovisual
bankbook
banknote (G)
bank note (W)
basketball
bas-relief
beforehand
billboard
birthrate
blood bank
blood count
blood poisoning
blood pressure
blood test
blood type
blood vessel
blueprint
boathouse
bodyguard
bombproof
bombshell
bondholder
bond paper
bookbinding
bookcase
book review
bookshop
boxcar
box office
box spring
briefcase
broadcaster
businesslike
businessman

bylaws
byline
byproduct (G)
by-product (W)
cardboard
carport
cash account
cashbook
cash register
chain letter
chainstore (G)
chain store (W)
checkbook
chinaware
choirboy
clapboard
classmate
classroom
clearinghouse
closeup (G)
close-up (W)
clubroom
coauthor
coeducation
coffee shop
committeeman
common sense (noun)
commonsense (adj.)
countdown
court-martial
courtroom
crosscurrent
cross-examination
cross-fertilize
cross-pollinate
cross-purpose
cross-reference
cross section
crossword
dateline
daybook
day letter
dining room
double entry

dry goods
east-northeast
en route
everybody
everywhere
ex officio
extracurricular
extra dividend
fairway
filmstrip
fireproof
first aid
flagstaff
foolproof
footnote
forthcoming
free trade
free will (noun)
galley proof
good will (kindness) (G)
goodwill (asset) (G)
goodwill (both) (W)
handwriting
headline
high frequency
horsepower
house organ
inasmuch
insofar
job lot
landowner
lawbreaker
layoff
letterhead
living room
loudspeaker
makeup
markdown (noun)
mark down (verb) (W)
midsummer
money order
moreover
network
nevertheless

newscaster
newsreel
night letter
noonday
northwest
notebook
note paper
notwithstanding
office boy
officeholder
offset
packinghouse
paperback
papercutter (G)
paper cutter (W)
parcel post
passbook
paymaster
payroll
per annum
percent
policyholder
postcard
postmark
postmaster
post office
racecourse
salesclerk
sales tax
school board
schoolhouse
shopwindow
signpost
stockbroker
stock exchange
stock market
stockpile
stopgap
subcommittee
subdivision
taxpayer
textbook
thereafter
time clock

timekeeper
timesaving
timetable
titleholder
title page
toastmaster
toll road
trademark
trade name
transatlantic
transcontinental
turnover

viewpoint
violet ray
wage earner
wavelength
wax paper
waybill
weekend
workday
x-ray (verb)
X ray (noun)
yearbook

Division of Words

Avoid all unnecessary divisions. Pronunciation is usually the best guide in determining how to divide words into syllables. An important principle to follow is that the part of the word left at the end of the line should suggest the part beginning the next line.

1. Do not divide monosyllables: *friend, through, stopped.*

2. Divide words of two syllables at the end of the first: *pave-ment, Eng-lish.*

3. Do not divide words of four letters or, if avoidable, those of five or six: *item, index, supper, needed.*

4. Do not divide a word on a single letter or on two letters: *able*, not *a-ble; omit*, not *o-mit; ratio*, not *rati-o*, or *ra-tio; only*, not *on-ly.*

5. In words beginning with prefixes, divide, if possible, on the prefix: *mis-pronounce, sub-sidize.*

6. Never let more than two consecutive lines end with a hyphen if it can be avoided.

7. Do not divide such suffixes as the following:

cial	*in*	spe-cial
tial		pala-tial
cion		coer-cion
sion		occa-sion
tion		administra-tion
cious		falla-cious

geous	*in*	gor-geous
gious		conta-gious
tious		frac-tious

8. Separate suffixes, as a rule, from the stem of the word: *hop-ing, dear-est.*

9. In general, the following endings make reasonable divisions: *able, ance, ant, ence, ent, ible, ical, tive.*

accept-ance	prefer-ence
account-ant	correspond-ent
consider-able	crea-tive

10. In general, divide a word between double consonants unless the stem *ends* in a double consonant.

embar-rass	*but*	assess-ment
forgot-ten		bill-ing
mil-lion		full-est
neces-sary		odd-ity
occur-rence		pass-able
refer-ring		profess-ing
win-ning		tell-ing

11. Words containing a single middle consonant are divided as follows:

   (a) If the preceding vowel is short and the syllable accented, let the consonant end the syllable: *bal-ance, pun-ish.*
   (b) If the preceding vowel is long, write the consonant with the following syllable: *le-gal, oppo-nent.*

12. Solid compounds should usually be divided between the members: *book-keeper, care-taker, date-line, forth-coming, type-write.*

13. When a hyphenated compound must be divided at the end of a line, divide on the hyphen: *forty-five, law-abiding, long-distance.*

14. Unless absolutely necessary, do not divide names of persons or other proper nouns.

15. Do not separate such titles as *Capt., Dr., Esq., Mr., Mrs., Rev., St.,* or abbreviations for degrees from names to which they belong.

16. Do not separate abbreviations for societies, radio stations, and the like: *YWCA, WBDO.*

17. Do not separate initials preceding a name.

18. Do not divide a word at the end of a page or paragraph if it is possible to avoid doing so.

19. Do not add another hyphen to words already hyphenated: not *self-con-trol*, but *self-control*.

20. When two vowels come together but are sounded separately, divide them into separate syllables: *gene-alogy*, *cre-ation*.

Use of Italics

1. Italics are often used to give emphasis to words or expressions. They should be used only for strong emphasis, never indiscriminately. To indicate italics, underline in manuscript the words to be so printed.

   I know you can't spend *all* your time comparing grammatical authorities. When one writes that a job requires ten *man-hours*, one should be aware that a large number of readers will perceive the term as a sexist slur.

2. Italicize all punctuation immediately following italicized words.

3. Italicize the words *Continued, To be continued, Continued on page,* and *To be concluded.*

4. Italicize the words, *See also, See* before a cross-reference in an index; also the words *For* and *read* in a list of errata placed at the beginning or at the end of a volume.

   See also legumes.
   For Rosevelt *read* Roosevelt.

5. Abbreviations of Latin words in common use are not usually italicized; as, e.g., etc., i.e., c. (ca. or circ.), viz., and vs. However, it is preferable not to abbreviate *versus*, as in "Yale versus Harvard," except in informal writing. For the use of *v.* in legal references, *see* pp. 109–110.

6. Italicize the following Latin abbreviations, words, and phrases used in literary and legal references:

   ad loc. (to the place)   *ibid.* (the same reference)
   et al. (and others)   *idem* (the same place)
   et seq. (and the following)   *infra* (below)
   fl. (lived)   *loc. cit.* (place cited)

op. cit. (work cited)   *sic* (thus)
passim (here and there)   *s.v.* (under a word or heading)
sc. (namely)   *vide* (see)

7. Use italics when a word is spoken of as a word. (*See also* p. 93.)

   The word *gay* now carries a different connotation from its meaning in Cornelia Otis Skinner's *Our Hearts Were Young and Gay.*

8. Foreign words and phrases not yet adopted into English should be underlined in letters and manuscripts and italicized in printed matter.

   Current Merriam-Webster dictionaries (*Webster's Third New International* and the *Ninth New Collegiate*) do not indicate, as did earlier editions, foreign words and phrases that may not yet be anglicized. In *The Random House Dictionary of the English Language,* the editors have distinguished between words and phrases considered to be anglicized and those considered to remain foreign by printing the latter in italic type. The following list of words and phrases are printed in roman type in *The Random House Dictionary,* indicating that they are anglicized and need *not* be underlined or marked for italics:

addendum	chef-d'oeuvre	en route
ad hoc	cliché	ensemble
ad infinitum	prima facie	entente
ad interim	procès-verbal	entourage
agenda	pro rata	entree
à la carte	protégé	entrepreneur
à la mode	quasi	ex officio
ante-bellum	quondam	exposé
ante meridiem	recherché	fete
a priori	communiqué	habeas corpus
apropos	confrere	habitué
artiste	contretemps	regime
attaché	coup	reveille
beau ideal	coup d'état	résumé
belles-lettres	cul-de-sac	soiree
billet-doux	debris	status quo
blasé	décolleté	subpoena
bloc	denouement	table d'hôte
bona fide	détente	hors d'oeuvre
cabaret	dilettante	in memoriam
camouflage	distrait	levee
canapé	dramatis personae	maître d'hôtel
carte blanche	éclat	mandamus
chargé d'affaires	elite	matériel

mélange	papier-mâché	post-mortem
melee	penchant	précis
ménage	per annum	tête-à-tête
morale	per capita	tour de force
mores	per contra	vice versa
naïve, naïveté	per diem	visa
noblesse oblige	porte-cochere	vis-à-vis
nom de plume	poseur	viva voce
opus	post meridiem	

Note that in spelling many of these once-foreign words and phrases, the accent marks used in the original language are retained in English.

9. Italics are used for the titles of long poems, works of art, long musical compositions, books, magazines, newspapers, pamphlets, plays, motion pictures, and radio and television series. *But:* The title of an episode in a television series is set in roman and enclosed in quotation marks.

El amor brujo
At Dawn We Slept
Popular Photography
Arizona Highways
Dynasty
Inside the Financial Futures Market

the *Birmingham Post-Herald*
the *Mona Lisa*
Romeo and Juliet
All Things Considered
The Mystery of Edwin Drood

The names of songs and short musical compositions, short stories and subdivisions of books, and magazine or newspaper articles are not italicized. They are set in roman and enclosed in quotation marks. (*See* p. 92.)

10. The names of ships, trains, aircraft, and spacecraft are italicized. However, the type of plane is not.

the M.S. *Nederland*
the *Washingtonian*
the carrier *Ticonderoga*

the shuttle *Columbia*
DC 10
Boeing 747

11. Legal usage italicizes all case names, including the "v.," and any procedural phrases in text of briefs, articles, books, and so forth, but never in footnotes.

Mapp v. Ohio
Elkins v. United States

In re Sumner
Ex parte John Chase
Lehman v. City of Shaker Heights
Ortega y Gasset v. Feliciano Santiago

The above examples are from *A Uniform System of Citation,* published by The Harvard Law Review Association, Cambridge, Massachusetts. For more detailed rules for legal usage, see that comprehensive manual. In a nonlegal context, italics are not used; as, the Sumner case.

The *GPO Style Manual* rules differ in some details.

The local legal printers will know the form preferred by a local court as to printed briefs. But consult local rules for the specific color required for brief covers.

12. Italicize the binomial (scientific) names of genera and species.

    Salix babylonica, Acer rubrum, Sinningia speciosa

    Do not italicize the names of genera without the species, or of groups of higher rank (classes, orders, families, tribes, and so forth); as, the family Leguminosae.

13. Italicize *Resolved* in resolutions and legislative acts, as well as *Provided* when used in the body of this matter.

    Resolved, That the President shall be authorized to represent this body at the convention to be held . . .
    Resolved by the Common Council of the City of Norwalk, That the sum of $40,000 be designated for the purchase of . . . : *Provided,* That . . .

14. In preparing matter for publication, use italics for a title following a signature: Stephen G. Albert, *Treasurer.*

15. Do not use italics for foreign titles or designations of foreign leaders; as, Emir, Principessa; or for names of foreign legislatures or institutions; as, the British House of Commons, the Riksdag, the Pinakothek, the Museo Napoleonico, Akershus Fortress.

CHAPTER SIX

Expressing Numbers

In general, the question of expressing a number in words or in figures is decided in terms of clarity and formality. In formal or semiformal writing, the tendency is to use words, while in business communications and popular magazines, figures are often used for easy comprehension.

Book

> The Teatro Puerto Rico has a concert hall of thirteen hundred seats and two movie theaters of three hundred seats each.

Letter

> The Teatro Puerto Rico has a concert hall of 1,300 seats and two movie theaters of 300 seats each.

1. ROUND NUMBERS

Spell out all round numbers and approximate amounts; as, *four or five feet, seven hundred miles, a thousand reasons, almost a million board feet of lumber, a man in his eighties.*

When round numbers greater than one thousand are spelled out, such as 1,850, use *eighteen hundred and fifty* or *one thousand eight hundred and fifty.*

The word *and* may or may not be used between tens and units. Modern usage seems to prefer omitting it; as, *three hundred five.*

Spell out round sums of money if the amount can be expressed in one or two words; as, *forty-five dollars, two hundred dollars, seven thousand dollars.* Use the dollar sign and spell out *million* and *billion* to express large amounts in even millions or tenths of millions; as, *$1.5 million, $8.7 million, between $10 million and $20 million.*

2. NUMBERS AT BEGINNING OF SENTENCE

Spell out all numbers at the beginning of a sentence, even when other numbers in the sentence are expressed in figures.

> Two carloads of new, sample-grade corn were received here today and sold at 85 to 99 cents a bushel.
> Twenty members were present at last month's meeting.

When a long number begins a sentence, change the wording so that the number appears later.

> *Not:* 1,625 pairs of shoes were destroyed in the fire.
> *Better:* The fire destroyed 1,625 pairs of shoes.
> *Not:* 135 employees will retire this year.
> *Better:* This year 135 employees will retire.

3. NUMBERS WITHIN A SENTENCE

Spell out numbers from one through ten, except in a series of related numbers.

> The two boys consumed 4 hamburgers, 2 cans of soda, and 6 cookies.
> The football team won 8 games and lost 2 last year.

In formal writing, numbers that can be expressed in one or two words are spelled out, but figures may be used in letters or reports.

> It is estimated that there may be up to thirty-nine bankruptcies per thousand businesses in this area. (Text of a book)
> The subsurface formation ranges between depths of 3 and 34 feet from the ground surface. (Text of a report)

Use figures to express definite amounts and longer numbers.

> The hotel received the record number of 3,138 requests for reservations this year.
> His house was sold for $191,500.
> This month 1,977,639 shares were traded, compared with 2,320,003 last month.
> The foundation unit cost per square foot varies from $15.50 to $88.30, depending on the building weight per square foot.

Related numbers or amounts within a sentence should be expressed entirely in figures or entirely in words unless doing so would cause confusion.

They employed 10 women for 3 weeks at $200 a week.
Or: They employed ten women for three weeks at two hundred dollars a week.

Avoid placing next to each other two numbers referring to different things:

Wrong: In 1981 15 states ratified the law.
Right: In 1981 fifteen states ratified the law.
Allowed: In 1981, 15 states ratified the law.
Wrong: 2 3-bedroom apartments, 3 $2 bets
Right: two 3-bedroom apartments, three $2 bets

When one number immediately precedes another, spell out one, preferably the one with the fewer letters; as, *ten 3-inch nails, 20 six-foot poles.*

4. DATES

In decades and centuries: Spell out numbers referring to decades and centuries; as, the *gay nineties,* the *nineteenth century.*

In years: In social correspondence, as in wedding invitations, express years in words, as *nineteen hundred and eighty-nine;* but in formal and legal documents, write *one thousand nine hundred and eighty-nine.*

In letters: Use figures, as a general rule, in the heading of a business letter to express the date; as, *January 27, 1986, not 1/27/86 or January 27th, 1986.*

In European usage and in military practice, the day precedes the month in letter headings; as, *2 May, 1986.*

In the body of a business letter, when the name of the month precedes the date, the date should be written in figures without *-st, -d,* or *-th.*

Make the appointment for January 22. (*Not* January twenty-second or January 22d.)

When the name of the month follows the date or when the name of the month is omitted, the date should be written in full or in figures with the ordinal abbreviation.

Make the appointment for the twenty-second of January *or* the twenty-second *or* the 22d of January *or* the 22d. (*Not* the 22 of January *or* the 22.)

Our representative will be in Boston on November 19, 20, and 21. Would it be convenient for you to see him on the 20th or the 21st?

Note the acceptable methods of writing dates:

May 1977 *or* May, 1977   May 25, 1977 (*not* May 25th, 1977)
June 6 to July 15, 1977 (*not* June 6, 1977 to July 15, 1977)
April, May, and June, 1987 (*but* May and June 1987 *or* May and June, 1987)

When abbreviating decades or dates, in informal writing, use an apostrophe to indicate the omission; as, *the Class of '68.*

In referring to a fiscal year, consecutive years, or a continuous period of two years or more, when contracted, the forms used are 1906–38, 1961–62, 1801–2, 1875–79 (*but* 1895–1914, 1900–1901). For two or more separate years not representing a continuous period, a comma is used instead of a dash (1945, 1949). If the word *from* precedes the year or the word *inclusive* follows it, the second year is not shortened and the word *to* is used instead of the dash; as, *from 1983 to 1986; 1985 to 1986, inclusive.*

In dates, A.D. precedes the year (A.D. 937); B.C. follows the year (254 B.C.).

In formal invitations, announcements, and acceptances, dates are invariably spelled out; as, *February Twenty-first, Nineteen Hundred and Sixty-nine,* or *February Twenty First, Nineteen Hundred and Sixty Nine.*

In legal documents, such as wills and deeds, dates are invariably written out; as, *the twelfth day of January, one thousand nine hundred and eighty-four.*

5. TIME OF DAY

Spell out the time of day in text matter.

(1) Use *a.m.*, *p.m.* or A.M., P.M. in connection with figures; as,

1:30 a.m.   1:30 p.m.   1:30 A.M.

Note that when the time is spelled out, the abbreviations a.m. or p.m. must not be used:

The train left at three in the afternoon.
Not: The train left at three p.m.

(2) Add zeroes to the even hour only if a time containing minutes appears in the same sentence.

> He will be on duty from 8:00 a.m. to 4:30 p.m.

6. STREETS

In the text spell out numbers of streets, avenues, wards, and districts; as, *Sixth Avenue, Thirteenth District, Ninth Ward.*

In writing streets and avenues, spell out the names of those up to twelve; as, *Fifth Avenue, Ninth Street.*

In correspondence express numbers above twelve in figures; as, *121 Street* or *121st Street.*

7. PAGE NUMBERS

Use figures for page numbers; as, *page 3, page 533.*

8. REFERENCES IN FOOTNOTES

In footnotes and in all bibliographical material, abbreviate a word designating a part when followed by a number.

Chap. III (pl. Chaps.)	col. 2 (cols.)
Vol. II (Vols.)	art. 14 (arts.)
Fig. 80 (Figs.)	p. 1 (pp.)
sec. 3 (secs.)	pp. 6f. (page 6 and the following page)
No. 1 (Nos.)	pp. 6ff. (page 6 and the following pages)
	pp. 5–8 (pages 5 to 8 inclusive)

Section is usually abbreviated in enumeration, except the first:

Section 1
Sec.   2
Sec.   3

In legal work, *Section* and *Sections* are abbreviated by the use of the symbols § and §§, respectively.

9. SUMS OF MONEY

For typographical appearance and easy grasp of large numbers, beginning with million, the word *million* or *billion* is used:

12 million (*not* 12,000,000); 12 billion
$2,750 million (*not* $2,750,000,000)
two and a half million dollars (*not* $2½ million)

300,000 (*not* 300 thousand)
amounting to 4 million
5 billion or 10 billion dollars' worth

(1) In bills and in other distinctly financial statements, the symbol for cents is used when given in cents only; as, *steers low, 25¢ to 40¢ lower.*

(2) Do not use both figures and words for sums of money except in commercial and legal documents. When both are used, parentheses follow the completed expression; as, *thirty dollars ($30)* or *thirty (30) dollars*, not *thirty ($30) dollars*. The custom of using both figures and words for sums of money is seldom used today in letters.

10. DECIMAL FRACTIONS

Use figures for expressing decimal fractions and percentages, but spell out percentages when they begin a sentence.

0.832; 10.5
The Saskatchewan official reports said 80 percent of the wheat in that province had been threshed.
Ten percent will be the profit.

In writing a decimal fraction not preceded by a whole number, a zero is placed before it except when the decimal fraction begins with a zero; as, 0.235, .0235.

In letters and formal writing, the word *percent* should be used instead of the symbol %. In commercial work, such as tabular matter, the symbol % is used.

11. FRACTIONS

Fractions standing alone or expressed in a single compound word are usually written out; as, *half* a mile, a *quarter* of an ounce, a *one-third* interest.

Fractions should be expressed in words or as decimals where possible; as, 20.5 miles, *not* 20 and a half miles or 20½ miles.

Written-out fractions used as adjectives must be hyphenated; as, a *two-thirds* vote, *one-half* inch; but when they are used as nouns, they are usually not hyphenated; as, *one sixth* of the estate, *two fifths* of the field. In business writing there is a growing tendency to use the hyphen for both the adjective and the noun; as, a *one-third* interest in the estate, *one-third* of the estate.

In general, a fraction expressed in figures should not be followed by *of a, of an.*

⅜ inch, *not* ⅜ of an inch   ⅔ cup, *not* ⅔ of a cup
0.5 percent, *not* ½ of 1 percent

It is incorrect to use *d*, *th*, and *ths* after fractions:

⁹⁄₁₀₀, *not* ⁹⁄₁₀₀ths   ¹⁄₁,₀₀₀, *not* ¹⁄₁,₀₀₀ths
¹⁄₃₂, *not* ¹⁄₃₂d part   ¹⁄₁₆, *not* ¹⁄₁₆th
Better: .06 inch, .004

Mixed numbers, when expressed in figures, should be typed with a space rather than a hyphen between the integer and the fraction; as, 23 3/4, *not* 23-3/4.

When fractions are used in giving specifications, the hyphen is used and the noun is always singular:

a 4½-inch pipe   a 1¼-inch belt   a .22-caliber rifle

When a fraction is the subject of a sentence, the verb agrees with the noun in the prepositional phrase.

Two thirds of his income *is* from real estate.
Two thirds of their incomes *are* from real estate.

With *one* as subject followed by a fraction, the verb is singular.

One and five-sixth yards is enough.
One and a half teaspoonfuls was the usual dosage.

12. AGES

In stating definite ages, usage differs. In general, figures should be used for ready comprehension; as, My age is 52 years, 6 months, 10 days; a boy 6 years old; 3-year-old colt; 2-month-old child.

In formal writing or when the age is indefinite, references to ages should be spelled out; as, *eighty* years and *four* months old; children between *six* and *fourteen*; a man in his *forties*.

13. RESULTS OF BALLOTS

These should be expressed by figures; as, 38 for, 25 against; yeas 56, nays 24.

14. DIMENSIONS

In text, to represent dimensions write 10 by 15 inches, *not* 10 × 15 inches *or* 10″ × 15″.

In technical work, use ′ for feet, ″ for inches, and × for *by:* 9′ × 11″. In ordinary writing, abbreviate but do not capitalize dimensions; as, 6 *ft.* 11 *in.*

15. Distances

Write in figures all measures of distances except a fraction of a mile; as, *16* miles, *12* yards, *3* feet; *but* one-half mile.

16. Measures

Enumerations of measure must be expressed by figures; as, *10* gallons, *4* quarts, and *3* pints; *60* bushels, *5* pecks. In ordinary writing, they are abbreviated; as, *6 lbs. 3 oz.*

17. Temperature

Use figures followed by the degree sign and the abbreviation *F.* for Fahrenheit or *C.* for Celsius; as, *32°F., 45°C.*

18. Weights

Enumeration of weight should be expressed in figures; as, *2* tons, *40* pounds, *10* ounces.

19. Metric system

Abbreviate after a numeral all designations of weights and measures in the metric system. The period may be omitted, according to the National Bureau of Standards.

20. Roman numerals

The following table represents Roman numerals commonly used:

1—I	6—VI	11—XI
2—II	7—VII	14—XIV
3—III	8—VIII	18—XVIII
4—IV or IIII	9—IX	19—XIX
5—V	10—X	20—XX
30—XXX	300—CCC	2,000—MM
40—XL	400—CCCC or	3,000—MMM
50—L	CD	4,000—MV̄
60—LX	500—D	5,000—V̄
70—LXX	600—DC	1928—
80—LXXX	700—DCC	MCMXXVIII
90—XC	800—DCCC	1930—
100—C	900—CM	MCMXXX
200—CC	1,000—M	1,000,000—M̄

Note: A dash above the numeral multiplies the value by 1,000: MV̄ = 4,000.

For the use of Roman numerals in outlines, *see* p. 71.

CHAPTER SEVEN

Spelling and Choosing Words

Rules for Spelling

Rules and examples that follow are those commonly accepted. However, there are exceptions to many rules, so that a writer who is in doubt should check words in an authoritative dictionary.

Dictionaries should also be compared in their listing for alternate forms. For example, Webster's explains that when another spelling or form is joined to the entry word by the word *also*, the spelling following it is a variant, less commonly used; when the entry is followed by the word *or* and then another spelling, the two forms or spellings are equally acceptable in standard practice:

woolly *also* wooly   gases *also* gasses (n. pl.)
canceled *or* cancelled   labeled *or* labelled

Final Consonants

1. With monosyllables and words accented on the last syllable when ending with a single consonant preceded by a single vowel double the consonant (other than *w*, *x*, or *y*) before a suffix beginning with a vowel.

bag   baggage   equip equipped
begin   beginning   impel impelled
bid   bidden   man   mannish

occur	occurred	sad	sadden
plan	planned	sit	sitting
refer	referring	wed	wedded
remit	remittance	wit	witty

Exceptions

infer	inferable, *but* inferred, inferring
transfer	transferable, *but* transferring, transferred

2. Final consonants when preceded by two vowels are not doubled in adding a suffix beginning with a vowel.

beat	beaten
congeal	congealing
retail	retailing
soak	soaking

3. Final consonants are not doubled when the word ends in more than one consonant.

conform	conformed	conforming
help	helped	helping

4. Final consonants may or may not be doubled when the accent is thrown forward. The American tendency is not to double the final consonant, British usage is to double it.

benefit	benefiting *or* benefitting, benefited *or* benefitted
cancel	canceling *or* cancelling, canceled *or* cancelled
travel	traveling *or* travelling, traveled *or* travelled

5. Adjectives ending with *l*, like other adjectives, add *ly* to form the corresponding adverbs.

accidentally	exceptionally	occasionally
casually	finally	really
coolly	legally	unusually

Prefixes and suffixes ending in *ll* generally drop one *l* in combination.

already	always
although	helpful
altogether	wonderful

6. Words ending in *n* keep that letter before the suffix *ness*.

barrenness	meanness
greenness	plainness
keenness	suddenness

7. Words ending in a double consonant usually retain both consonants before suffixes.

assess	assessment	shrill	shrilly
embarrass	embarrassment	success	successful

Final E

8. Words ending in silent *e* usually omit the *e* before suffixes beginning with a vowel.

abridging	encouraging	pleasing
acknowledging	forcible	salable
arguing	giving	subduing
arrival	guidance	tracing
blamable	hoping	truism
changing	judging	typing
coming	lovable	using
deplorable	loving	wiring
desirable	managing	writing
dining	mistaking	

9. When words end in soft *ce* or *ge*, keep the *e* before *able* and *ous*.

advantageous	noticeable
changeable	outrageous
chargeable	peaceable
courageous	pronounceable
enforceable	serviceable
manageable	traceable

10. Keep final *e* in the present participle of *dye, singe, tinge, eye,*

dyeing	singeing
eyeing	tingeing

11. When words end in *oe*, keep the *e* before a suffix beginning with any vowel except *e*.

canoeing
hoeing
toeing

12. When words end in silent *e*, keep the *e* before a suffix beginning with a consonant.

baleful	management
encouragement	movement
extremely	ninety
lonely	useful
lovely	

Exceptions

acknowledgment	duly
argument	judgment
	truly

13. Verbs ending in *ie* change the termination to *y* before adding *ing*.

die, dying (*but* died)   lie, lying (*but* lied)   tie, tying (*but* tied)

Final Y

14. Words ending in *y* preceded by a consonant change *y* to *i* before a suffix, unless the suffix begins with *i*.

busy   busier   business
defy   defiant   defies
mercy   merciful   merciless

But

carry   carrying
hurry   hurrying
study   studying
thirty   thirtyish

15. Words ending in *y* preceded by a vowel generally keep the *y* before a suffix.

buyer   buying
delayed   delaying
obey   obeying

Exceptions

daily   paid
laid   said

16. Monosyllabic adjectives usually keep *y* when adding a suffix.

dry   dryly
sly   slyly

17. Follow the well-known rhyme in spelling words with *ie* and *ei*.

I before E
Except after C
Or when sounded as A
As in n*ei*ghbor and w*ei*gh

ei used after *c*

| ceiling | deceit | receipt |
| conceive | perceive | receive |

ie used after all letters except *c*

achieve	fiend	niece	shriek
apiece	frontier	pierce	sieve
believe	grief	relieve	yield
chief	mischief	reprieve	

Exceptions

| counterfeit | forfeit | leisure | seize |
| foreign | height | neither | weird |

ei sounded as *a*

feign	reign
heinous	their
neighbor	weight

Words Ending in C

18. Words ending with a vowel plus *c* remain unchanged before *a, o, u,* or a consonant.

frolicsome   critical

Before an added *e, i,* or *y,* the letter *k* is inserted if the *c* sound remains hard.

frolicked   panicky

Nothing is added after *c* if the *c* sound becomes soft.

criticism   toxicity

19. Words ending with a consonant plus *c* usually remain unchanged before any suffix, but occasionally a *k* is inserted: usually *arc, arced, arcing*, but sometimes *arcked, arcking*.

Words Ending in S or S-Sounds

20. When words end in *s* or an *s*-sound (*ss, x, ch, sh, z*), the plural is formed by adding *es* to the singular.

annex	annexes
church	churches
dish	dishes
hostess	hostesses
quartz	quartzes

Variations in American and British Spelling

21. Note the variations in American and British usage in the following: (1) Words ending in *or*.

American	British	American	British
arbor	arbour	humor	humour
behavior	behaviour	labor	labour
candor	candour	misdemeanor	misdemeanour
clamor	clamour	neighbor	neighbour
endeavor	endeavour	odor	odour
favor	favour	parlor	parlour
flavor	flavour	rumor	rumour
harbor	harbour	vigor	vigour
honor	honour		

Note that *discoloration, horror, invigorate, mirror, pallor, tenor, terror*, and *tremor* do not take *u* in British spelling.

Note that adjectives formed from *clamor, humor, labor, odor, rigor*, and *vigor* do not take *u* in British spelling.

clamorous	laborious	rigorous
humorous	odorous	vigorous

(2) Words ending in *er*.

American	British	American	British
center	centre	meter	metre
maneuver	manoeuvre	reconnoiter	reconnoitre

(3) Words ending in *ise* and *ize*.

Most words ending in this sound take *ize*. Some may be spelled either *ize* or *ise*. American usage generally prefers *ize*. The following spellings are those given in Webster's:

advise	compromise	exercise	patronize
amortize	demoralize	extemporize	penalize
anglicize	despise	familiarize	recognize
apologize	devise	fertilize	satirize
authorize	disfranchise	franchise	scrutinize
baptize	disorganize	harmonize	specialize
capitalize	dramatize	merchandise	supervise
centralize	economize	mobilize	surmise
characterize	emphasize	modernize	surprise
chastise	enterprise	monetize	sympathize
civilize	equalize	naturalize	utilize
colonize	excise	organize	visualize

Using the Dictionary

When you are unsure of the spelling of a word, you may find it difficult to locate the word in the dictionary. English spelling is confusing because many letters and combinations of letters sound a good deal alike. The solution is to try the various possible equivalents for each sound you hear when you say the word.

Pronounce the word slowly and divide it into syllables. List the possible spellings for each syllable by consulting the following chart.

General sound	Examples	Approximate equivalents
long a (ā)	mate, lain, gay	a, ai, ay
	feign, bouquet, whey	ei, et, ey
	cliché	é
broad a (ä) *or*	father, pause, qualm	a, au, al
circumflex o (ô)	foster, bought	o, ough

long e (ē)	cedar, seek	e, ee
	feat, ceiling, yield	ea, ei, ie
f	flee, laugh, phobia	f, gh, ph
long i (ī)	aisle, pile, stein, high, by, lye	ai, i, ei, igh, y, ye
short i (ĭ)	depict, embryonic	i, y
j	jet, page, ledge	j, ge, dge
k	pike, capital, bisque	k, c, que
long o (ō)	dome, roam	o, oa
ow	flower, about	ow, ou
r	rate, wrist	r, wr
s	cost, descent, rice	s, sc, ce
sh	shoe, chute	sh, ch
	suspicion, conscience	ci, sci
	mission, elation	ssi, ti
z	amazing, surmise	z, s

You should also check the following suffixes that sound alike: *-able* and *-ible;* *-ant* and *-ent;* *-ance* and *-ence;* *-cial* and *-tial;* *-cious* and *-tious;* *-osity* and *-ocity.*

Remember, too, that a consonant is usually doubled only after a short vowel sound (a, e, i, o, u), as in *planning, repellent, imminent, allotting, rebuttal.*

Suppose you wanted to look up *cynosure.* The word would begin with either *s* or *c.* The long *i* sound could be *ai, i, ei, igh, y, ye.* The rest of the word would probably be *-nosure.* You would try *si, sei, sy, ci,* and *cei* without finding the word, but *cy* would bring success.

Similarly, *idiosyncrasy* contains several possible combinations. Thinking of *ideology,* you would try *ideo,* perhaps, as well as *idio.* The next syllable could be *sin, syn, cin,* or *cyn,* and the last two syllables might be *cracy, crasy, krasy,* or *kracy.* Of course, you will generally find the word before you reach the last syllable, but a systematic approach will help you to analyze a word and shorten the search.

Choosing the Correct Word

When choosing the word that best expresses the intent, some writers and speakers mistake one word for another similar one. Note the differences in the pairs and groups of words that follow.

For lively discussions of the misuse of words, see *The Elements of Style* by William Strunk, Jr., and E. B. White (Macmillan), *The Careful Writer* and other books by Theodore M. Bernstein (Atheneum), *The*

Writer's Art by James J. Kilpatrick (Andrews, McMeel & Parker Inc.),
On Language by William Safire (Times Books), and *On Writing Well*
by William Zinsser (Harper & Row).

Words Often Confused

accede	to adhere to an agreement
exceed	to surpass
accept	to receive
except	to exclude
adherence	attachment
adherents	followers
adapt	to adjust
adept	proficient
addition	something added
edition	the whole number of copies published at one time
adverse	opposed
averse	disinclined
affect (vb.)	to influence, to change
effect	to accomplish (vb.); result (n.)
afterward, afterwards	both forms are correct
all right	the correct form
alright	no such spelling
all ready	entirely ready (The work is *all ready* for you.)
already	action has occurred (I have *already* finished the work.)
all together	in a body (The family is *all together*.)
altogether	entirely (You are *altogether* right.)
allude	to refer to indirectly
refer	to mention something definitely
allusion	an indirect reference
delusion	an error of judgment
illusion	an error of vision

almost (adv.)	nearly
most	an adj., an adv. of comparison, a pronoun: most people, most beautiful, most of them
altar (n.)	a sacred place of worship
alter (vb.)	to change
amateur	one who engages in a pursuit, study, science, sport as a pastime
novice	one new in a business or in a profession
amoral	nonmoral
immoral	dissolute
unmoral	having no moral perception; synonymous with nonmoral
among	use *among* when reference is to more than two
between	use *between* when reference is made to only two persons
amount	bulk, the sum total referring to number
number	refers to something counted
quantity	refers to something measured
anecdote	a narrative of a particular incident
antidote	a remedy to counteract poison
anywhere	no such word as *anywheres*
appraise	to value
apprise	to inform, to notify
apprize	to put a value on; seldom used, same as *appraise*
apt	suitable, appropriate, skilled
liable	legally bound; implies undesirable consequences
likely	possible
ascent	act of rising
assent	consent
assay	to test and to analyze, as ore; to estimate
essay (vb.)	to try, to attempt
attorney	strictly applies to one transacting legal business

lawyer	applies to anyone in the profession; also, one legally appointed by another to transact business for him
avocation	a minor occupation pursued especially for enjoyment
vocation	a regular calling or profession
balance	the difference between the debit and credit side of an account
remainder	the comparatively small part left over
berth	a place in which to sleep in a railroad sleeping car or on a ship
birth	act of being born
beside	at the side of
besides	in addition to
biannual	twice a year; synonymous with semiannual
biennial	every two years
bouillon	a clear soup
bullion	uncoined gold or silver in bars or ingots
breath (n.)	respiration
breathe (vb.)	to inhale and exhale
bring	to convey toward (the speaker)
take	to carry from (the speaker)
calender	a machine for finishing paper or cloth
calendar	record of time
cannon	a large gun
canon	a law; a rule; a clergyman belonging to the staff of a cathedral or collegiate church
canvas (n.)	strong tent cloth
canvass (vb.)	act of soliciting for orders, votes, and so forth
capital	the seat of government of a state or country; money invested in a business
capitol	a building in which a state legislative body meets; with cap., the building in which the U.S. Congress meets in Washington
casual	happening by chance
causal	relating to a cause or causes

censer	an incense pan
censor	a critic; to criticize
censure	to blame
cession	the act of ceding, that is, a granting or a surrender of something, especially the transfer of territory from one country to another
session	a term or a meeting place; as of a court, legislature, or any organized assembly
character	sum of qualities that constitute the true individuality of a person
reputation	what others think of a person
cite	to summon to appear before a court, to quote by way of authority or proof, to refer to
sight	a view
site	a place
client	a person using the services of a lawyer or other professional person
customer	a person who purchases a commodity or service
close	to shut; to bring to an end
clothes	wearing apparel
cloths	fabrics
coarse	rough
course	a direction of going, action; part of a meal
colleague	an associate in a profession or a civil or ecclesiastical office
partner	a member of a partnership, joint owner in business
collision	a clash
collusion	secret agreement to defraud
commence	to begin; more formal than begin
comments	remarks
compare	to bring things together to note points of difference or similarity
contrast	to bring things together to note points of difference

continual	frequently recurring; refers to time and implies close succession (*continual* rains)
continuous	uninterrupted; refers to time and space and implies continuity (*continuous* heartbeat)
council	an assembly or group for conference
counsel	advice, legal adviser
credible	worthy of acceptance
creditable	praiseworthy
credulous	ready to believe on uncertain evidence
customary	established by custom, conforming to common usage
habitual	according to habit
usual	frequent, ordinary
decease	death
disease	illness
device	mechanical appliance
devise	to contrive, to give by will
discredit	to destroy confidence in
disparage	to speak slightingly of, to undervalue
disinterested	lack of self-interest
uninterested	not interested, indifferent
disqualify	to render unfit
unqualified	not fitted
dying	ceasing to live
dyeing	coloring
emerge	to rise from, to come into view
immerge	to plunge into, to immerse
emigration	the moving from a country
immigration	the moving into a country
eminent	outstanding, high, lofty
imminent	threatening to happen soon
empty	having nothing in it (an empty bottle)
vacant	having nothing on it or in it (vacant land; a vacant apartment)
endorse	in America, preferred to *indorse*

envelop (vb.)	to put a covering about
envelope (n.)	a wrapper
error	an act involving a departure from truth or accuracy
mistake	a misunderstanding
exceedingly	very greatly
excessively	too greatly
exceptional	unusual
exceptionable	open to objection
excite	to stir up emotionally
incite	to stir into action
expect	to regard as likely to happen
suspect	to doubt the truth of
extant	still existing
extent	measure, length
famous	celebrated
noted	eminent, well known
notorious	unfavorably noted
few	used in reference to number
less	used in reference to quantity
flammable	synonyms meaning capable of being easily ignited
inflammable	
formally	ceremoniously
formerly	in times past
forth	forward
fourth	the next after *third*
guarantee	to secure; preferred in the verb sense
guaranty	financial security; preferred in the noun sense
hanged	of a person
hung	of an object
healthful	health-giving, as of climate
healthy	in good health
wholesome	producing a good effect, as of food
hire	to employ, to obtain the use of

lease	to grant by lease, to hold under a lease
let	to give the use of, to be let or leased
human	pertaining to mankind
humane	benevolent
hypercritical	too critical
hypocritical	insincere
imply	the speaker implies
infer	the hearer infers
impossible	not possible
impracticable	not possible under present conditions
indict (ĭn dīt′)	to charge with an offense
indite	to write, to compose and write
ingenious	clever
ingenuous	frank, naïve
lay	to set down
lie	to recline
lean	having little fat
lien	a legal claim
leave	to depart from
let	to allow, to permit
legible	easy to read
eligible	qualified to be chosen
lessee	a tenant
lessor	one who gives a lease
loose	free
loosen	to free
lose	to mislay
majority	more than half (sing. or pl., according to use)
plurality	the largest number of votes cast for one person, a greater number than any other but less than half of the votes cast
marital	pertaining to marriage
martial	pertaining to war, military
(mär′ shəl)	
marshal	to arrange; an official

medal	a badge of honor
meddle	to interfere
miner	a worker in a mine
minor	underage; inferior in extent, importance, or size
moral (mȯr əl) (adj.)	virtuous, right, and proper
morale (mə ral) (n.)	state of mind (the *morale* of the students)
new	recent
novel	unusual
oculist	one who treats eyes
optician	one who makes eyeglasses
optometrist	one who measures the vision
ordinance	law, prescribed practice or usage
ordnance	military supplies
overdo	to do too much
overdue	past due
partially	in some degree
partly	in part
partition	a division
petition	a formal written request, a prayer
party	a body of persons; refers to a group, not to a single person (except in law)
person	an individual
persecute	to oppress, to subject to persistent ill-treatment
prosecute	to sue
personal	individual, private
personnel	the staff of an organization
plaintiff	a party to a lawsuit
plaintive	mournful
practical	that which can be done advantageously; sensible, not theoretical (can refer to persons or things)

practicable	that which can be done (used to refer to things)
precede	to go before
proceed	to begin
proposal	something offered for acceptance or rejection
proposition	something offered for discussion, assertion
respectfully	courteously
respectively	each in the order given
resume	to put on anew, to begin again
résumé	a summing up
role	a part or character in a play
roll	a list; to revolve
salary	a fixed periodical payment made to a person employed in other than manual or mechanical work
wages	workman's or servant's periodical pay
sample	a part of anything presented for inspection
specimen	a part, or one of a number, intended to show the quality of the whole
seasonable	timely, in keeping with the season
seasonal	periodical, affected by the seasons
specie	coin or coined money, usually of gold or silver
species (sing. and pl.) (spē´ shēz)	sort, variety
stable	firmly established, as *stable* price; barn
staple	produced regularly or in large quantities; a commodity for which the demand is constant
staid (adj.)	sedate
stayed	remained, postponed
stationary	not moving; fixed
stationery	writing material
suit	a set, as of clothes; a legal action; wooing; to please

suite	a retinue; a number of things constituting a set, series, or sequence, as a suite of rooms
talesman	a person summoned to make up the required number of jurors
talisman	a charm
tantamount	equivalent in value, meaning, or effect (His statement was *tantamount* to a confession.)
paramount	highest in rank or jurisdiction
temporal	limited by time; pertaining to the present life, distinguished from the sacred or eternal
temporary	lasting for a time only
unquestionable	indisputable
unquestioned	that which has not been questioned
waiver	the giving up of a claim
waver	to hesitate

Foreign Words and Phrases

(Selected from *The Random House Dictionary of the English Language*)

Latin Words and Phrases

annus mirabilis	Wonderful year
arbiter elegantiae	A judge in matters of taste
bona fides	Good faith
carpe diem	Enjoy the present
casus belli	A cause justifying war
causa sine qua non	An indispensable condition
cave canem	Beware of the dog
caveat emptor	Buy at your own risk
cui bono?	For whose advantage, to what end?
de facto	In reality, actually existing
de gustibus non est disputandum	There is no disputing about tastes
de mortuis nil nisi bonum	Concerning the dead say nothing but good

Dei gratia	By the grace of God
Deo gratias	Thanks to God
Deo juvanti	With God's help
Deo volente (D.V.)	God willing
Deus vobiscum	God be with you
dis aliter visum	It seemed otherwise to the gods
Dominus vobiscum	The Lord be with you
dulce et decorum est pro patria mori	Sweet and seemly is it to die for one's country
ecce homo	Behold the man
ex cathedra	Officially, with authority
ex more	According to custom
facile princeps	Easily the first
fidus Achates	Faithful Achates; trusty friend
gaudeamus igitur	Let us be joyful
genius loci	The spirit of the place; guardian deity
hic et ubique	Here and everywhere
hic sepultus	Here lies buried
hinc illae lacrimae	Hence those tears
hoc anno	In this year
humanum est errare	To err is human
in extremis	At the point of death
in hoc signo vinces	By this sign you will conquer
in loco parentis	In the place of a parent
in medias res	Into the midst of things; into the heart of the matter
in omnia paratus	Prepared for all things
in perpetuum	Forever
in propria persona	In one's own person
in rerum natura	In the nature of things
in situ	In its place; in proper position
in statu quo	In the state in which it was before
in toto	Altogether; entirely
in transitu	In transit
ipso jure	By the law itself
jure divino	By divine law
jus canonicum	Canon law
justitia omnibus	Justice for all
labor omnia vincit	Labor conquers all things
laborare est orare	To work is to pray
laus Deo	Praise be to God
loco citato	In the place cited
locus in quo	Place in which

locus sigilli	The place of the seal
loquitur	He (or she) speaks
mens sana in corpore sano	A sound mind in a healthy body
meum et tuum	Mine and thine
miles gloriosus	A braggart soldier
mirabile dictu	Wonderful to say
mirabilia	Miracles
modus operandi	A mode of operating
morituri te salutamus	We who are about to die salute thee
motu proprio	Of one's own accord
multum in parvo	Much in little
mutatis mutandis	The necessary changes having been made
mutato nomine	The name having been changed
nemine contradicente	No one contradicting
nemine dissentiente	No one dissenting
nemo me impune lacessit	No one attacks me with impunity
nihil	Nothing
nil admirari	To wonder at nothing
nil desperandum	Nothing to be despaired of
nolens volens	Whether willing or not
non possumus	We are not able
nunc	Now
obiit	He died; she died
O tempora! O mores!	O times! O customs!
omnia vincit amor	Love conquers all
opere citato	In the volume cited
otium cum dignitate	Leisure with dignity
pari passu	With equal pace; without partiality
passim	Here and there
pater patriae	Father of his country
paucis verbis	In few words
pax vobiscum	Peace be with you
persona grata	An acceptable person
pleno jure	With full authority
primus inter pares	First among equals
pro bono publico	For the public good or welfare
pro Deo et ecclesia	For God and the church
pro forma	As a matter of form
pro memoria	For memory
pro tempore	Temporarily; for the time being
quantum sufficit	As much as suffices
quo animo?	With what spirit or intention?
quo Fata vocant	Whither the Fates call

quo jure?	By what right?
quo modo?	In what way?
quod erat demonstrandum	Which was to be shown
requiescat in pace	May he (or she) rest in peace
scripsit	He or she wrote (it)
sculpsit	He or she sculptured (it)
secundum	According to
semper idem	Always the same
semper paratus	Always ready
seriatim	In a series
sic passim	So throughout
sic semper tyrannis	Thus always to tyrants
sic transit gloria mundi	Thus passes away the glory of the world
sine die	Without fixing a day for future action or meeting
sine qua non	Something essential
summum bonum	The highest or chief good
suo jure	In one's own right
suo loco	In one's own or rightful place
suum cuique	To each his own
tempora mutantur, nos et mutamur in illis	Times change and we change with them
tempus fugit	Time flies
timeo Danaos et dona ferentes	I fear the Greeks even when they bear gifts
ubique	Everywhere
ut dict.	As directed
vade mecum	Go with me; companion
vae victis	Woe to the conquered
vale	Farewell
verbatim et literatim	Word for word and letter for letter

French Words and Phrases

à bon marché	At a bargain
à gauche	To the left-hand side
à propos de rien	Apropos of nothing
affaire de cœur	A love affair
au contraire	On the contrary
au fait	Expert, having practical knowledge of a thing

au revoir	Till we see each other again
autre temps, autres moeurs	Other times, other customs
avec plaisir	With pleasure
bête noire	Something that one especially dislikes or dreads
bon jour	Good day; hello
bon soir	Good evening; good night
catalogue raisonné	A classified or descriptive catalogue
c'est-à-dire	That is to say
c'est la vie	Such is life
chacun à son goût	Everyone to his own taste
chef de cuisine	Head cook
cherchez la femme	Look for the woman
compte rendu	Report, account
coup de grâce	A death blow
coûte que coûte	Cost what it may
dégagé	Unconstrained; without emotional involvement
de trop	Too much; too many
dernier ressort	The last resource
Dieu avec nous	God with us
Dieu défend le droit	God defends the right
Dieu et mon droit	God and my right
en plein jour	In full daylight, openly
en rapport	In sympathy or accord
fait accompli	An accomplished fact
femme de chambre	A chambermaid, a lady's maid
fête champêtre	An outdoor festival
garde du corps	A bodyguard
gardez la foi	Keep the faith
grand monde	The world at large; refined society
honi soit qui mal y pense	Evil be to him who evil thinks
ici on parle français	French is spoken here
jeu de mots	Play on words, pun
jeu d'esprit	A play of wit or fancy
j'y suis, j'y reste	Here I am, here I stay
le roi est mort, vive le roi	The king is dead! Long live the king!
le style, c'est l'homme	The style is the man
le tout ensemble	The whole (taken) together
lettre de cachet	A sealed or secret letter, usually containing orders for imprisonment
ma foi	Really!
mal de mer	Seasickness
mal du pays	Homesickness

mise en scène	Stage-setting; surroundings; environment
mon ami	My friend
monde	World; society
mot juste	The exact or appropriate word
moyen âge	The Middle Ages
n'est ce pas?	Isn't that so?
n'importe	It does not matter
nom de guerre	An assumed name
objet d'art	A work of art
peu de chose	A small matter
pièce de résistance	The principal meal; the principal event (of a series)
pied-à-terre	A temporary lodging
pis aller	The last resort or resource
quand même	Nevertheless
qui s'excuse, s'accuse	He who excuses himself accuses himself
raison d'état	For the good of the country
raison d'être	Reason for being
salle à manger	Dining room
sans doute	Without doubt
sans gêne	Without embarrassment
sans pareil	Without equal
sans peine	Without difficulty
sans peur et sans reproche	Without fear and without reproach
sans souci	Carefree
tant mieux	So much the better
tant pis	So much the worse
tout à fait	Entirely
tout à l'heure	Instantly
tout le monde	Everyone
voilà	See! Look!

Pronunciation

1. Many words include letters that should not be pronounced. In the following, do *not* pronounce the italicized letter:

ba*s*-relief	indi*c*tment
com*p*troller	qua*l*m
fore*h*ead	sa*l*mon
indi*c*t	vi*c*tuals

2. Many words include letters that should be pronounced and often are not. In the following, pronounce the italicized letter:

accident*a*lly	occasion*a*lly
accompani*m*ent	partic*u*larly
arc*t*ic	per*h*aps
can*d*idate	po*e*m
gen*e*rally	proba*b*ly
ge*o*graphy	re*a*lize
govern*m*ent	sev*e*ral
hist*o*ry	su*r*prise
kep*t*	temper*a*ment
leng*th*	us*u*ally
lib*r*ary	yes*t*erday
Niag*a*ra	

Note that the words in the following list are mispronounced because a letter or a syllable is incorrectly added:

athlete (*not* athelete)	hindrance (*not* hinderance)
elm (*not* elum)	realtor (*not* realitor)
helm (*not* helum)	umbrella (*not* umberella)

CHAPTER EIGHT

Abbreviations

Modern usage advocates the spelling out of most words in letters and in literary text. Abbreviations are commonly used in tabulations, technical matter, and routine writing.

For capitalization of abbreviations, *see* pp. 46–48; for punctuation after abbreviations, *see* pp. 69–70.

There is considerable variation in the use of periods and in capitalization (as, *mph, m.p.h., Mph,* and *MPH*), and styling other than those given in this dictionary are often acceptable.

Webster's Ninth New Collegiate Dictionary

Plurals of Abbreviations

Most abbreviations form the plural by adding *s* to the singular form; as, *bds., mfrs., mos.*

Some abbreviations are the same in both singular and plural; as, *ft., kg., s.* (shillings), *deg., enc.*

Some abbreviations form their plurals by doubling the letter that represents the singular of the abbreviation; as, *MM.* (Messieurs), *pp.* (pages), *SS.* (Saints).

Some uncapitalized abbreviations form their plurals by adding an apostrophe and *s* to the singular form; as, *b.o.'s* (buyer's options), *b.v.'s* (book values), *g.a.'s* (general averages).

Capitalized abbreviations usually form their plurals by adding *s;* as, *Ph.D.s, YWHAs.*

Possessives of Abbreviations

The singular possessive is formed like other possessives by the addition of an apostrophe and *s*; as, *CE's, Jr.'s*. The plural possessive is formed like other plural possessives by the addition of an apostrophe to abbreviations whose plurals end in *s*; as, *Jrs.', Ph.D.s'*.

Geographical Names

1. Use the official abbreviations for states and regions administered by the United States. ZIP Codes should be used in envelope addresses but not in text. Leave two spaces between the state abbreviation and the ZIP Code.

2. Alaska, Guam, Hawaii, Idaho, Iowa, Maine, Ohio, and Utah are never abbreviated except in envelope addresses.

Ala.	AL	Mont.	MT
Alaska	AK	Nebr.	NB
Ariz.	AZ	Nev.	NV
Ark.	AR	N.H.	NH
Calif.	CA	N.J.	NJ
Colo.	CO	N. Mex.	NM
Conn.	CT	N.Y.	NY
D.C.	DC	N.C.	NC
Del.	DE	N. Dak.	ND
Fla.	FL	Ohio	OH
Ga.	GA	Okla.	OK
Guam	GU	Oreg.	OR
Hawaii	HI	Pa.	PA
Idaho	ID	P.R.	PR
Ill.	IL	R.I.	RI
Ind.	IN	S.C.	SC
Iowa	IA	S. Dak.	SD
Kans.	KS	Tenn.	TN
Ky.	KY	Tex.	TX
La.	LA	Utah	UT
Maine	ME	Vt.	VT
Md.	MD	Va.	VA
Mass.	MA	V.I.	VI
Mich.	MI	Wash.	WA
Minn.	MN	W. Va.	WV
Miss.	MS	Wis.	WI
Mo.	MO	Wyo.	WY

3. In general, do not abbreviate geographical names except to gain space in tabular matter: *Fort* William Henry, *Port* Jervis, *Mount* Vernon.

4. In place names, abbreviate *Saint*.

St. Helena	St. Paul
St. John	Sault Ste. Marie
St. Louis	St. Charles

5. Use the abbreviated form *U.S.* for United States when preceding the word *Government* or the name of a Government organization but *not* in association with the name or names of other countries. *U.S.* is used as an adjective but is spelled out when used as a noun. (*GPO Style Manual*)

U.S. Navy	U.S.–NATO assistance
U.S. Army	*but* Army of the United States
U.S. attorney	*but* foreign policy of the United States
	British, French, and United States governments

6. Use the following abbreviations for Canadian provinces and territories:

Alta.	Alberta	N.W.T.	Northwest Territories
B.C.	British Columbia	Ont.	Ontario
Man.	Manitoba	P.E.I.	Prince Edward Island
N.B.	New Brunswick	Que. *or* P.Q.	Province of Quebec
Nfld.	Newfoundland	Sask.	Saskatchewan
N.S.	Nova Scotia	Y.T.	Yukon Territory

Names of Firms and Corporations

7. When writing the words *Company, Brother, Brothers, Limited, Incorporated,* and *Corporation* in firm or corporate names, follow the company usage:

The Aetna Casualty and Surety Company
Macmillan Publishing Company
Simon and Schuster, Inc.
James River Corporation
Devine Bros., Inc.
Warehouse Wines & Spirits, Ltd.

(1) Use the character &, called an ampersand, only if the firm's name consists of the names of persons or the company itself uses the ampersand.

Village Bank & Trust Co.
Weed & Duryea Co.
Volkswagen Authorized Sales & Service
D & B Computing Services
Curtiss & Crandon, Realtors

(2) In footnotes and bibliographies use *Co.*, *Bro.*, and & when they form part of the name of a firm.

(3) The character & should never be used to connect two names in text matter unless a company or firm name is intended:

Galileo and Copernicus
Picasso and Cézanne
Lord & Taylor (firm name)

8. In writing the names of firms, follow the usage of the firm addressed; do not abbreviate the given name unless it is abbreviated by the firm itself.

Theo. Bedford Co.   Chas. M. Jonny, Inc.
Charles Hunt & Co.   William G. Freiburg Ltd.

Titles

Titles Preceding Personal Names

9. Use the following abbreviations for titles preceding personal names: Mr., Messrs., M. (Monsieur), MM. (Messieurs), Mrs., Ms., Mme., Mlle. (Madame, Mademoiselle; plurals are Mmes. and Mlles.; in a French context they are written without periods, whether singular or plural), St. (Saint) and Ste. (feminine Sainte, Fr.).

10. In formal usage such as invitations and announcements it is preferable to spell out titles, such as *Honorable, Governor, Lieutenant Governor, Reverend, Professor.*
The Honorable Shirley Temple Black, Governor Mario Cuomo, Professor Arthur D. Butterfield

11. In writing salutations, titles should not be abbreviated except for
Mr., Mrs., Ms., and *Dr.*

Dear Professor Harris: Dear Mr. Bailey:
Dear Colonel Jones: Dear Mrs. Ward:
Dear Dr. Vetter: Dear Ms. Kunin:

12. In writing *doctor, general, professor,* and the like without the
surname, no abbreviation should be used.

The doctor will be here tomorrow.
I hope, General, that you will accept the invitation.

13. The title of *doctor* is given to holders of high university degrees
in any faculty; as, *Doctor of Divinity, Music, Medicine, Literature,
Law, Philosophy,* and so forth.
   Abbreviations for scholastic degrees are not used in the United
States in combination with such personal titles of address as *Mr.,
Dr.,* or *Honorable.*

John McKay, A.B., *not* Mr. John McKay, A.B.
Jane Holmes, A.M., *not* Hon. Jane Holmes, A.M.

14. In the case of *Reverend* usage varies. The following are considered
correct (*see* pp. 47–48, 310–313):

Rev. Dr. Ramsay *or* Rev. Mr. Ramsay
Rev. Helen Miller
Reverend President Henry Wentworth
The Right Reverend Bishop Keith
The Reverend Diane Smith, D.D.
The Reverend Professor Carlos P. de Leon y de Heredia

Reverend should never be used as follows:

The Reverend Brown   Reverend Brown

   In writing abbreviations for academic degrees and religious orders after a name, observe the following sequence:

First   Religious orders
Second   Theological degrees
Third   Other doctorate degrees
Fourth   Honorary degrees in chronological order of their bestowal

The Right Reverend John Smith, D.D., Ph.D., LL.D., L.H.D.
The Very Reverend Thomas O'Brien, S.J., S.T.D., Litt.D.

Titles Following Personal Names

15. Use the following abbreviations after personal names:

Esq. This title is used mainly by lawyers in the United States. It should not be written with any other title.

Vincent Gallogly, Esq., *not* Mr. Vincent Gallogly, Esq.

Junior. In formal use such as wedding invitations, this word is written out. In newspapers, business correspondence, and in signatures, it is abbreviated to denote a son whose name is the same as his father's. It is then usually capitalized and preceded and followed by commas:

Philip Grant, Jr., *or* Philip Grant Jr.

The plural is formed by pluralizing the surname or by adding *s* to the abbreviation:

The Philip Grants, Jr. (formal)   The Philip Grant, Jrs. (informal)

The possessive is formed as follows (no comma follows the abbreviation):

Philip Grant, Jr.'s check   The Philip Grant, Jrs.' tickets
        (singular)   (plural)

The abbreviation *Jr.* should not be used unless the surname is preceded by initials or by a first name, as *P. E. Grant, Jr.* or *Philip Grant, Jr.*, not *Grant, Jr.* or *Mr. Grant, Jr.*

The abbreviation may also be used when a first name or initials are preceded by a title, as *Dr. Philip Grant, Jr.*

Although *Jr.* is usually dropped after the death of the father of the same name, this is a matter of preference.

Second. A young man, not a son, whose name is the same as that of an older living relative, such as a cousin or an uncle, may use II or 2nd (or 2d) after his name to identify him and thus avoid confusing him with the relative. Also, if he is named for his grandfather, whose name differs from that of the young man's father, he may use II or 2nd (or 2d).

Third. If the name of a grandson is the same as that of his grandfather and his father, the numeral III or 3rd (or 3d) without periods may be written after his name. Commas are not used with the Roman numeral, but they may or may not be inserted before and after the ordinal number.

Philip Grant III *or* Philip Grant 3rd (*or* 3d)

Senior. This, or its abbreviation, *Sr.*, is unnecessary and is seldom used after a man's name. Sometimes, to avoid confusion with a daughter-in-law, a widow may prefer to use *Sr.* after her name.

Dates

16. Do not abbreviate the names of the months except when necessary. Spell out the names of the months in the heading of a letter.

   When a date follows a month, use cardinal figures in text matter as well as in headings: *on May 12; on Friday, May 12.* Ordinal numbers, or figures with ordinal endings, are used when a date appears alone or before a month.

on the twelfth of May   on the 12th of May
on the 12th or 13th we will be shipping . . .

Do not abbreviate the date in text as follows: 5/12/88.

   When necessary because of space, abbreviate the names of the months as follows: Jan., Feb., Mar., Apr., Aug., Sept., Oct., Nov., Dec. Do not abbreviate May, June, and July.

   In tabular matter, the following may be used:

Ja.	My.	S.
F.	Je.	O.
Mr.	Jy.	N.
Ap.	Ag.	D.

When the days of the week must be abbreviated beyond the usual forms, the following may be used without periods:

Su   M   Tu   W   Th   F   S

References to Parts of Books

21. Write out references to chapters, pages, verses, and notes occurring in the text; but in parentheses, footnotes, cut-in notes, side notes, and tables, abbreviate as follows:

art. (arts.) article   pl. (pls.)   plate
ch. (chs.) chapter   pt. (pts.)   part

fig. (figs.)	figure	sec. (secs.)	section
p. (pp.)	page	vol. (vols.)	volume

Note that the Roman numeral with capital letters is used with these abbreviations except in the case of *p.* and *pp.*

Common Abbreviations

In the following list of abbreviations, generally accepted forms are given. For a more complete list, see *Webster's Third New International Dictionary, Webster's Ninth New Collegiate Dictionary,* or *The Random House Dictionary of the English Language.*

In Webster, abbreviations are listed together in a separate section; in *The Random House Dictionary,* they are entered alphabetically in the body of the text.

AA	Alcoholics Anonymous; American Airlines, Inc.
AC	air-conditioning; alternating current; athletic club
A/C, a/c	account
ACDA	Arms Control and Disarmament Agency
ack.	acknowledge, acknowledgment
actg.	acting
ad, advt.	advertisement (*plural* ads)
A.D.	(*anno Domini*) in the year of the Lord
ADC	Aid to Dependent Children
adj.	adjective; adjustment
Adj. Gen., A.G.	Adjutant General
ADM	Admiral, Admiralty
admin.	administration
ADP	automatic data processing
adv.	adverb
ad val., a/v	(*ad valorem*) according to
adv. chg.	advance charges
advg.	advertising
AF	Air Force, audio frequency
AFDC	Aid to Families with Dependent Children
AFL-CIO	American Federation of Labor and Congress of Industrial Organizations
agcy.	agency
agt.	agent
AID	Agency for International Development

AK	Alaska (ZIP Code abbreviation)
aka, a.k.a.	also known as
AL	Alabama (ZIP Code abbreviation)
Ala.	Alabama
ALGOL	algorithmic language used in programming computers
alt.	altitude; alternate
Alta.	Alberta, Canada
A.M., M.A.	Master of Arts
a.m., A.M.	(*ante meridiem*) before noon
AMA	American Management Association; American Medical Association
amb.	ambassador
AMEX	American Stock Exchange
amt.	amount
anon.	anonymous
ans.	answer
AOA	Administration on Aging
AP	Associated Press; additional premium; American plan
APO	Army Post Office
app.	appendix; applied; appointed; approved
approx.	approximate
appt.	appointed; appointment
apt.	apartment (*plural* apts.)
AR	Arkansas (ZIP Code abbreviation)
A.R.	accounts receivable; annual return
ARC	American Red Cross
ar.	arrival; arrive
Ariz.	Arizona
Ark.	Arkansas
asap	as soon as possible
assn.	association (*plural* assns.)
asso., assoc.	associate; associated
asst.	assistant
asstd.	assented; assorted
AST	Atlantic Standard Time
att.	attach; attachment
attn.	attention
atty.	attorney (*plural* attys.)
at. wt.	atomic weight
aux.	auxiliary
AV	audiovisual
avdp.	avoirdupois
Ave., ave.	avenue
avg.	average

AZ	Arizona (ZIP Code abbreviation)
B.A.	Bachelor of Arts
bal.	balance
bar.	barometer; barometric
BASIC	Beginners' All-purpose Symbolic Code (computer programming language)
bbl.	barrel (*plural* bbls.)
B.C.	before Christ; British Columbia, Canada
bd.	board; bond
b.d.	bank draft; bills discounted
B/E, b.e.	bill of exchange
beg.	begin; beginning
B/F	brought forward
bk.	bank; book (*plural* bks.)
bkg.	banking; bookkeeping; breakage
B/L	bill of lading (*plural* BS/L)
bldg.	building
B.L.S.	Bachelor of Library Science; Bureau of Labor Statistics
Blvd.	Boulevard
BO	back order; body odor; box office; branch office; broker's option; buyer's option
BOQ	bachelor officers' quarters
bor.	borough
B.O.T.	Board of Trade
bot.	bottle
BP	blood pressure
b.p., bp	boiling point
B.R.	bills receivable
Br.	British; Branch; Brother (*plural* Bros.)
Brig. Gen.	Brigadier General
Brit.	Britain; British
B.S.	Bachelor of Science; Bureau of Standards
b.s., B/S	balance sheet; bill of sale
B.t.u., Btu	British thermal unit
bu.	bushel(s)
bull.	bulletin (*plural* bulls.)
bur.	bureau
bus.	business
b.v.	book value
B.W.I.	British West Indies
bx.	box (*plural* bxs.)
BX	base exchange (Air Force)
C, C.	Celsius; Centigrade

c, c.	canceled; case; century; coupon; cent; copyright; cost
c., ca.	(*circa*) about
CA	California (ZIP Code abbreviation)
C.A.	Chartered'Accountant; chief accountant; capital account; credit account; current account; commercial agent
CAB	Civil Aeronautics Board
CACM	Central American Common Market
CAD	computer-aided design
cal.	calendar; calorie; caliber
Calif.	California
Can.	Canada; Canadian
canc.	cancel; canceled; cancellation
cap.	capitalize; capacity
Capt.	Captain
car.	carat
CARE	Cooperative for American Remittances to Everywhere, Inc.
cat.	catalogue
CATV	Community Antenna Television
CBC	Canadian Broadcasting Corporation
CBD	cash before delivery
CBI	Cumulative Book Index; computer-based instruction
CBS	Columbia Broadcasting System
cc, cc.	carbon copy; cubic centimeter(s)
CCU	cardiac care unit
CD	certificate of deposit; Congressional District; Civil Defense
CDR, Cdr.	Commander
C.E.	Chemical Engineer; Chief Engineer; Civil Engineer
c.e.	(*caveat emptor*) at buyer's risk
CEA	Council of Economic Advisers
cen.	central; century
CEO	chief executive officer
cert., ct., ctf.	certificate; certification; certified
CF	carried forward
cf.	compare; see
cfm	cubic feet per minute
CFR	Code of Federal Regulations
cfs	cubic feet per second
cg.	centigram(s)
C.H., c.h.	Clearing House; Courthouse; Custom House
Ch.	China; Chaplain; Church; Chapter

chap.	chapter
chem.	chemical; chemist; chemistry
chg.	change; charge
Chmn.	Chairman
chron.	chronological
CIA	Central Intelligence Agency
Cía.	(*compañía*) company
Cie	(*compagnie*) company
CIO	Congress of Industrial Organizations
cir.	circle; circular; circuit; circumference
cit.	citation; cited; citizen
civ.	civil; civilian
CLU	Chartered Life Underwriter
cm	centimeter
CO	Colorado (ZIP Code abbreviation)
C/O	Certificate of Origin
c/o	care of; carried over
Co., co.	company (*plural* cos.); cash order
COBOL	Common Business-Oriented Language (computer programming language)
C.O.D., c.o.d.	cash on delivery
C. of C.	Chamber of Commerce
Col.	Colonel; Colombia
col.	column; colony
coll.	collateral; collection; college
colloq.	colloquial
Colo.	Colorado
com., comm.	commerce; commission; committee; common
Comdr.	Commander
Cong., C.	Congress; Congressional; Congregational
Conn.	Connecticut
cont., contd.	continued
cor.	corner; correct; corrected
Corp.	Corporation; Corporal
corr.	corrected; corresponding; correspondence
cor. sec.	corresponding secretary
cp.	compare; coupon
CPA	Certified Public Accountant
CPB	Corporation for Public Broadcasting
CPCU	Chartered Property and Casualty Underwriter
CPFF	Cost Plus Fixed Fee
CPI	Consumer Price Index
Cpl.	Corporal

cpm	cycles per minute
CPO	Chief Petty Officer
CPS	Certified Professional Secretary
cps	cycles per second
CSC	Civil Service Commission
CST	Central Standard Time
CT	Connecticut (ZIP Code abbreviation)
ct.	cent; county; court (*plural* cts.)
ctn.	carton
ctr.	center
cu.	cubic
cu. ft.	cubic foot or feet
cu. in.	cubic inch or inches
cum.	cumulative
cur.	currency; current
cu. yd.	cubic yard
CWO	Chief Warrant Officer
c.w.o.	cash with order
cwt.	hundred-weight
cyl.	cylinder; cylindrical
D	five hundred; Democrat; Democratic
d.	date; day; depart; died
D.A.	District Attorney
db.	decibel
d.b.a.	doing business as (name of firm)
DC	District of Columbia (ZIP Code abbreviation)
D.C.	District of Columbia; Doctor of Chiropractic
d.c., dc	direct current
dd	dated; delivered
D.D.	Doctor of Divinity
D.D.S.	Doctor of Dental Surgery
DE	Delaware (ZIP Code abbreviation)
D.E.	Doctor of Engineering
deb.	debenture
Dec.	December
dec.	deceased; decrease
def.	defendant; defense; defined; definition; deferred
deg.	degree(s)
Del.	Delaware
del.	delegate; delete
dely.	delivery
Dem.	Democrat; Democratic
dep.	depart; department; deposit; depot; deputy

dept.	department; deponent
der.	derivation; derivative
det.	detachment; detail; determine
dft.	defendant; draft
dia., diam.	diameter
diag.	diagram
Dir.	Director
dis.	discharge; discount; distance
disc.	discount
dist.	distance; district; distribution
div.	dividend; division (*plural* divs.)
D.J.	disc jockey; district judge; Doctor of Jurisprudence
DJIA	Dow-Jones Industrial Average
D.Lit(t).	Doctor of Letters; Doctor of Literature
DOA	dead on arrival
DOB	date of birth
doc.	document
DOD	Department of Defense
DOE	Department of Energy
dom.	domestic; dominion
DOT	Department of Transportation
doz.	dozen(s)
DP	displaced person (*plural* DPs); data processing
dp.	depart
Dr.	Doctor (*plural* Drs.)
D.S., D.Sc.	Doctor of Science
DST	Daylight Saving Time
DTP	diphtheria, tetanus, pertussis
DTs, D.T.s	delirium tremens
D.V.M.	Doctor of Veterinary Medicine
E	English; east; earth
ea.	each
EB	eastbound
econ.	economic(s); economy
ed.	editor; edition (*plural* eds.)
Ed.D.	Doctor of Education
EDP	electronic data processing
EDT	Eastern Daylight Time
E.E.	Electrical Engineer
EEC	European Economic Community (Common Market)
EEG	electroencephalogram (-graph)
EEOC	Equal Employment Opportunity Commission
e.g.	(*exempli gratia*) for example

EKG	electrocardiogram (-graph)
elev.	elevation
enc., encl.	enclosure
end.	endorsed; endorsement
Eng.	England; English
engr.	engraved; engraver; engineer
Ens.	Ensign
env.	envelope (*plural* envs.)
EOM, E.O.M.	end of month
EP	European plan
EPA	Environmental Protection Agency
equiv.	equivalent
ERA	Equal Rights Amendment
ESL	English as a second language
ESP	extrasensory perception
esp.	especially
Esq.	Esquire
EST	Eastern Standard Time
est.	estate; estimate
ETA, e.t.a.	estimated time of arrival
et al.	(*et alii*) and others
etc.	(*et cetera*) and so forth
et seq., seq.	(*et sequentia*) and the following
ETV	educational television
Eur.	Europe; European
ex.	example; exchange; express; export; experiment
exch.	exchange; exchanged
exec.	executive
exor.	executor
exp.	expense; experiment; export; express
expy.	expressway
ext.	extension; exterior; external; extra; extract
F., Fahr.	Fahrenheit
f.	family; female; and the following one; French; frequency
FAO	Food and Agriculture Organization of the United Nations
f.a.s.	free alongside ship
FBI	Federal Bureau of Investigation
FCA	Farm Credit Administration
FCC	Federal Communications Commission
FDA	Food and Drug Administration

FDIC	Federal Deposit Insurance Corporation
Feb.	February
Fed.	Federal; Federated; Federation; Federal Reserve Bank; a federal officer
fem.	feminine
FET	federal excise tax
ff.	and the following (pages); folio
FHA	Federal Housing Administration
FICA	Federal Insurance Contributions Act
FIFO	first in, first out
fig.	figure (*plural* figs.); figuratively
Fin.	Finland; Finnish
FIT	federal income tax
FL	Florida (ZIP Code abbreviation)
fl.	floor; florin; fluid
Fla.	Florida
FM	frequency modulation
fm.	fathom; from
FMC	Federal Maritime Commission
fn.	footnote
FNMA	Federal National Mortgage Association (Fannie Mae)
F.O.	field office; Foreign Office
F.O.B., f.o.b.	free on board
F.O.C.	free of charge
fol.	folio; following
FOR	free on rail or road
FORTRAN	Formula Translation (computer programming language)
FOT, f.o.t.	free on truck
4 WD	four-wheel drive
frwy.	freeway
f.p., fp	freezing point
FPC	Federal Power Commission
f.p.m., fpm	feet per minute
FPO	Fleet Post Office
fps, f.p.s.	feet per second; frames per second
FR	full rate (cable)
Fr.	Father; France; French; Frau
fr.	franc; from
freq.	frequency; frequent(ly)
FRG	Federal Republic of Germany
Fri.	Friday

FRS	Federal Reserve System
FT	full-time
ft.	feet; foot; fort
FSLIC	Federal Savings and Loan Insurance Corporation
FTC	Federal Trade Commission
furn.	furnished; furniture
fut.	future; futures (exchange)
FWD	front-wheel drive
fwd.	forward
FX	foreign exchange
FYI	for your information
G.	German; gulf
g.	gram; gravity; acceleration of gravity
GA	General Agent; General Assembly; Georgia (ZIP Code abbreviation)
Ga.	Georgia
G.A., g.a.	general average
gal.	gallon (*plural* gals.)
GAO	General Accounting Office
GATT	General Agreement on Tariffs and Trade
G.B.	Great Britain
GD	general delivery
GDR	German Democratic Republic
Gen.	General
gen.	gender; general(ly); genus
geog.	geographer; geographic; geography
geol.	geologic; geologist; geology
Ger.	German; Germany
GIGO	garbage in, garbage out
Gk.	Greek
gloss.	glossary
G.O.P.	Grand Old Party (Republican)
Gov.	Governor (*plural* Govs.)
govt.	government
G.P.	General Practitioner
gp.	group
GPA, g.p.a.	grade point average
gpm, g.p.m.	gallons per minute
GPO	Government Printing Office
gps, g.p.s.	gallons per second
Gr.	Grecian; Greece
gr.	grade; grain; gram; gross

grad.	graduate(d)
gram.	grammar; grammatical
GRAS	generally recognized as safe
GRE	graduate record examination
gr. wt.	gross weight
GSA	General Service Administration; Girl Scouts of America
GT	gross ton(s)
Gt. Brit.	Great Britain
gtd., guar.	guaranteed
GU	Guam (ZIP Code abbreviation)
h.	harbor; hour(s); house; husband
hab. corp.	habeas corpus
HCL	high cost of living
HD	heavy-duty
hdwe.	hardware
Heb.	Hebrew
HF	high frequency
hf.	half
hgt.	height
HHS	Department of Health and Human Services
hist.	historian; historical; history
H.M.S.	His (Her) Majesty's Service or Ship
Hon.	Honorable (*plural* Hons.)
HP, hp	horsepower
HQ	headquarters
H.R.	House of Representatives
HST	Hawaiian Standard Time
ht.	height
HUD	Department of Housing and Urban Development
Hung.	Hungary
hwy.	highway
Hz	hertz
I	island, isle
IA	Iowa (ZIP Code abbreviation)
ibid.	(*ibidem*) in the same place
ICBM	intercontinental ballistic missile
ICC	Interstate Commerce Commission
ICFTU	International Confederation of Free Trade Unions
ICJ	International Court of Justice
ICU	intensive care unit
ID	Identification; Idaho (ZIP Code abbreviation)

id.	(*idem*) the same
i.e.	(*id est*) that is
IFC	International Finance Corporation
IL	Illinois (ZIP Code abbreviation)
ILA	International Longshoremen's Association
ILGWU	International Ladies' Garment Workers Union
Ill.	Illinois
ill.	illustrated; illustration
imp.	imperfect; import; imprimatur
IN	Indiana (ZIP Code abbreviation)
in.	inch(es)
Inc.	Incorporated
inc.	income; incoming; increase
incl.	including; inclusive
incog.	incognito
Ind.	Indiana
ind.	independent; industrial; industry
init.	initial
in re	in regard to
INS	Immigration and Naturalization Service
ins.	insurance
Inst.	Institute; Institution
inst.	installment; instant
instr.	instructor
int.	interest; interior; international
Intl.	International
intro.	introduction; introductory
inv.	invested; invoice
invt.	inventory
IOU	I owe you
ips, i.p.s.	inches per second
IQ, I.Q.	intelligence quotient
i.q.	(*idem quod*) the same as
IRA	individual retirement account
IRBM	intermediate range ballistic missile
Ire.	Ireland
irreg.	irregular
IRS	Internal Revenue Service
is., isl.	island; isle
iss.	issue
It.	Italy; Italian
ital.	italic; italicize
J.	Judge; Justice (*plural* JJ.)

J.A.	Judge Advocate
JAG	Judge Advocate General
Jan.	January
jct.	junction
J.D.	Doctor of Laws
jnt. stk.	joint stock
jour.	journal
J.P.	Justice of the Peace
Jpn.	Japan; Japanese
jt.	joint
junc.	junction
K	Kelvin
k	kilo; kindergarten; kosher; 1,000 (technical)
Kans.	Kansas
kc	kilocycle
kg.	kilogram(s)
kgps, kg/s	kilograms per second
kl	kiloliter(s)
km	kilometer(s)
kph, k.p.h.	kilometers per hour
KS	Kansas (ZIP Code abbreviation)
kw	kilowatt(s)
kwh	kilowatt-hour
KY	Kentucky (ZIP Code abbreviation)
Ky.	Kentucky
L	fifty; Latin
L.	Latin; law; (*libra*) pound(s) sterling
l.	lake; left; length; lire; liter(s)
LA	Los Angeles; Louisiana (ZIP Code abbreviation)
La.	Louisiana
lab.	laboratory
lang.	language
lat.	latitude
lb.	pound (*plural* lbs.)
L/C	letter of credit (*plural* Ls/C)
lc, l.c.	left center; lower case
LCDR, Lt. Cmdr.	Lieutenant Commander
Leg.	Legislative; Legislature
leg.	legal
LF, L.F., lf, l.f.	low frequency

lg.	large
L.I.	Long Island
Lieut., Lt.	Lieutenant
liq.	liquid
lit.	literally; literature
ll.	lines
LL.D.	Doctor of Laws
loc.	local; location
loc. cit.	(*loco citato*) in the place cited
long.	longitude
Lt., Lieut.	Lieutenant
Lt. Cmdr.	Lieutenant Commander
Lt. Col.	Lieutenant Colonel
Ltd., ltd.	limited
Lt. Gen.	Lieutenant General
Lt. Gov.	Lieutenant Governor
lv.	leave(s)
LWV	League of Women Voters
M	(*mille*) 1,000; million (technical); Monsieur (*plural* Messrs.)
m, m.	mark(s); meter(s)
m.	married; masculine; mile(s); mill(s); minute; month
MA	Massachusetts (ZIP Code abbreviation)
M.A.	Master of Arts
mach.	machine; machinery
Maj.	Major
maj.	majority
Maj. Gen.	Major General
Man.	Manhattan; Manitoba, Canada
man.	manager; manual
Mass.	Massachusetts
mat.	matinee; maturity
max.	maximum
M.B.A.	Master of Business Administration
MBS	Mutual Broadcasting System
mc	megacycle
M.C.	Master of Ceremonies; Member of Congress
MD	Maryland (ZIP Code abbreviation)
Md.	Maryland
M.D.	Doctor of Medicine
mdse.	merchandise
ME	Maine (ZIP Code abbreviation)

M.E.	Managing Editor; Mechanical Engineer; Mining Engineer
meas.	measure; measurement
mech.	mechanic; mechanical
med.	medical; medicine; medium
Messrs., MM.	Messieurs
met.	metal; meteorological; metropolitan
Mex.	Mexican; Mexico
mfd.	manufactured
mfg.	manufacturing
mfr.	manufacture; manufacturer
mg	milligram
Mgr.	Manager; Monseigneur; Monsignor
mgt., mgmt.	management
MHz	megahertz
MI	Michigan (ZIP Code abbreviation)
mi.	mile(s); mill(s)
Mich.	Michigan
mid.	middle; midshipman
mil.	mileage; military; million
min.	mineral; minimum; minute(s)
Minn.	Minnesota
misc.	miscellaneous
Miss.	Mississippi
M.I.T.	Massachusetts Institute of Technology
mk.	mark (*plural* mks.)
mkt., mar.	market
ml	milliliter
Mlle	Mademoiselle (*plural* Mlles)
mm	millimeter
MM.	Messieurs
Mme	Madame (French)
Mmes	Mesdames (French)
MN	Minnesota (ZIP Code abbreviation)
mng.	managing
MO	Missouri (ZIP Code abbreviation)
Mo.	Missouri
mo.	month (*plural* mos.)
m.o.	mail order; *modus operandi*; money order
mod.	moderate; modified
Mon.	Monday
Mont.	Montana
MP	Member of Parliament; Military Police; Mounted Police

mp, m.p.	melting point
mpg, m.p.g.	miles per gallon
mph, m.p.h.	miles per hour
MS	Mississippi (ZIP Code abbreviation)
MS, ms.	manuscript (*plural* MSS or mss.)
m/s	meters per second
Ms.	Miss or Mrs. (*plural* Mss.)
M.S., M.Sc.	Master of Science
msg.	message
Msgr.	Monsignor
msgr.	messenger
M. Sgt., M/Sgt.	Master Sergeant
MST	Mountain Standard Time
MT	Montana (ZIP Code abbreviation)
mt.	material; mountain (*plural* mts.)
mtg.	meeting; mortgage
mun.	municipal
m.v.	market value
M.V.D.	Motor Vehicle Department; (Russian) Ministry of Internal Affairs
N.	Navy; noon; north
n.	name; net; new; noon; note
n/30	net in 30 days
n.a.	no account (banking); not applicable; not available
NAACP	National Association for the Advancement of Colored People
NAS	National Academy of Sciences
NASA	National Aeronautics and Space Administration
nat., natl.	national
NATO	North Atlantic Treaty Organization
naut.	nautical
nav.	naval; navigation
NB	Nebraska (ZIP Code abbreviation); northbound
N.B.	New Brunswick, Canada
N.B., n.b.	(*nota bene*) note well
NBC	National Broadcasting Company
NBS	National Bureau of Standards
NC	North Carolina (ZIP Code abbreviation)
N.C.	North Carolina
n.c.	no charge
NCO	noncommissioned officer

ND	North Dakota (ZIP Code abbreviation)
n.d.	next day's delivery; no date
NE	northeast
N.E.	New England
NEA	National Editorial Association; National Educational Association
Nebr.	Nebraska
neg.	negative(ly)
Neth.	Netherlands
Nev.	Nevada
N.F.	Newfoundland, Canada; no funds
NG, N.G.	National Guard
n.g.	no good
N.I.H.	National Institutes of Health; not invented here
NH	New Hampshire (ZIP Code abbreviation)
N.H.	New Hampshire
NJ	New Jersey (ZIP Code abbreviation)
N.J.	New Jersey
NL	night letter
NLRB	National Labor Relations Board
NM	New Mexico (ZIP Code abbreviation)
N. Mex.	New Mexico
No., no.	North; northern; number (*plural* nos.)
n.o.c.	not otherwise classified
nol. pros.	(*nolle prosequi*) to be unwilling to prosecute
non. pros.	(*non prosequitur*) he does not prosecute
non seq.	(*non sequitur*) it does not follow
Nor.	Norway; Norwegian
NORAD	North American Air Defense Command
Nov.	November
NOW	National Organization of Women
N.P.	neuropsychiatric; Notary Public
NPR	National Public Radio
NRC	Nuclear Regulatory Commission
N.S.	not specified; Nova Scotia, Canada
NSC	National Security Council
N.S.F.	National Science Foundation; not sufficient funds
nt. wt.	net weight
n.u.	name unknown
nuc.	nuclear
NV	Nevada (ZIP Code abbreviation); not voting; no value

N.V.D., nvd	no value declared
NW	Northwest
NWT	Northwest Territories, Canada
NY	New York (ZIP Code abbreviation)
N.Y.	New York
NYC, N.Y.C.	New York City
NYSE	New York Stock Exchange
NZ	New Zealand
O.	ocean
OA, o/a	on account
OAS	Organization of American States
ob, OB	(*obiit*) he/she died; obstetrician; obstetrics
obs.	obsolete
obit.	obituary (*plural* obits.)
O/C	overcharge; over the counter
oc.	ocean; overcharge
Oct.	October
O.D.	Doctor of Optometry; officer of the day
o.d.	on demand; overdose; overdraft
OE	Old English
OED	Oxford English Dictionary
OEO	Office of Economic Opportunity
ofc., off.	office; officer; official
OH	Ohio (ZIP Code abbreviation)
OK	Oklahoma (ZIP Code abbreviation)
Okla.	Oklahoma
OMB	Office of Management and Budget
Ont.	Ontario, Canada
op.	(*opus*) work
OP, o.p.	out of print
op. cit.	(*opere citato*) in the work cited
OPEC	Organization of Petroleum Exporting Countries
opp.	opposite
opt.	optional
OR	operating room; Oregon (ZIP Code abbreviation)
Oreg.	Oregon
org.	organization
orig.	original(ly)
OS, o/s	out of stock
OSHA	Occupational Safety and Health Act
O/T	overtime
OW, o.w.	one way (fare)

oz.	ounce(s)
p.	page (plural pp.); per; peseta; peso; pressure
PA	Pennsylvania (ZIP Code abbreviation)
P.A.	power of attorney; press agent; purchasing agent
Pa.	Pennsylvania
pa.	paper
p.a.	per annum (by the year)
Pac.	Pacific
PAC	political action committee
Pan Am	Pan American Airways, Inc.
par.	paragraph; parallel
pat.	patent(ed)
Pat. Off.	Patent Office
PC, P.C.	private corporation
pc.	parsec; piece (plural pcs.)
pct.	percent
pd.	paid
P.E.	Professional Engineer
pet.	petroleum
pf., pfd.	preferred (securities)
PFC, pfc.	private first class
Pg.	Portugal; Portuguese
Ph.D.	Doctor of Philosophy
PHS	Public Health Service
P.I.	Philippine Islands
PINS	person(s) in need of supervision
PJ	Presiding Judge
pkg.	package (*plural* pkgs.); parking
pky.	parkway
pl.	place; plate; plural
plf.	plaintiff
PLO	Palestine Liberation Organization
PLS	Professional Legal Secretary
Plz.	Plaza
PM, P.M., p.m.	(*post meridiem*), afternoon; prime minister
Pm., prem.	premium
pmt.	payment
p.n.	promissory note
P.O.	petty officer (Navy); Post Office
p.o.d.	payment on death; pay on delivery
POE, p.o.e.	port of embarkation; port of entry
Pol.	Poland; Polish

pol.	political; politician; politics
pop.	population
Port.	Portugal; Portuguese
pp.	pages
p.p.	parcel post
ppd.	postpaid; prepaid
P.Q.	Province of Quebec, Canada
PR	public relations; Puerto Rico
pr.	pair; price; printed
PRC	People's Republic of China
pref., pf.	preface; preference; preferred
prem.	premium
Pres.	President
prin.	principal
prob.	problem
prod.	produce(d); product
prof.	professional; professor (*plural* profs.)
pron.	pronoun; pronounced
prop.	property; proposition
Prot.	Protestant
pro. tem.	(*pro tempore*) temporary
prov.	province; provisional
PS, P.S.	postscript (*plural* PSS)
pseud.	pseudonym
psf, p.s.f.	pounds per square foot
psgr.	passenger
psi, p.s.i.	pounds per square inch
PST	Pacific Standard Time
psych.	psychology
pstg.	postage
pt.	part; payment; pint; point; port
PTA, P.T.A.	Parent-Teacher Association
ptg.	printing
PU	pickup
pub.	public; publication; published; publisher
PUD	pickup and delivery
Pvt.	Private (Army and Marines)
pwr.	power
PX	post exchange (military) (*plural* PXS)
Q.	Quebec; Question
q.	quart; quarter; quasi; question; quire
Q.E.D.	(*quod erat demonstrandum*) that which was to be proved
Q.M.	Quartermaster

qr.	quarter; quarterly
qt.	quart (*plural* qts.)
Q.T., q.t.	quiet, as in *on the Q.T.*
qty.	quantity
quad.	quadrangle; quadrant
q.v.	(*quod vide*) which see
qy.	query
R.	registered trademark; Republican
r.	received; right; road; ruble; rupee
R.A.	Regular Army; Royal Academy
RADM	Rear Admiral
R & D	Research and Development
R.C.	Roman Catholic
rcpt.	receipt (*plural* rcpts.)
rd.	road; rod; round
re	regarding
R.E.A.	Rural Electrification Administration
rec.	recipe; record(ed)
recd.	received
Rec. Sec.	Recording Secretary
ref.	referee; reference; refining; refunding
refr.	refrigerate(d); refrigerator
reg.	register(ed); regular; regulation
Rep.	Representative; Republic; Republican
rep.	repair; repeat; report(er)
req.	required; requisition
res.	residence; resolution
ret.	retired; return
Rev.	Reverend (*plural* Revs.)
rev.	revenue; review; revised; revolution
Rev. Stat.	Revised Statutes
RF, r.f.	radio frequency
R.F.D.	rural free delivery
RI	Rhode Island (ZIP Code abbreviation)
R.I.	Rhode Island
R.I.P.	(*requiescat in pace*) rest in peace
rm.	ream; room
R.N.	Registered Nurse; Royal Navy
rom.	roman type
ROTC	Reserve Officers Training Corps
rpm, r.p.m.	revolutions per minute
RPO	Railway Post Office
rps, r.p.s.	revolutions per second
rpt.	report

R.R.	railroad; rural route
R.S.V.P.	(*répondez s'il vous plaît*) please reply
rte.	route
Rt. Hon.	Right Honorable
Rt. Rev.	Right Reverend
Rus.	Russia; Russian
Ry.	Railway
S.	Saint; Senate; Signor
s.	second; silver; stock
s/a	subject to approval
S.A.	Salvation Army
S. Afr.	South Africa
S. Am.	South American
S & L	Savings and Loan
Sask.	Saskatchewan, Canada
Sat.	Saturday
SB	southbound
S.B.	Bachelor of Science
SBA	Small Business Administration
SC	South Carolina (ZIP Code abbreviation)
S.C.	South Carolina
Sc.D.	Doctor of Science
sch.	schedule; school
Script.	Scripture
SD	South Dakota (ZIP Code abbreviation)
S. Dak.	South Dakota
SE	Southeast
SEATO	Southeast Asia Treaty Organization
SEC	Securities and Exchange Commission
sec.	second(s); section; security
secy.	secretary (*plural* secys.)
sel.	select(ed); selection
Sen.	Senate; Senator (*plural* Sens.); Senior
Sept.	September
seq.	(*sequens*) the following (*plural* seqq.)
ser.	serial; series; service
SFC	Sergeant First Class
Sgd., S.	Signed
Sgt.	Sergeant
sh.	share(s) (*plural* shs.); sheet
shpt.	shipment
shtg.	shortage
sic	so written; thus
sig., Sig.	signal; signature; Signor

sine die	without a day set for meeting again
sing.	singular
S.J.	Society of Jesus (Jesuits)
sld.	sailed; sealed; sold
sm.	small
S.M.	Master of Science
So., S.	South; Southern
s.o.	shipping order
Soc.	society; sociology
SOP	standard operating procedure
SP	Shore Patrol
Sp.	Spain; Spanish
sp.	special; species; specific; spelling
spec.	specification (*plural* specs.); specimen
Sq	squadron
sq.	square
Sr.	Senior; Sister
SR	sedimentation rate; shipping receipt
SRO, S.R.O.	single-room occupancy; standing room only
SS	Saints; same size; Social Security; steamship
SSA	Social Security Administration
SSG, S.Sgt.	Staff Sergeant
St.	saint (*plural* SS)
st.	state; street
Sta.	Station
stat.	statistics; statutes
S.T.D.	Doctor of Sacred Theology
std.	standard
Ste.	(*Sainte*) saint (feminine)
stge.	storage
stk.	stock
Stk. Exch.	Stock Exchange
Stk. Mkt.	Stock Market
Sun.	Sunday
sup.	superior; supply; *supra*
supp.	supplement(ary)
Supt.	Superintendent
sur.	surface; surplus
surg.	surgeon; surgical
surv.	survey; surveyor
svc., svce.	service
svgs.	savings
s.v.p.	(*s'il vous plaît*) if you please
Sw., Swed.	Sweden; Swedish

sw.	switch
sym.	symbol; symmetrical
syn.	synonym; synonymous
syst.	system
T.	tablespoon(s); township (*plural* Twps.)
t.	teaspoon(s); temperature; ton(s)
T.B.	trial balance
tbsp.	tablespoon(s)
TD	Treasury Department; touchdown
TDY	temporary duty
tech.	technical; technician
tel.	telegram; telephone
temp.	temperature; temporary
Tenn.	Tennessee
ter.	terrace; territory
Tex.	Texas
thou.	thousand
Thurs.	Thursday
TID	(*ter in die*) three times a day
TL	total loss; truckload
TLC	tender loving care
TM	trademark
tn.	ton; town; train
TN	Tennessee (ZIP Code abbreviation)
tr.	translated; transpose; trust; trustee
trans.	transaction; translated; translation; transportation
treas.	treasurer; treasury
T.Sgt., TSgt.	Technical Sergeant
tsp.	teaspoon
Tues.	Tuesday
Turk.	Turkey; Turkish
TV	television; terminal velocity
TVA	Tennessee Valley Authority
TWA	Trans-World Airlines, Inc.
twp.	township
TWX	teletypewriter exchange
TX	Texas (ZIP Code abbreviation)
U., Univ.	University
UA	United Airlines; United Artists
UAW	United Auto Workers
UC	undercharge; uppercase
UFO	unidentified flying object (*plural* UFOs)
UFT	United Federation of Teachers

ugt.	urgent
UHF	ultrahigh frequency
UK	United Kingdom
UL	Underwriters Laboratories
UMW	United Mine Workers
UN, U.N.	United Nations
unam.	unanimously
UNESCO	United Nations Educational, Scientific, and Cultural Organization
UNICEF	United Nations International Children's Fund
UPI	United Press International
UPS	United Parcel Service
U.S.	United States
U.S.A.	United States of America
USA	United States Army
USAF	United States Air Force
USAR	United States Army Reserve
USCG	United States Coast Guard
USDA	United States Department of Agriculture
USES	United States Employment Service
USIA	United States Information Agency
USMC	United States Marine Corps
USN	United States Navy
USO	United Service Organizations
USSR	Union of Soviet Socialist Republics
UT	Utah (ZIP Code abbreviation)
UW	underwriter
v	volt
v.	verb; verse; versus; volume
VA	Veterans Administration; Virginia (ZIP Code abbreviation)
Va.	Virginia
V.A.	Veterans Administration
VAdm	Vice Admiral
val.	value
var.	variety; various
VAT	value-added tax
VDT	video display terminal
vel.	velocity
vert.	vertebrate; vertical
VF	very high frequency
V.I.	Vancouver Island, Canada; Virgin Islands
vic.	vicinity
Vice Adm.	Vice Admiral

Vice Pres., V.P.	Vice President
VIP	very important person (*plural* VIPs)
vis.	visibility; visual
viz.	(*videlicet*) namely
vol.	volcano; volume; volunteer
V.P.	Vice President
vs., v.	versus; against; verse
V.S.	Veterinary Surgeon
VT	Vermont (ZIP Code abbreviation)
Vt.	Vermont
vv	verses; vice versa
W	West; Western
w.	watts
WA	Washington State (ZIP Code abbreviation)
Wash.	Washington State
WB	Westbound
Wed.	Wednesday
whole.	wholesale
whs.	warehouse
WI	Wisconsin (ZIP Code abbreviation)
W.I.	West Indies
Wis.	Wisconsin
wk.	week (*plural* wks.)
W.O.	Warrant Officer
WP	word processing
wpm	words per minute
wps	words per second
WR	warehouse receipt
wt.	weight
WV	West Virginia (ZIP Code abbreviation)
W. Va.	West Virginia
WY	Wyoming (ZIP Code abbreviation)
Wyo.	Wyoming
XL	extra large; extra long
XS	extra small
YB	yearbook
yd.	yard
YMCA	Young Men's Christian Association
YM-YWHA	Young Men's and Women's Hebrew Association
YOB	year of birth
YT	Yukon Territory, Canada
YWCA	Young Women's Christian Association

YWHA	Young Women's Hebrew Association
Z, z.	zero; zone
ZI	Zone of the Interior
ZIP	Zone Improvement Plan
zpg	zero population growth

PART TWO

PART I

CHAPTER NINE

Goals, Attitude, and Advancement

Goal. As a secretary who has ability and ambition, you should set yourself a goal. By considering what job you hope to have in five or ten years, you can think about what skills must be acquired, what further education may be needed, and what experience will contribute to your preparation for this advanced position.

Whether your goal is to become secretary to the president or to become an executive yourself, you must learn the chain of command and who does what in the organization where you are employed. It is important to remember names and how to spell them, and to recognize executives when meeting them in the corridor or in the elevator and say, "Good morning, Mrs. Smith," "Hello, Mr. Ditrio." Speaking to an officer of the company is only being courteous. Executives don't like to be ignored as if they were invisible.

Skills. The basic skills of language, typing, and shorthand should be polished every day. You yourself can judge if you are doing your best. While 150-words-a-minute shorthand and one-on-one dictation may not be required, shorthand can be invaluable in reporting meetings, taking telephone messages, keeping one's own notes and reminders, and noting directions for action. Knowing shorthand gives you an advantage over someone who doesn't.

Typing skills are as important with word processors as with typewriters. The fewer corrections needed, the quicker the job is done, and the more time is available for attending to other tasks.

A good secretary proofreads his or her work, either alone or by reading it back to another secretary. A device on the word processor known as speller verification can spot typographical errors, but unfortunately it cannot detect incorrect punctuation, omitted words and sentences, or wrong figures. Consequently, you must read for sense as well as look for typos. And where figures, dates, or sums of money are concerned, great care must of course be taken to ensure accuracy.

It may be in the area of language skills that you can make your most valuable contribution to the work of the office. Your command of spelling, punctuation, and grammar can be an enormous help to an employer. Many managers are skilled in their technical specialties but are unable to express their ideas coherently on paper. Their correspondence, memoranda, and reports may be poor reflections on their ability unless a secretary makes needed corrections. If you can write simple, clear sentences and organize thoughts into paragraphs, you can relieve your employer of many routine communications as well as assist in other aspects of the work.

You need to develop the ability to read and use instruction manuals in order to utilize the sophisticated equipment now used in many offices. You should be able to use more than one kind of calculator or word processor, noting similarities and differences and adapting to the differences.

Professionalism. In progressing toward your goal, you must develop and demonstrate professionalism. The term *professionalism* in this sense means a serious attitude toward the work, knowledge of your job, willingness to use your knowledge in a constructive manner, and pride in maintaining high standards of performance.

The secretary's ability and self-confidence can project the efficiency of the organization. Since you are often the first person a customer encounters, it is important that the experience be positive. A pleasant voice, appropriate dress, a confident manner, and willingness to be of service are important in making a good impression for yourself as well as for your employer.

Appropriate dress may vary from one setting to another. It is desirable to look attractive, for your own self-esteem and for the atmosphere of the office. Cleanliness, personal grooming, and avoiding clothes that are too tight or too revealing are obvious considerations. The degree of chic will depend on your own taste and income, on your exposure to the public, and on the type of work done in your office. Some employers prefer the secretary to be more conservatively dressed than others might. In a lawyer's office, for example, the secretaries are likely to wear suits and dresses that are more tailored than what might be expected in the advertising department of a popular magazine.

For women, simple blouses and skirts, and classic suits and dresses can be varied with colorful accessories and simple jewelry. You can develop skill in assembling color-coordinated outfits that look smart without spending all your salary on clothes. Try to buy a complete outfit at one time so that it fits in with clothes you already have. There are a number of magazines for working women that offer tips on buying and coordinating clothes for the office. Above all, each item of clothing must be clean and well pressed to look professional. While it is desirable to dress in fashion, it is not necessary to follow trends that are unbecoming to you or to spend more than you can afford in competition with fellow workers. However well dressed you may be, it is your personality and the quality of your work that will bring about your promotion to a more responsible position.

Similarly, makeup and hairstyles should be becoming and unobtrusive. Theatrical makeup and unusual hair coloring would seldom be appropriate in business situations. If you are unsure of your own taste, you may find a role model in an older secretary or in someone whose job you aspire to. By observing those who look professional and attractive, you can improve your own appearance. This also holds true for male secretaries, who should dress conventionally and avoid extreme hairstyles.

Mentor. As in other fields, a secretary can benefit from having a mentor. This person may be an immediate superior or a person in another department. He or she would probably be someone older who has been with the organization longer and knows how promotions are achieved. A mentor can suggest ways to improve your performance, how to prepare for more responsibility, and when to ask for it. A mentor can demonstrate suitable dress, effective presentation of ideas, attention to detail, and proper timing. What is involved is not imitation but adaptation of behavior to achieve results.

Perhaps no mentor is available to you. In some offices no one is willing to share "*my* wealth of information." In that case you can gather pertinent information from the department concerned or the person directly in charge of an area. Office politics may rule out guidance from someone higher up, but this won't prevent you from observing how promotions are gained. Just be sure your work product is nearly perfect, your behavior ethical and dignified, and your attitude cooperative.

Attitude. It is imperative that you arrive on time for work, ready to start without needing to spend time on makeup or drinking coffee, and take only the specified lunch period. A serious worker does not prepare to leave well before closing time, so as to rush out before the others. The point is to try to get all work finished in time but, if necessary, to be prepared to stay until the job is done. A serious attitude toward work includes devoting sufficient time to complete it correctly. Willingness to make an extra effort is an indication of ambition and your desire to cooperate with the employer.

Loyalty to your employer is a high priority. What a secretary does or says is a reflection of the employer. You should not gossip about your work or your employer's responsibilities, but you should be alert to pick up any information that might be useful to your department. You tell nothing that has not been announced.

This presupposes that your employer is right. Where there is mutual respect, loyalty comes as a matter of course. There are cases of an insecure employer who blames his mistakes on his secretary or asks him or her to do something dishonest or unethical. Then the best approach is to decline respectfully and start looking for another job. Association with someone you cannot respect will make the job too unpleasant to endure if you have any other option at all. Good secretaries are usually in such great demand that a more agreeable situation can be found. After all, the working hours are a major part of your life, and even a high salary cannot compensate for an atmosphere that makes you miserable. Working is a pleasure when you feel appreciated, when you are learning and growing, so that the days seem short.

A professional attitude includes behavior toward co-workers. A secretary needs the cooperation of others, and you must be willing to help others when possible. Of course, the favor should be returned; it is expected that cooperation will go both ways. You have to be able to get along with individuals you might not choose as friends. It isn't worth getting the better of someone in an argument if it leaves bad feelings. Try to keep personalities out of discussions, and you can make the office atmosphere a bit pleasanter. Your job may depend on your ability to get along with some difficult co-workers.

Your own good judgment is invaluable. You must know when to bring matters to your employer's attention. You must know when to interrupt and when a matter can wait. You must sense when a joke is inappropriate and when a light touch can defuse a situation. Judgment is learned, even from mistakes. Having made a mistake, you learn not to repeat it.

It is best to keep your personal life outside the office. Except for matters that must be shared, such as a death in the family or similar upsetting events, sharing intimate matters with co-workers can be embarrassing if circumstances change. And office romances are best avoided. The unpleasantness of gossip is often painful to the participants, especially if the romance goes sour.

When you have become your employer's right hand, so to speak, you can anticipate what he or she will need in many situations. You can be prepared with data for a meeting, with check requests or cash advance requests when required, with telephone numbers when needed, as well as extra supplies that might be necessary for a conference. Ideally, the secretary knows the employer's job well enough to be the assistant, hence the position of administrative secretary or assistant. Pay should then be commensurate with the responsibilities, not with the length of service alone.

Some employers feel threatened if the secretary is too quick, too efficient. They feel unable to share the work with a secretary. They dole out tasks and keep a tight grip on everything. If a secretary demonstrates capability, he or she should be given as much responsibility as he or she can handle. Doing so will free the employer to do planning or specialized work the secretary cannot do.

An employer may not know how to use a secretary. Such a person wants to be waited on, even if the secretary is busy. It seems to make him or her feel important. Rather than take a few steps to speak to someone in another office, this employer asks the secretary to stop work and place a telephone call or perhaps call someone for needed information. It may be possible to suggest that the task you are engaged in won't be finished when needed if you are interrupted. Perhaps you can ask if the request can wait until you have completed your present task. If this is not acceptable, the employer probably will not change, and you can only do your best to provide the service requested.

On the other hand, many managers feel it saves time to place and answer their own phone calls. They recognize that the secretary has his or her own work to do, and they interrupt only when necessary.

If there is mutual respect, an employer and secretary can work well together without irritating each other. The relationship has been called an office marriage, with good reason. A romantic tie is not implied but a working partnership that is efficient and demonstrates mutual admiration. As in a long marriage, the secretary and employer make allowances for occasional shortcomings, realizing that goodwill is always there and both are interested in doing a good job. When this is the case, a secretary does not mind getting coffee for the employer or a visitor or being asked to make copies of a document. He or she is glad to facilitate the business at hand rather than feeling demeaned by such requests.

Advancement. If the day comes when a job is no longer challenging, when the work is so routine that it seems effortless or boring, it is time to think of making a change. You may wish to take on more responsibility. Now is the time to prepare a presentation to be given when your employer has a free moment. You should be ready to describe the work you do, to show samples, and to indicate what you would like to do. You should ask to be considered for the job you want if it is in your own department. (If it is in another area, you can make a similar presentation to the appropriate person.) You should mention how long you have been in your present position and the extent of your knowledge about the company. This is a selling effort, one of selling yourself and your skills. If you have practiced your presentation, dressed yourself carefully, and chosen the right moment, success may well be yours.

However, it may happen to be a time when there is no opening or the company is cutting back on staff. Or someone else may have been selected for the opening. There are often unfair decisions and disappointments. If the first effort is not successful, there will be other opportunities. You should not be resentful if your first request is not granted. It may take time to reach the desired goal, and to be a survivor one must sometimes be disappointed. But it is necessary to risk to rise in the world.

In some large companies, openings are posted on bulletin boards, and the secretaries apply for jobs they want. The skills required and the department concerned are mentioned. It would be useful to find out what the job is like from the person who is leaving before you apply. You might prefer to keep your present position rather than move to a department that would not be congenial. Or the job might sound interesting, a challenge you would be glad to accept. In that case you would surely apply.

Changing jobs. If after a few months' time no opening or advancement is offered, you may consider moving to another department or another organization. The skills and knowledge acquired in one company can be valuable in another. Unless there is a compelling reason for remaining in one part of the country, this might be a time to think of looking for a job in another city or even another country. Personal growth can come from the stimulation of a new job or from moving to a different area. Secretarial work is a portable skill, needed everywhere. It can provide entry into another field, a whole new world of interest. One might go from a sales department to a real estate office, to a doctor's or a publisher's office. Public service is an area of interest to many, and social service agencies have their supporters. Learning about a new field and meeting new associates can lend another dimension to one's life.

By obtaining newspapers from other cities, perhaps in the local library, you can read the Help Wanted advertisements and note the jobs available and the prevailing salaries. You should also check the real estate pages to get an idea of living costs in another area before moving. In the library, too, are books and magazines dealing with many kinds of work in other areas of the country and abroad. You can learn about other people's experiences, and all this information is free. (*See* p. 402, Getting a Job.)

You can also seek information from acquaintances in other fields, in secretaries' organizations, and other business connections. Networking, that is, making connections with others in your field, can turn up opportunities you otherwise would have missed.

It might be possible to transfer to another branch of your present organization in another location. Doing so would preserve your seniority, and the years of prior employment would apply to any pension or retirement benefits. But if you are in your early twenties and have been with a company only a few years, you need not concern yourself unduly with retirement benefits but rather with opportunities for growth.

It is easier, of course, to get another job when one is currently employed. Unless you have substantial savings, it is comforting to have a regular paycheck while you are answering advertisements. Interviews can be scheduled for the lunch hour or perhaps in the early morning. It may be awkward to let it be known that you are considering a new job, so discretion should be used.

There is also the possibility of becoming an entrepreneur, whether offering word processing services or organizing a small business that will use the expertise acquired in previous employment. There are many magazine articles and books devoted to this subject.

Advancement depends on having initiative, good skills, confidence, and an attractive personality. The secretary who is determined to make good will succeed. With diligence, willingness to take a chance, and a reasonable amount of good luck, you can go as far as you wish. By setting a goal and making wise choices in your selection of jobs, you can enjoy your work, earn a good salary, and make a real contribution.

CHAPTER TEN

Office Machines

Today's offices may be equipped with the latest electronic gadgets or may still rely on the typewriter and telephone, depending on the size and profitability of the enterprise. While it is not practical to describe in detail the array of equipment now available, a brief description of some of the machines you may encounter is provided.

The manual typewriter has been replaced by the electric typewriter. Among the desirable features of the electric typewriter are the keys for carriage return and for easy correction of errors, the possibility of using varied typefaces, and the uniform appearance of the typed product. And of course much less effort is required when using the electric machine, since only a light touch is needed. Consequently, time is saved and the results are more attractive.

Next in appeal is the electronic typewriter, which has many of the convenient features of a word processor. It can return the carriage automatically at whatever right margin you have set, either when a word ends or a hyphen is typed. You can automatically center headings, align columns of figures on the decimal point, type data flush left or flush right—all by touching a key or two. Electronic typewriters offer a memory, ranging from a page or two up to thirty or more. Some electronic typewriters will interface with a computer, allowing almost unlimited memory capacity.

Word Processor. The word processor may be a freestanding apparatus or simply one program of a computer. A "dedicated" word processor includes the same components as a computer but has programs for word processing only. A computer can employ many kinds of programs and has much more capability, and it is therefore more expensive. A dedicated word processor would be appropriate for offices that produce mainly correspondence, reports, and other textual documents. Writers, reporters, and lawyers find word processors invaluable because of the convenience in editing, updating, and storing documents. Legal documents can be adapted to various uses without tedious retyping.

The Computer. The computer consists of a keyboard much like that of a typewriter; a VDT (video display terminal) or CRT (cathode ray terminal), which looks like a television screen and permits you to see what you are keyboarding; and the CPU (central processing unit), which is the brain of the computer. In the central processing unit are thousands of electronic circuits contained in tiny silicon chips. Information is processed in the CPU, which also houses the computer's memory and stores programs, operating instructions, and other necessary information.

The information keyboarded and appearing on the screen will vanish when the machine is turned off. Therefore it must be stored for reuse. The storage may be on a floppy disk, which is removable, or on a hard disk, which is in a permanent container and is connected to the computer. The floppy disk comes in several sizes. A 5¼-inch disk can hold up to 80 pages of data; a double-density disk will hold many times that amount. The hard disk can store up to 150 times the amount stored in a floppy disk and can be accessed much faster, making the hard disk more useful for business purposes requiring greater capacity.

The computer uses one of three types of printers. The dot matrix printer produces letters that consist of tiny dots. While it is legible and can print graphics, it is not considered suitable for business correspondence. A more attractive (and more expensive) printer uses the daisy wheel, which offers a variety of typefaces and letter-quality printing. Another type is the laser printer, which works somewhat like a copier, using laser beams. This type of nonimpact printer can print graphics as well as a variety of type sizes and styles. The product is letter quality, and the laser printer is much quieter than the other types.

In general, using a computer is not difficult. After turning on the machine, you load a program into the CPU by inserting a floppy disk into the disk drive, or you can select a program on the hard disk. When the screen lights up, you look over the menu and choose the appropriate operation. Using the keyboard, you key in the information (you are "inputting"), and it is shown on the screen. When you have completed the task, you print it out or store it—or both.

Learning to use a computer may intimidate someone accustomed to a typewriter. The action is so much faster, and in the beginning the frustration level is high. Be patient and persevere, however; the convenience and ease of using the computer will win you over. It is important to remember that the computer will react to whatever signal it receives. If you make an error in your input, that is what the computer will record. Most computers have an "oops" key, which enables you to correct a mistake if you act promptly. This could save you from unintentionally deleting hours of work.

Learning on the job can be exhausting, since regular work has to be done even while you are learning to use a new machine. For this reason it is desirable to have a period devoted solely to how to use the computer. You will find that you learn faster and remember more readily without the distraction of regular tasks. Many vendors of computers and dedicated word processors offer courses of instruction with the purchase of equipment, as well as follow-up consultation.

The disadvantage of using computers is the cost of purchasing the equipment and training personnel to use it. However, the computer is essential to most businesses because of the time saved and the convenience of maintaining records in memory to be displayed automatically or printed out as desired. Specialized sales promotions and reports can be generated quickly and easily, and handwritten documents of many kinds can be eliminated. The elimination of hand-copying can greatly reduce errors. (Of course, an error in input will remain, so that accuracy still depends on the operator.)

While word processing is one feature of the computer, much more capacity is available. The computer can be used for data processing, accounting, budgeting, mailing list management, financial modeling and forecasting, telecommunications, electronic mail, and business graphics. Uses of the dedicated word processor and computer appear in Chapter 11.

Copiers. In most offices, copiers have replaced carbon paper in producing copies of correspondence and other text. The copier is fast, easy to use, and can produce the desired number of copies with the touch of a button. Various kinds of paper can be used, including letterhead stationery.

The copier prints through the use of light rather than by impact, that is, striking the paper with a hammer or using a ribbon or dots. The document is placed facedown on the copier. A strong light shines on it, creating a pattern of electrical charges, which are imprinted on a rotating drum. The drum revolves through a tray of powder that clings to the charged imprint on the drum. The image created by the powder is then transferred to another piece of paper, thus producing the copy. While most machines use black powder, some accept other colors as well.

Many copiers employ microprocessors, which make the machines easier to use and maintain. The microprocessors are similar to computers and are programmed to tell you by means of signal lights when the machine is ready for use, when it needs more toner, and when there is a problem that prevents the machine from operating. Some machines use disposable cartridges for the toner, making it possible to add toner without soiling your hands or clothes; cartridges also permit the use of colored toner. Some machines are able to use several colors at once to produce copies close to the colors of originals.

Some copiers can reproduce in various sizes, enlarging or reducing as needed, and some can copy on both sides of the paper. It is also possible to add a sorter, which saves time by collating documents of many pages. Automatic feeders permit you to load a report and do something else while the pages are automatically fed, copied, and collected. Useful for copying lengthy documents are bins that hold a large quantity of paper. Some machines even trim paper and staple documents together when programmed to do so. Of course, the more capability the machine has, the more expensive it is.

Copiers are useful for providing multiple copies of memoranda, reports, and correspondence. They make copies of checks, invoices, deposit slips, budgets, and many other records. The reduction feature is convenient for copying budgets and other large financial planning documents. Various business forms can be created and reproduced in quantity. The copier has become an indispensable machine in our business and personal lives.

One problem some offices have is the excessive use of copiers for personal records. To keep costs down, some offices have found it necessary to use locking devices or to require personal signatures when the copier is used. The machine is expensive in itself, and the maintenance contract is an additional cost. If employees abuse the use of the copier, the number of copies that can be made before the drum or other components of the machine must be replaced is reduced.

Facsimile Machines. While computers can transmit text and data, the facsimile machine can also send exact copies of letterheads, charts, graphics, and even photographs from one location to another. Using the telephone lines, the fax machine transmits electronically to another such machine. You must have a line dedicated to the facsimile machine, and you must know the number of the receiving machine. You insert the document in the machine, dial the number of the machine at the other end, and give the order to transmit. The document is sent at once. To be sure that all pages of a long document have been received, you can use the same telephone line to call the person on the receiving end.

An automatic fax machine can be loaded before you leave the office, and the documents will be transmitted automatically during the night, when telephone rates are lower. Similarly, material can be received automatically; a buzzer or bell sounds when something is being sent to you.

While large companies often have their own facsimile machines, smaller companies can use facilities offered by office services in many cities. These services provide facilities that may be too expensive for the occasional needs of smaller organizations. At a cost of a few dollars, exact copies of contracts, financial data, graphics, and so forth, can be sent to a facsimile machine in another location. A "mailbox" with its own facsimile number can be maintained, so that the office service will receive data for you and telephone you when messages are received. Other services provided include telex (*see* below), twenty-four-hour access to mailboxes, metered mail, and shipment and receiving of packages on a twenty-four-hour basis, including gift wrapping. There is a modest service charge.

Telex. This service is similar to facsimile in speed of transmission, but only correspondence can be sent. The data must be keyed into the machine by an operator. Telephone lines are used. For confidential material, codes can be used. The telex machine can be left on to receive messages during times when the office is closed, if desired, as well as during working hours. Doing so means paying for an open telephone line, of course.

Office Organization. The office machines used today have relieved secretaries of many repetitive chores. Improved equipment has made it possible for secretaries to accomplish more in a shorter time. As a result, in many companies two or three managers now share one secretary. In other situations a secretary becomes more of an administrator, with dictation being handled by machines and transcribed in a central location. The secretary is then free to organize the work of the office.

CHAPTER ELEVEN

Word Processing and Data Processing

Word Processing

One of the benefits of the electronic revolution has been the development of word processors at prices available to most businesses and many individuals. The convenience and the timesaving aspects alone make word processors preferable to electric typewriters for most purposes. The possibility of combining other functions with typing has expanded the capability of the secretary. The word processor is fast and accurate and requires only a light touch. It can be used to print documents of any length and, depending on the printer, in many different typefaces.

Word processing means that text is manipulated electronically. The dedicated word processor has been developed solely for this use. It cannot run the variety of programs (called "software") available for computers, but it can do some chores better than some computers because it is specialized. The same components are used for both: the visual display terminal (VDT, which is like a video screen); the central processing unit (CPU, the brains of the computer); the keyboard; and the printer.

Using a keyboard much like a typewriter's, you type (or "keyboard") the letter, report, financial data, or whatever you are working on. The words and figures appear on the screen, so that you can see as you type and make any corrections as you go. A moving dot or arrow of light, called a cursor, moves just ahead of the last character typed. The cursor shows where the next character will appear or where a correction is being made. When you have finished keyboarding the document, you give it a name and store it. (In some programs you name or number the document before creating it.) If you don't store it, your work will vanish when the machine is turned off. An index of stored documents is made automatically, so that they can be retrieved.

The document is stored either on a floppy disk or on a hard disk. The floppy disk is a delicate storage unit that is placed in a slot in the disk drive when in use. When not in use, it must be kept in its jacket, handled carefully, and stored away from dust, heat, or anything magnetic. The hard disk is attached to the computer and has much greater capacity than a floppy disk. These disks are included in the term *magnetic media.*

If you are inputting a long document, it is advisable to take the time to store after every few pages. When you have completed the document, you should make a backup copy on another disk as a precaution against possible loss.

The CPU implements your commands of correcting, moving, inserting, deleting, printing, and storing your text. In an office where many word processors are in use, the CPU and printer probably will be shared. A personal computer in a small office or at home will have its own CPU and printer.

Uses. The principal uses of word processors are for correspondence, memoranda, reports, and other text. Reporters and writers use word processors for composing. Correcting and editing are easily accomplished, and the finished work can be stored, printed, or transmitted from one computer to another.

Special Features of Word Processors

Automatic Wordwrap. Instead of your having to touch a carriage return key, the cursor moves automatically to the next line when the programmed right margin is reached. If justification (an even right margin) is desired, spaces will be entered when the document is printed out, so that all lines are the same length. (This presents a more formal appearance but may create undesirable "rivers" of vertical blank spaces in the text. A good compromise is half-justification, available in some programs.)

Editing. One of the greatest conveniences in word processing is the ability to make corrections and changes without retyping the entire document. After you have finished keyboarding the letter or report or chapter, you can scan it on the screen, spotting most errors as you go. If you have included a wrong letter in a word, you can simply type the correction in the same space. No erasing, no more retyping. The offending letter is gone without a trace. If you wish to add or delete a word, a line, a paragraph, or a page, it is done in a flash, using the appropriate keys. When you insert new material, space opens up as needed. When something is deleted, the text is moved automatically to fill the empty spot. An additional feature is the capacity to copy or move whole paragraphs or pages to another location. This of course saves much retyping.

Editing can be done on stored material. Suppose you have input a rough draft for your employer. After proofreading it, you store it and print it out. He or she reads it over, makes changes in spacing, moves paragraphs around, deletes or adds a phrase, and hands it back to you. You bring the stored draft back to your screen and make the corrections as specified. You can scan the new material or use the spelling aid to make sure no other errors have crept in, but pages on which no changes have been made do not need to be proofread again. The time required to produce the new version is much less than that needed before word processing, and the possibility of creating more errors when retyping has been eliminated. You then store the new version under the same name, unless for some reason the original draft is likely to be needed. In that case, you give the corrected version a new name, perhaps adding only a letter or number to the original name. You can thus distinguish between the two versions and can retrieve either as needed. You can print out the corrected version and make extra copies simply by giving commands to the printer.

The ease with which corrections can be made not only is timesaving but avoids tiresome repetition. It enables the author of a report to make whatever changes are desired, without a long wait for retyping and guilt for causing extra work.

Spelling Aid. Most word processing programs have a spelling aid feature, a dictionary containing thousands of words. Some programs are activated before you start the document; some are used after you finish. A signal sounds when the cursor encounters an unfamiliar combination of letters, and you check to see if a word is misspelled. You can add any terms used regularly in your work that may not be included in the dictionary. The next time the new term appears, the program will accept it. Of course, you must still double-check punctuation, dates, and figures. The machine cannot be relied on to correct these.

Global Search. If your work frequently requires you to produce the same documents but with some changes, the search feature is a great time-saver. For example, you have stored the standard form, and you bring it to the screen. You ask the machine to find a particular name and replace it with another name throughout the document. Thus you might request changing G. W. Jones to M. B. Smith. You could also ask the machine to find an individual word, phrase, or sentence; to pause; and then to permit you to let it stand, change it, or delete it. You might change 1987 to 1990 or the spelling of "endeavour" to "endeavor." The search feature will find every instance where the change is needed, and the new term will be inserted automatically. Or the machine may pause and a message will appear on the screen, asking if you wish the term replaced or not. You have the option of replacing all instances automatically or of choosing which ones to change. In this way you can be sure all necessary changes are made, and it is unnecessary to retype the entire document.

Printing Commands. The automatic features of the word processor make it easy to use spacing and headings to increase the attractiveness and readability of your work by simply giving the appropriate commands. A heading can be centered automatically by giving the instruction to the machine. You can change margins within a document if you wish, setting off a paragraph to give it prominence. You can specify how many characters per inch. If your printer can accommodate the command, you can specify underscoring or italic or boldface type. Some printers allow subscripts and superscripts as well. You can insert page numbers, chapter titles, and running heads or feet at the top or bottom of pages, and even add foreign accent marks if available. These commands are stored, and the printer will follow them. Some word processors provide a function for automatic outlines and footnotes as well.

Automatic Tabulation. Another handy feature is automatic tabulation. For columns aligned on the decimal point, you decide where the columns are to be. Then instead of having to allow extra spaces for numbers of varying lengths, you set the tab at the decimal point. After you tab to the decimal point, you type the number and it starts backward from the decimal point. After you have typed the decimal point, the numbers resume forward. You then tab to the next decimal point setting and continue in the same manner. The numbers are automatically aligned.

The columns could similarly be aligned on the right, the left, or centered in the text. You simply set the tab at the desired point and key in the data. It will be aligned as you specify.

Form Letters. When the same letter or memorandum is to be sent to a number of persons, a stop signal can be inserted in the space for the individual's name and address or in any other part of the letter. A separate list of the names, addresses, special phrases, or other data you wish inserted is then prepared. Instructions can be given to the printer to merge this list with the form letter containing the blanks. The individual letters or memoranda will be printed out as desired.

Merging Paragraphs. Another use for the word processor is the storage of paragraphs for replying to routine correspondence. These paragraphs can be numbered and printed out for easy reference. Then, to suit the occasion, the letter can be assembled from the pertinent paragraphs. In effect, you write a program instructing the word processor to pick up designated stored paragraphs in the order desired. The letter will be printed out without the necessity of retyping any of the paragraphs.

Glossary. You can also store sentences and phrases for frequent use. This stored text is called a glossary. For example, you might store your employer's name and title, so that you need only touch the appropriate key for those lines to appear automatically. A standard sentence, such as "We are looking forward to seeing you again at the annual convention," can be programmed, so that it appears automatically when you touch one key, eliminating the need to type the entire sentence. Similarly, you may wish to incorporate text or data from other stored documents. By giving suitable commands you can summon that text from storage, either to the screen or to the printer.

Other features may include the ability of the word processor to be used as an adding machine or calculator, or to manipulate characters vertically within a column.

There are also programs that permit you to make graphs, which can be printed in color if the printer has that capability.

Machine-to-Machine Communication

Word processing machines equipped with a communications function can transmit a document to a compatible communicating machine without a printed version. This makes possible the rapid delivery and accuracy of copy. The process enables documents of any length to be sent at high speed between locations using telephone lines. It can provide needed information much faster than either conventional mail or courier service. This process is referred to as electronic mail. (*See* pp. 201–202, Electronic Mail.)

In offices having workstations connected to a remote computer, a document can be prepared by one person, reviewed by someone else in another location, and prepared for signature by someone at a third workstation, not necessarily in the same building. This can be done by storing the document in the remote computer, from which it can be retrieved at the second workstation. There it can be edited, if desired, and stored again. At the third location the document is printed, signed, and dispatched.

Accounting

A personal computer can be used in accounting. Software is available to handle all the usual accounting functions: general ledger, accounts receivable, accounts payable, payroll, and inventory control. Some programs are integrated, so that an entry posted in one part of the program is entered automatically in other appropriate accounting areas. When transactions are made in accounts receivable or payroll, the computer can automatically post the appropriate corresponding entries to the general ledger chart of accounts. Trial balances can be obtained, as well as other aspects of the accounting function. Some programs will produce budgets, balance sheets, payroll summaries, and even check writing.

Spreadsheet. An electronic spreadsheet program makes possible detailed financial planning. Such a program provides a ledgerlike layout that may be 60 columns in width and 250 lines long. Using these columns and rows, you can set up a budget for one year or several. By listing all income and probable expenditures, you can determine where funds are most needed and where cuts might be made. The computer does all the calculations for you in a flash, eliminating the need for laborious addition or subtraction.

These entries are linked, so that a change in one entry is reflected throughout the spreadsheet. By proposing changes in some entries, you can readily see the result in all other categories.

An annual budget can be set up and manipulated at will. You can then consider how making a major purchase or reducing one budget item might affect other aspects of an operation.

You can store the treasurer's report prepared for a monthly meeting. The following month you can retrieve it, make the appropriate additions, and print it out, thus avoiding the retyping of headings and other constant information. Only the monthly changes need to be added, and any calculations required are performed by the computer.

Data Processing

Data processing means dealing with information by means of a computer. Whether the computer is storing sales records, the names and records of hospital patients, the inventory of a hardware store, or the contracts for highway construction, the data are being filed in much the same way. A video terminal is used to enter the data, a processing unit manipulates the data, a storage system houses the data, and a printer provides "hard copy," the visible paper record of what has been stored. In a large company the system would be located in a data processing unit.

Data are stored in "fields." Fields make up "records," and records make up "files." A common analogy is the checkbook. Each piece of information on the check is considered a field: the date, amount, payee, and so on. Each check recorded is a record, and the checkbook is the file. When a file is set up, as in opening a checkbook, it has an identity. The specific data are stored in the fields, and each transaction is a record.

Data Control. One of the critical aspects of data processing is data control. It is necessary to decide how best to organize the information coming into the data processing center. Information is of course vital to every organization, whether a social club or a giant corporation. Such data include lists of actual and potential members/customers, cost and sales figures, information about vendors, transportation costs, records of supply sources—in fact any data that might be useful in making decisions. To analyze the operation of an organization, past performance needs to be examined, successes and failures studied, and statistics on various aspects of the operation made available. There must be a way to project alternative courses of action. In order to retrieve the necessary data in usable form, careful consideration must be given to organizing the data.

Once the manner of organization has been decided on, the data must be converted via keyboard to magnetic tape or disk. The staff of the data processing center is responsible for scheduling and production of reports as required, as well as collating and sorting the printed data.

In a small office the secretary may in effect operate a data processing unit. The data stored would be all the letters, memoranda, schedules, reports, and other information affecting the operation of the office. You may be able to use a program already available to store your entire output. Chapter 17, on filing, offers some examples of ways to store and retrieve documents.

Electronic Calendar. You can set up a weekly calendar for months or even years ahead. Whether you use it for planning or as a reminder system, it will show at a glance what activities will occur where and when. Any pertinent information can be included, with a list of persons who need to be informed. Multiple calendars can be maintained. Some programs can match the calendars of several executives to determine an open time for a joint meeting or conference. A separate calendar can be used to schedule conference rooms or special facilities or equipment.

You can keep a record for each day of the cost of travel, meals, entertainment, telephone calls, and any other expenses for which you or your employer will be reimbursed. When you are ready to prepare an expense account, the data will be ready to use. If your organization uses a special form for expense accounts, you can enter the form on your computer and store it. Then when you have the data, you will be able to call up the form, enter the information, and print it out.

(*See also* Chapter 13, Reminder Systems.)

Electronic Mail

Your computer can serve as a substitute for the U.S. Postal Service if your organization subscribes to an electronic mail service such as MCI Mail, GTE's Telemail, or Western Union's Easylink. Services such as The Source and CompuServe provide electronic mail as well as information services. (*See* pp. 202–203.)

To send mail electronically, after you compose your letter or other text on the computer, you call one of the electronic services by a telephone connected to your computer. You must identify yourself by giving your assigned ID number and the password in order to "go on-line," that is, be able to access the electronic service. You can then address the letter or other communication to one or more recipients. You send the letter to the service with appropriate mailing directions. When the recipient turns on his or her computer and calls the electronic service, the computer announces that there is mail waiting. This mail can be scanned to show the sender's name, the date, the subject, and so forth. The recipient can then decide which is most urgent and retrieve the mail in any order desired. It can be stored and read later or printed out right then on the computer's printer.

The speed and convenience of electronic mail can be worth the cost. The sender pays for a local telephone call plus computer time charged by the service. Both sender and receiver must be members of the service. Computer time is charged according to the time of day at the sender's location, with the hours between 8 A.M. and 6 P.M. being the most expensive. The service also makes a monthly service charge, regardless of the extent of your usage.

Not all word processing software is equally convenient or economical for electronic mail. Among the desirable features are the following: the ability to scan and read the mail you receive, so that you can spot the important items first; an address file of the names and ID numbers of correspondents; and the ability to compose before you go online with the electronic service. There are more possibilities becoming available all the time, and you can choose the software best adapted to your use.

Electronic mail is convenient for routine communications between offices. A message can be left for someone at any hour and can be answered at any hour. This possibility can help to eliminate "telephone tag," the situation in which Mr. White calls Mrs. Brown; Mrs. Brown is busy, and he leaves a message. Mrs. Brown calls back, and Mr. White is at lunch; she leaves a message. Meanwhile, no progress is made. And if different time zones are involved, it can be a time-saver to have an answer this morning to last night's request for information.

If your company has a network of computers and telephone terminals, you can communicate with them without joining an electronic service, whether the network is within a building or spread over several states. The various areas in the building are connected by cables, and with suitable software you can send messages directly through the system to designated persons in the other areas. Each person receiving mail has a password to ensure that only the person addressed has access to that mail. (A secretary may have access to his or her employer's password in order to manage the mail.) Similarly, branches of the company located in other cities may be connected by means of leased telephone lines; in this way you can send electronic mail and receive replies from your computer.

Information Services

Using the computer, you can do research without leaving the office. By accessing one of the information networks you can obtain printouts of an astonishing variety of information. There are general databases, such as The Source and CompuServe, that offer news, sports, technological information, stock market prices, business and management reference sources, and much more. CompuServe offers an electronic encyclopedia. Dow Jones News Retrieval provides background information from financial journals dating back several years. It also provides news, weather, movie reviews, and online shopping.

Lexis is a service devoted to the law. It provides files containing the full text of court decisions, statutes, regulations, and other legal material.

Nexis provides the full text of newspapers and magazines for several past years.

Dialog is an enormous database that offers about two hundred different research areas, from agriculture and engineering to medicine, foundation grants, technological data, and labor statistics. It provides in-depth material previously available only to research librarians in large organizations.

The convenience of having up-to-date information immediately available has made the electronic databases popular and profitable. No longer do you need to spend hours in a library if you have access to one of these valuable services. For listings of more than three thousand online bibliographic and nonbibliographic databases, consult the *Directory of Online Databases*, available in many libraries. You can then select the information service most useful for your purposes. (*See* p. 400, Computer and Databases.)

CHAPTER TWELVE

Using the Telephone to Best Advantage

Good Manners. Much of the advice given to secretaries on the use of the telephone is actually a reminder to use everyday good manners. This means that you answer the telephone after the first ring, if possible. Your voice is pleasant, your manner assured and agreeable, your enunciation distinct. You always have a pen or pencil and pad ready to take messages. The messages you take are accurate and complete: the time the call was received, the last name of the caller spelled correctly (initials, too, if a common name), the caller's telephone number. You transfer calls graciously when it is necessary. You ask someone to cover your telephone when you must be away from your desk, and you leave a pencil and pad for messages.

If a call becomes disconnected, you hang up at once. If you originated the call, you call again, apologizing for the interruption, and the conversation is continued. If someone else has placed the call, you leave the line free for the caller to call back.

Always bear in mind that your telephone is for business use. Keep calls brief and refrain from personal calls as much as possible.

Attitude. Excellent transcribing of shorthand and typing are essential, but a good secretary has the additional skill of correct telephone practice. Your ability to handle calls to and from your employer can give a highly favorable impression of the office (or a distinctly unfavorable one) to callers who never meet you in person.

You realize that the ring of the telephone is not simply an interruption. Handling telephone calls is a very important part of your work. Often you are the first person in the organization who speaks to the prospective customer or client. Your courtesy and competence obviously reflect something of the organization to the caller. The careless handling of a telephone call could lose an important client or sale, for the business world is made up of individuals, many of them overworked and pressed for time. A secretary's unpleasantness could be the last straw to a caller, or your graciousness could make all the difference. Everyone likes to come in contact, even by telephone, with a cheerful person who is genuinely interested in being of service.

As a competent secretary you learn all you can about the areas handled by your own and other departments, so that you can quickly and correctly transfer calls meant for others. You say to the caller, "I'm sorry, but this matter is not handled by our department. Shall I have your call transferred to Mr. Green in the shipping department?" You then signal the operator on the switchboard, slowly and several times, to ask him or her to transfer the call. When the operator has come on the line, you say, "Will you please give this call to Mr. Green in the shipping department." Or you may say to the caller if you think it is suitable, "Ms. Bidwell handles requests for catalogues. If you wish, I'll be glad to take your name and address and see that you are sent our latest price list." Circumstances differ, but the attitude of the secretary should always be cooperative and agreeable.

Voice. Your voice will sound best if you sit erect, so that you can breathe properly. You should speak loudly enough to be heard, enunciating clearly, and you *never* speak with something in your mouth, such as gum, a cigarette, or a pencil. Your voice is pitched low, and you speak at a reasonable speed, adapting your speech pattern to the general custom in your area. The inflection of your voice will indicate your emotional reaction, just as a monotone would indicate a lack of concern. You try to be patient and sympathetic to all callers and never permit yourself to argue, closing a conversation when all the pertinent facts have been stated. In general, your voice will reveal an alert, vital person who is both capable and agreeable.

Answering Incoming Calls. You answer by identifying yourself or your office. You may say, "Miss Brown speaking," or "Retail Sales, Marian speaking," according to the formality of the office. If you answer someone else's telephone, you say, "Mrs. Smith's office, Miss Brown speaking." Then the caller knows at once if he has dialed correctly, and he can proceed with the business of the call.

You use a title for each person you speak to: "Thank you, Mrs. Green," "Good-bye, Mr. Harris." When the name is not known, you may say, "Yes, sir" or "Yes, ma'am." (Women are not pleased to be addressed as "dear" or "honey," and "madam" sounds pretentious in most circumstances.) You do not use expressions such as "yep" or "nope," "uh-huh" and "bye-bye." You avoid any impression of overfamiliarity.

Executive's Line. In a large number of business and government offices, executives place and receive their own calls. This policy has been adopted both as a matter of courtesy and as a time-saver for the caller and the person being called. In-Dialing (*see* p. 211) permits calls to be completed without the intervention of either an operator or a secretary.

Screening the Executive's Calls. When you do screen calls for your employer, you answer, "Mrs. Smith's office, Miss Brown speaking." The caller usually identifies himself and asks to speak to Mrs. Smith. "Yes, Mr. Jones, just a moment please." You then announce the call to your employer, and Mrs. Smith picks up the telephone and says, "Hello, Mr. Jones."

If Mrs. Smith is not free to take the call, does not wish to speak to Mr. Jones, or is not at her desk, the secretary may say, "I'm sorry, Mr. Jones. Mrs. Smith has someone with her just now (or "Mrs. Smith has just stepped out of her office" or "Mrs. Smith is away from her desk just now"). May I give her a message?" You might also offer, "Perhaps I can give you the information you need."

Sometimes a caller is unwilling to give his name or any indication of the matter he wishes to discuss. You will insist politely but firmly that you cannot disturb Mrs. Smith if you do not have this information. If the caller still declines to state his business, you may say, "I'm sorry, sir. Mrs. Smith is busy on another line. If you cannot tell me who is calling, it might be best to write her a letter and mark it 'Personal.' I will bring it to her attention at once."

Your job is of course to help your employer in every way you can. As you become accustomed to the work of the office, there are many types of information you can supply to callers, with the agreement of your employer, to save her having to answer all queries. You never forget that you are the secretary, that Mrs. Smith is the executive, and that your position depends on her. The haughty secretary who gives the impression that it is only through his or her kindness that the public may approach the employer is as foolish as the self-important secretary who considers himself or herself too busy to be courteous to people who telephone.

You sometimes may feel like the traffic controller of a busy airport, but you can learn to cope with interruptions without undue stress and even enjoy it. When you place a call for your employer, you tell the other secretary or executive, "Mrs. Smith of So-and-So Corporation is calling" (or "Mrs. Prunella Smith" when several executives of So-and-So Corporation have the same last name). If it should be necessary to ask someone to wait, you remember to say, "Thank you for waiting." Habitual courtesy makes business much pleasanter, and the secretary can always be sure he or she has not been unintentionally rude either to the important corporate officer or to the employer's childhood friend.

Answering Two Telephones. If two phones ring at once, you answer one, ask to be excused for a moment ("please"), and place that call on hold or put down the receiver gently. You then answer the second call. If it can be handled briefly, do so. It may be better to call that person back, to avoid keeping the first caller waiting. Frequent use of "please" and "thank you" helps to smooth the way in every situation. Having returned to the first call, you attend to the matter in question and call back the second caller as soon as possible. "I am sorry to have kept you waiting, Mrs. Ellsworth. May I help you now?"

Wrong Number. If the caller has reached a wrong number, you reply, "I'm sorry, there is no Mr. Black here. What number are you calling?" You never indicate that this is the umpteenth wrong number today and that you are exasperated by so many interruptions. When you yourself dial incorrectly or use an obsolete number, you apologize: "I'm sorry. I must have the wrong number. Please excuse me." If the wrong number you have called is long distance, you immediately notify the long-distance operator, so that an adjustment may be made for the charge.

Discretion. As in other areas of your work, discretion is very important where the telephone is concerned. When your employer is making or receiving an important call, you ask visitors to wait in another room, if possible. You refrain from making disturbing noises, and if the call is personal or confidential, you find something to do in another room and keep others away.

If a message must be given to your employer while she is using the telephone, you type or write it clearly on a slip of paper and place it where she can see it. She can then decide whether or not to break off the call for a moment.

When you are telephoning and you must speak to someone else, you cover the mouthpiece or put the call on hold so that the caller need not eavesdrop inadvertently. You are always careful not to make a remark that might be embarrassing if it were overheard.

Long-Distance Calls. Before placing a long-distance call, you may wish to ask your employer if it is to be made person-to-person or station-to-station. If a person may not be readily available, as in a large organization or in a hotel, the call should be made person-to-person. Calls to extension numbers, to a particular department, to a room number in a hotel, and so forth, are always person-to-person whether or not it is requested. Charges on this basis start only when the individual called answers the telephone, while station-to-station charges begin the moment the number is reached. Since charges for person-to-person calls are higher than for station-to-station calls, the circumstances of each long-distance call should be considered separately.

Record of Calls. You should keep a record of long-distance calls made, jotting down the date and number called after each call has been completed. You can then verify each call listed on the monthly telephone bill.

Placing the Call. When calling station-to-station, you can dial directly in most areas. (See the opening pages in the local telephone directory for area code numbers and instructions.) Where this service is not available, the secretary dials 0 (for Operator) and says, "I would like to place a call to [city and state]. The number is area code 311 555-2368. We will speak with anyone who answers. This number is ———."

Many person-to-person calls can be made by dialing directly. (See the local telephone directory for instructions, if necessary.) If this service is not available, the secretary dials the long-distance operator and says, "I would like to place a call to Mr. John Doe in ———. The number is area code 311 555-2368, extension 525 [if any]."

You should keep your list of telephone numbers up-to-date and have the correct number at hand when placing a call. If for some reason you do not have the number needed, you can dial the area code plus 555-1212 for Information within that Numbering Plan Area. A list of cities and area codes is in the front pages of each local directory. There is a charge for calls to out-of-state directory assistance.

(*See also* p. 211, Expanded Direct Distance Dialing and Wide Area Telephone Service.)

Credit Card Calls. Many executives use credit cards for making business calls when traveling. A credit card can be obtained by calling the local telephone company's business office. When placing the credit card call, the caller dials 0 (zero) and the area code and number desired. When the operator comes on the line, the caller tells him or her, "This is a credit card call. My card number is ———." The charges are applied to his account, and the call goes through.

Overseas Calls. You can dial many overseas calls directly, which of course is less expensive than if the assistance of an operator is required. To place an overseas call, dial 011 (the International Access Code), then the two- or three-digit country code, then the one- to five-digit city code, and finally the local number. For example, to place a call to Rome, Italy, dial 011 39 6 and then the local number. If direct dialing service is not available in your area, you should dial 0 (Operator) and give the country, city, and local telephone number. If your call does not require special operator assistance, you will receive the low dial rate.

Should you make your call on a person-to-person, collect, credit card, or billed-to-a-third-number basis, use 01 for the International Access Code and dial the country code, city code, and local number as above. After the call is dialed, the operator will come on the line to ask the name of the person you are calling or your credit card number.

Calls to the Bahamas, Bermuda, Canada, Puerto Rico, and the U.S. Virgin Islands may be dialed directly in the same manner as long-distance calls within the United States. Calls to Mexico require the International Access Code + 52 + the city code + the local number. If International Dialing is not available in your area, see instructions in your local telephone directory.

Calls to Ships. When large ships or yachts are in port, they can be reached through the steamship lines that operate them. Some yachts have their own telephone numbers and can be called at-anchor in home port. Their numbers may be listed under "Yacht _____" in the local telephone directory. Ships at sea can be reached through the marine operator. The following information will be needed: the name of the ship, the name of the person called, the number of his stateroom if known, and the name and telephone number of the person making the call.

Calls to Moving Vehicles. Calls can be made through a mobile service operator to cars or trucks equipped with mobile service. Some trains and airplanes also provide this service.

Conference Calls. Several persons may be connected simultaneously, either locally or by long distance. If your office has this equipment, you can arrange with the participants so that they are all available at the appointed time. The long-distance operator can also make the arrangements when given the telephone numbers of the persons involved.

Collect Calls. When toll charges are to be paid by the person being called, you say to the operator, "I wish to make a collect call to Mr. _____ in [city and state]. His number is [area code plus local number]. Mrs. Prunella Smith of So-and-So Corporation is calling."

Typical rates for long-distance calls will be found in the front of the telephone directory. Collect calls may also be made to some foreign countries. Additional information can be obtained from the International Information Service by dialing a number given in the telephone directory.

Special Services

The local telephone directory contains explanations in its opening pages of the services available in the area and how to make use of them.

PBX. This stands for private branch exchange, which makes connections automatically for both incoming and outgoing calls.

In-Dialing. This service, also called Inward Dialing, enables individuals to receive calls directly without the assistance of a PBX operator.

Direct Distance Dialing. This service is widely available. Each telephone is given a number to be called directly, both locally and long distance. An extension on your desk enables you to answer your employer's telephone if she wishes or if she is away from her desk.

To make an outside call, an access code digit, 9, is dialed first before the area code and individual number. A trunk line to the office as a whole enables someone outside the office to call an individual whose number is not known, so that his office operator can make the connection. However, the use of direct dialing has eliminated the need for much of the operator's work and has speeded the connection.

Expanded Direct Distance Dialing. The person making the call dials long-distance person-to-person calls directly. The operator comes on the line only to obtain the called person. An access number, 0 (zero), is used before the area and local number; as, *0-311-555-2368.*

Wide Area Telephone Service (WATS). This permits a telephone user to dial long-distance calls within one or more of the six regions into which the United States is divided for a flat rate per month or on a measured-time basis per month. The result is considerable savings in long-distance billing for a customer with a high volume of calls. For example, a New York City customer could have for a flat rate per month an unlimited number of calls throughout Vermont, New Hampshire, Massachusetts, Rhode Island, Connecticut, New Jersey, Delaware, and eastern Pennsylvania. WATS lines are so designated on the telephone set, and these lines should be used only for WATS calls.

Reminder Systems

The types of reminder systems used will depend on your responsibilities. If you help your employer with income tax matters, social security payments, withholding taxes, and the like, the regular dates when payments are due must be kept in mind. If you are responsible for arranging a monthly departmental luncheon, for example, the necessary reminders to department members must be taken into account. In a school principal's office, the secretary often sets up the monthly calendar for custodians and must bear in mind the events that occur regularly. Thus, the secretary of any office must decide which reminder systems best suit the situation and will operate simply and effectively.

Using a Diary. One type of diary is the book that provides a page for each day. You keep one for your employer and one for yourself. In the employer's, you enter appointments and important days to remember, so that he or she can avoid making conflicting appointments. You watch that diary closely for appointments he or she may have made without mentioning them to you.

In your diary are noted the days on which checks must regularly be sent, orders placed, reservations made, and so forth, as well as reminders for your employer and the appointments he or she is to keep. As the check is sent, the order placed, the reservation made, each reminder is checked off in such a way that it is still legible. Thus the diary serves as a record of what has been done during the day, to prevent oversight and to be referred to later if necessary. The pages are turned over, rather than being torn off and destroyed like those of a calendar.

A list of diary items that go on from year to year may be kept: birthdays and anniversaries of the employer's family, regular meetings of boards of directors, clubs, committees, and so forth; renewal dates for automobile licenses, club memberships, subscriptions to periodicals; tax dates, dates for mortgage payments, and the like. As soon as the diaries for the coming year are received, you enter all recurring items for the following year under the appropriate dates. At the time, adjustments for weekends and holidays can be made, to avoid scheduling appointments or work to be done when the office will not be open. As you hear of additional appointments and things to be done, you can note them in the diaries.

It is important to note in advance any time-consuming tasks, so that either you or your employer will have sufficient time available to get the job done on time without undue strain. The advance notice can be placed in your diary so that you can get together the needed material for your employer. Underline important dates and deadlines in red to avoid oversight.

In case of large sums needed for payments, an advance notice on the employer's diary may be helpful.

Some executives need to keep a full record of each telephone call and caller, each luncheon conference, and, in fact, every transaction of any kind. As the secretary of such an executive you keep a continuing record of each telephone call received, with the name of the caller, and each telephone call placed by your employer. The names of persons he or she lunches with are recorded, as well as the names of those who stop by his or her office, whether by appointment or informally. Each morning you give this informal record, neatly typed, to your employer. He or she then dictates the matters discussed with each person. These memoranda are kept permanently, serving both as proof of contacts made and as data for periodic time studies.

Of course, all diaries are to be considered confidential and will not be left lying open for curious visitors to examine.

Tickler Files. Tickler cards are useful for recurring items. Matters that you attend to may be handled in this manner. A box and index cards are generally used, with a tabbed guide for each month and daily guides behind the current month guide. Memoranda are written on cards and filed according to the date when a reminder is needed.

A monthly deadline for items for the employees' newspaper, for example, might be noted on a card and moved each month, instead of making twelve cards or twelve entries in the diary. Pertinent information can be typed on the card, so that in your absence anyone could make sure the task is completed. Tickler cards are also useful for matters to be followed up at some indefinite time. If the employer says he or she wishes to review a certain account or perhaps study the progress of a particular stock at some future date, you may note this intention on a card and move it from time to time until the matter has been taken care of.

Appointments should be noted in a diary or on a calendar, not in a tickler card file. You should refer to the diary each afternoon to note the appointments for the next working day; the tickler file should be consulted each morning.

You can note routine tasks as they occur to you, and reminders of these can be placed in the tickler file; then the work can be kept up-to-date by your substitute when you are absent or away on vacation.

Follow-up Files. One of the most useful reminders for any secretary is the follow-up file. Items suitable for this purpose are correspondence or memoranda still to be answered, matters referred to the employer by others in the organization for handling or comment, and matters requiring action by a certain date.

You make an extra copy for the follow-up file when you transcribe a letter or memorandum. The office copying machine may be used to make a follow-up file copy when the matter has been received from another department, to avoid placing an original document in the follow-up file. Other items for the follow-up file would be notes and material being collected for a speech or report. These may be kept in an envelope or clipped together and placed in the follow-up file. At a suitable time, perhaps two weeks before the speech or report is needed, you place the material on your employer's desk with a memorandum stating the purpose of the material and when the speech or report is due.

If the number of follow-ups is relatively small, one file folder may be sufficient. Copies of letters or memoranda may be marked with the follow-up date and filed chronologically, with the next ones to be handled on top.

When a considerable number of items are to be followed up, a file drawer and one or more sets of folders can be provided. Use a folder for each month and thirty-one folders for the days of the month. Another folder can be included for "Future Years."

Reminder Notebook. Another kind of reminder system is that kept in a looseleaf notebook. The volume of reminders needed will determine the size of the notebook used. One page for each business day may be required or perhaps only one per month. In some cases a separate page will be useful for each matter, while in others a line or two will suffice for each reminder and each page may carry several reminders. Colored tabs may be used to separate the months to permit ready reference. In some kinds of work a seasonal reminder may be needed rather than a monthly arrangement.

Monthly	*Seasonal*
* Remind Mr. Smith to pay fire insurance premium	* Reorder calendar pages for desk calendars
* Start collecting material for third quarter report	* Order Christmas cards if they are to be imprinted
* Pay parking garage fee	* Reserve hotel space for fall sales conference

When the reminder has served its purpose, it may be checked off or discarded.

Reminding Your Employer. In the latter part of the day or early each morning, a typed schedule of the coming day's appointments may be placed on your employer's desk. All pertinent information should be listed (who, where, when), and before the hour of the appointment you should give your employer the caller's file (if any) and other useful material.

Before a report is due or when a request must be answered, you place on your employer's desk the file or material for the report, information pertinent to the request, or any other useful data, together with a memorandum stating what needs to be done and when it is due.

Electronic Calendar. If you have a computer terminal, you can prepare schedules for yourself, your employer, or the whole department. Programs are available that enable you to set all the dates in the computer's memory for months or years in advance. You can then make up whatever categories are useful and enter data of many kinds.

Each category would be assigned a letter or number that is applied to each entry; for example, all meetings of the same kind would use the same symbol: S for Sales Meetings. The symbol enables you to retrieve the information by category. You may set up categories for conferences and conventions, for sales meetings, for particular projects. You could include due dates for payments of various kinds or keep vacation records for all members of the department. You can include all appointments for your employer and yourself, all telephone calls to be made, or whatever other reminders are necessary, as well as expense account items.

You can then call up to the screen each day's schedule of things to be done. One program has a category of items to be done that goes on from day to day until you delete it. Otherwise, each day's listings remain on the schedule as written.

It may be useful to print out the week's schedule so that you can see at a glance when time is free to add another appointment.

You can sort your data by any category, such as dates for all sales meetings or due dates for all payrolls; you can print out a list of deadlines for a project; you can summon up all expenditures you have listed in order to prepare an expense account. Properly used, the electronic calendar can save much time and drudgery.

Procedures Manual. You should maintain a notebook of procedures to be followed in the various aspects of your work. Include all forms you use, with a note of explanation stating how many copies are to be made and where each is to be sent or filed. List all chores you regularly perform, even watering plants. Note how often each is done—daily, weekly, or whatever. If it is necessary to rent or buy equipment or supplies, note which vendors are used. If regular servicing of equipment is required, note the schedule for each machine. Keep a list of the serial numbers of all equipment in the event that repairs are needed. Which company handles such repairs? Are there guarantees on file, and if so, where?

If you set up meetings, note when announcements are sent out; who receives them; what arrangements must be made regarding permissions needed for use of space, furniture, equipment, and so forth; whether refreshments are to be offered and how they are provided.

Include any information that might be useful to someone who substitutes for you during your vacation or other absence. Where is the index of your files? Is a special procedure needed to access your electronic calendar? How do you get a cash advance for your employer? During what hours?

While it would be nice to have all data well organized and arranged logically with an index, you may never have time for that. Rather than use lack of time for an excuse, you can make notes in individual paragraphs, perhaps highlighting in color the various subjects. Then you can place the paragraphs in your notebook in sections under such headings as Meetings, Repairs, Daily Tasks, and the like. It's better to have a less-than-perfect manual than to risk delays because no one else knows how things are done or where you have filed something important.

You should review the manual periodically to make sure it is accurate and up-to-date. While some secretaries like to feel indispensable, it is a disservice to your employer and the organization to try to "carry it all in your head." Information about the functioning of the office is not your personal property. Many others might be inconvenienced in your absence if you have not made it possible for someone else to carry on the work.

CHAPTER FOURTEEN

Form for Business Letters

General Instructions for Typing

Appearance. Letters should be attractively placed on the page, neither crowded nor unnecessarily spread out. The suitable size of stationery should be used, if possible. For a short letter, fifty words or less, a small sheet would be preferable. A longer letter would fit better on a larger sheet. Double spacing is used only for short letters, whatever the size of the stationery. If the body of the letter is double-spaced, the inside address and the address on the envelope should also be double-spaced.

At least four lines should be left below the date before typing the salutation or the inside address. Depending on the length of the letter, the usual spacing is six or eight lines between date and inside address. A crowded appearance detracts from the appeal of a letter, and too many lines crammed on a page may suggest to the reader that he or she just hasn't time to go through all this now.

White space around paragraphs rests the eye and gives the reader an opportunity to skim the entire letter, picking out the important points. Many business letters are glanced at by the addressee and referred to others for action. If a suitable margin is left for comments, time can be saved by several people.

Continuation Pages. When a letter being typed reaches two inches from the bottom, the balance of the letter must be carried over to another page. If the inside address is to be typed below the letter, the stopping place for the body of the letter will be at least three inches from the bottom. If a paragraph is started at the bottom of a page, at least two lines should be included, and at least two lines should be carried forward to a continuation page, preceding the complimentary close. If possible, a full paragraph should be carried over to the second page, but always more than a line or two. The second page must never carry only the complimentary close and signature.

When a letter exceeds one page, blank sheets (stationery without letterhead) are used for the pages after the first. Each new page must carry a page heading to provide identification if pages become detached from a letter. On the sixth line down from the top of the page, the page number is enclosed in hyphens. The name of the addressee is placed on the next line, and the date is given on the following line. The letter is resumed three lines down from the date.

-2-
Mrs. Lucille Warner
July 14, 19—

Although it is clear that our original plan cannot be followed in its entirety, I believe that much of it still applies. Please let me have your comments as soon as possible.
Sincerely yours,

Nina N. Pugh
Vice President

NNP:ds

Extra Copies of a Letter. Extra copies of a letter may be needed. If the addressee is to be informed, the names of persons to receive copies are shown on the original: *cc: Mr. Smith, Mrs. Barrett.* If the names of recipients are not shown on the original, these names are typed on the file copy or on a separate sheet to be attached to the file copy.

If the same letter is sent to a number of persons, the procedure is handled easily by a word processor. The form letter and the list of recipients are keyed into the word processor with appropriate instructions. If a typewriter is being used, the letter is first typed without inside address and salutation. Copies are made on the office copying machine, and the individual addresses and salutations are added as required. Unless separate files are maintained for all recipients, one file copy of the letter may suffice, with the names and addresses of all recipients typed on a separate sheet and attached to the file copy.

The Format of Business Letters

The format of business letters is usually decided by the organization. However, the typist should be familiar with the possible styles, since these may differ with the length of the letter or with its tone.

Block Style. In the full block form, the date, inside address, salutation, all paragraphs of the letter, complimentary close, signature, and added data all begin at the left margin.

While this may at first appear too unbalanced to be attractive, it is quick and easy to produce and offers a simple and easy-to-read format. This style has been widely adopted by individuals and organizations. (*See* p. 239.)

Modified Block Style. The date forms the right margin, and the inside address is typed block style. The paragraphs are typed in block form. The complimentary close is typed near the center of the page, two spaces below the body of the letter, with the signature aligned with it. (*See* p. 240.)

Modified Semi-Block Style. Same as modified block style except that paragraphs are indented five spaces. (*See* p. 241.)

Simplified Letter. This format eliminates the need for courtesy titles, awkward salutations, and the complimentary close. It focuses attention on the subject of the letter. Developed by the Administrative Management Society, it has been adopted by many large corporations in the United States. While its appearance might give the impression of being impersonal, it actually directs attention to the reader.

The simplified letter is useful when writing to the following: companies, government agencies, and other organizations in which the name of an individual respondent is not known; an individual whose professional or courtesy title (Mr., Mrs., Miss, Ms., Dr., and so forth) is not known; an individual whose name, profession, and preference for a courtesy title are known but whom the writer wishes to address in an informal manner by including a simplified salutation (for example, Mrs. Doane, Mr. Sadowsky) in the first sentence of the first paragraph. (*See* p. 242.)

Note: No punctuation marks are used at the ends of the lines of typed headings or inside address, except in official Government correspondence. A colon follows the salutation, and a comma follows the complimentary close.

The Parts of Business Letters

Business letters follow a definite order that is convenient for the reader and the typist. Although the placement and the punctuation of letter parts may differ, the arrangement follows a standard pattern.

1. Letterhead (or heading)
2. Date (unless centered under letterhead)
3. File number (when used)
4. Personal or Confidential (when used)
5. Inside address
6. Attention line (when used)
7. Salutation (when used)
8. Subject line (when used)
9. Body of letter
10. Complimentary close (when used)
11. Signature
12. Additional data
13. Postscripts
14. Mailing instructions

The salutation and the complimentary close are omitted in the simplified letter.

1. Form for Headings. Most business letters are written on letterhead stationery. Many executives also have personal stationery to be used for private correspondence, and this may carry the business address but not the firm name. Such stationery would be used, for example, for correspondence connected with civic affairs or trade organizations in which the writer serves as an officer. While this position and correspondence may be a result of his or her being a company executive, letters of this type would not concern the company or be referred to others in his or her office.

On stationery without a letterhead, the headings should be written in the following order: street address, name of city or town, state or province name using the two-letter post office designation, ZIP Code, and date.

19 West 44th Street
New York, NY 10018
July 18, 19—

2. Date. The date (month, day, year) may be placed in one of several positions, depending on the letterhead:

(1) At the left margin four or six spaces above the inside address, depending on the size of the paper and the length of the letter. This style is commonly used with the block style or the simplified letter form.

(2) Centered two lines below the letterhead if the letterhead is in the upper left corner of the sheet or if the letterhead is centered.

(3) Three lines below the letterhead if the letterhead is on the right side of the sheet. The end of the date line then forms the right margin of the letter.

3. File Number. An executive may wish to have the correspondent refer in his answer to a particular person or department. This request, in the form of a file number, should then be included in the correspondent's answer.

Placement of the file number: Such a line may be placed below the date and above the inside address on the left.

[Letterhead]

July 25, 19—

File C-4923

Mr. Henry Banks
The Ideal Fitting Company
65 East Front Street
Northport, CT 06832

If a file number has been included, it must be carried over to the heading on all continuation sheets.

-2-
Mr. Henry Banks
July 25, 19—
File C-4923

4. Personal or Confidential. The words *Personal* and *Confidential* should not be used as attention-getting devices. *Personal* indicates that only the addressee is expected to read the letter. *Confidential* means that the letter may be opened and read by the addressee and/or anyone authorized to do so.

Personal or *Confidential* is typed three spaces above the inside address (or the salutation when the inside address is placed at the lower left margin—*see* below). The word is typed in full capitals and underlined. If either *Personal* or *Confidential* is used in the letter, it must be used on the envelope as well. It is typed in full capitals and underlined, two or three lines below the return address.

5. Inside Address. In a business letter the inside address, containing the title, name, and address of the recipient, is usually placed at the left margin above the body of the letter. In both business and official letters less formal in tone, the inside address may be written at the left margin below the signature.

Numerical street names may be written with the endings *st, d, rd,* and *th* or as numbers only.

414 West 121st Street *or* 414 West 121 Street
138 - 25th Drive *or* 138 - 25 Drive

The names of avenues and streets expressed in one word should be written out, but when the avenue or street names are expressed in more than one word, figures are preferred. In formal communications the numerical names of streets and avenues are written in full.

Fifth Avenue (*not* 5th)
163 West 78th Street
Fifteen West Twenty-fifth Street (formal)

In the inside address the names of cities should not be abbreviated, but the names of states may be given in full or the two-letter post office abbreviation may be used. To be consistent and to save time the post office abbreviations may be used throughout (exceptions to this rule appear on p. 144).

If the letter is being sent to a foreign country, the name of the country is typed on a separate line, with initial capital letters only in the letter but with full capitals on the envelope.

In letter	*On envelope*
Señora Luis Cabeza	Señora Luis Cabeza
129 Avenida Sforza	129 Avenida Sforza
Lima	Lima
Peru	PERU

Titles in Inside Address

Use of *Messrs*. (Abbreviation of *Messieurs*). This title, seldom used today, is most often written when addressing professional partnerships, such as architects or lawyers, when one or more of the partners is known to be living. *Messrs*. is not used when the terms Company, Corporation, or Incorporated (Inc.) are included in the firm's name.

Correct: Messrs. Smith and Jones (a professional firm)
Incorrect: Messrs. Blank Typewriting Company
Incorrect: Messrs. American Packing Corporation
Incorrect: Messrs. Jones and Smith, Inc.

Messrs. is never used in the salutation.

The title *Miss*, rather than *Mrs.*, is used in addressing a woman when the writer is uncertain of her correct title. The abbreviation *Ms.* may also be used.

Business Titles. In business letters it is correct to use a business title on the same line as the personal title or on the line below. The choice will depend on which arrangement gives the better balance.

Mr. Louis R. Drake
Treasurer, Chickering Brothers

Dr. Daniel Jenkins, Secretary
Wentworth Memorial Fund

Dr. Katherine Dimmitt, Director
Personnel Department

Mr. Paul Stewart
Secretary to the Mayor

Dr. Virginia Johnson
Superintendent of Schools

When the use of a business title gives a top-heavy appearance to a letter, as in the following example, it may be omitted unless it is particularly needed for identification.

Mr. William D. Ward
Director, Statutory Relations
Financial Division
Aetna Life Insurance Company
151 Farmington Avenue, YF54
Hartford, CT 06156

The business title should not precede the name.

Incorrect:

Secretary Daniel Rago
Treasurer T. J. Wiedemann
Chairman Kathleen Achorn

Professional Titles. A title referring to professional standing may precede the name. An addressee who has no professional title should be addressed as *Mr., Mrs., Ms.,* or *Miss* as the case may be.

President Henry Adler
Exville College
    or
Dr. Henry Adler
President, Exville College

or

The President of Exville College

Dr. Janet Blake
Dean, School of Education
or
Ms. Janet Blake
Dean, School of Education
or
Dean Janet Blake
School of Education

When an individual has a doctor's degree the address may read:

Dr. John H. Livermore
Dr. Marian Baker

If the person also has the rank of professor, the address may read:

Professor John H. Livermore
Professor Marian Baker

Alternatively, the style used may be:

Dr. John H. Livermore
Professor of Chemistry

Dr. Marian Baker
Professor of Biology

Two titles meaning the same thing are not used together.

Correct: Dr. Alfred Young *or* Alfred Young, M.D.
Incorrect: Dr. Alfred Young, M.D.

A lawyer is usually addressed as:

Suzanne Salzer, Esq. *or*
Suzanne Salzer
Attorney-at-Law

6. *Attention Line.* When the writer wishes to bring his letter to the attention of a certain person or department, he may do so by using an attention line. This usually is written between the inside address and the salutation, with a double space above and below it. The words "Attention of" are seldom used today, although some firms still retain

"Attention" (followed by a colon). Today the name of the person or the department is usually considered sufficient. Note that the use of an attention line does not affect the salutation, which agrees with the inside address.

Hollywood Sportswear
1041 North Highland Avenue
Claremont, CA 91711

Mr. John Doe

Gentlemen:

Ryan & O'Brien
Gibbs Building
Sarasota, FL 33577

Mr. George Blank
Sales Department

Gentlemen:

7. Salutation. The following are correct forms for business and professional letters:

Dear Sir: (*Dear Sirs* is not used in the United States.)
Dear Madam: (sometimes followed by title; e.g., *Dear Madam Chairman*)
Gentlemen: (generally used in addressing firms and organizations)
Ladies: (*Mesdames* is seldom used in business correspondence.)
Dear Mr. Bryan: (informal American, formal British usage)
My dear Mrs. Bryan: (formal American, informal British usage)
Ladies and Gentlemen: (in addressing committees or organizations composed of men and women)
To Whom It May Concern or *TO WHOM IT MAY CONCERN:* (used in correspondence intended to have the effect of a legal notice)

For the forms used in correspondence with Government officials, see pp. 291–310.

Gentlemen. Use this salutation when writing to a board, a committee, or a firm composed of men or of men and women, or if it is not known whether the organization or group includes women.

Ladies. Use this salutation when addressing a board, a committee, or a firm composed exclusively of women.

Use of Name. Whenever an individual name of a correspondent is known to the writer, it should be used rather than the title alone.

Mr. Allan Douglas, Manager

or

Mr. Allan Douglas
Manager, Lakewood Hotel

If the individual name of a correspondent is not known to the writer, he should be addressed by the correct title of the position he holds, as *chairman, director, registrar, secretary,* and so forth.

Addressing Organizations When an Individual Name Is Not Used.

Associations, clubs, and societies

Address:	The Secretary
	Lakewood Men's Club
Salutation:	Dear Sir:
	or
Address:	The Lakewood Men's Club
Salutation:	Gentlemen:
Address:	The Secretary
	Lakewood Women's Club
Salutation:	Dear Madam:
	or
Address:	The Lakewood Women's Club
Salutation:	Ladies:
Address:	The Lakewood Parents Association
Salutation:	Ladies and Gentlemen:
Address:	The Lakewood Improvement Society
Salutation:	Gentlemen:
	or
	Ladies and Gentlemen:

Boards, bureaus, departments, offices

Address:	President, Board of Medical Examiners
Salutation:	Dear Sir:
	or
Address:	Board of Medical Examiners
Salutation:	Gentlemen:
Address:	Martha Blakelock Travel Bureau
Salutation:	Gentlemen:

Address:	Chief, Bureau of Ordnance
Salutation:	Dear Sir:
	or
Address:	Bureau of Ordnance
Salutation:	Gentlemen:
Address:	Chief, Police Department
Salutation:	Dear Sir:
	or
Address:	Lakewood Police Department
Salutation:	Gentlemen:
Address:	The Postmaster
	Lakewood Post Office
Salutation:	Dear Sir:

Committees

Address:	The Chairman, Building Committee
	Lakewood Men's Club
Salutation:	Dear Sir:
	or
Address:	The Building Committee
	Lakewood Men's Club
Salutation:	Gentlemen:
Address:	The Chairman, Membership Committee
	Lakewood Women's Club
Salutation:	Dear Madam:
	or
Address:	Membership Committee
	Lakewood Women's Club
Salutation:	Ladies:
Address:	The Program Committee
	Lakewood Community Center
Salutation:	Gentlemen:
	or
	Ladies and Gentlemen:

Companies

Address:	James Stone (company name)
Salutation:	Gentlemen:
Address:	Martha Wentworth (company name)
Salutation:	Gentlemen:

Address:	Messrs. Kerr and Bates (a professional partnership such as a firm of architects or lawyers)
Salutation:	Gentlemen:
Address:	Kerr and Bates (a company or corporation name that has lost its personal significance)
Salutation:	Gentlemen:
Address:	Kerr and Bates (a professional partnership composed of women)
Salutation:	Ladies:
Address:	N. R. Brockman & Company
Salutation:	Gentlemen:
Address:	Barbara's Dress Shop (company name)
Salutation:	Gentlemen:
Address:	Barbara's Dress Shop (firm composed of women)
Salutation:	Ladies:

Addressing Private Individuals. As the street, city, and state are understood to follow the name, these are omitted except in the first example, and because the same complimentary close may be used in letters to each of the following individuals, it will not be repeated. The wording of the salutations and the complimentary closes in the first example is, first, formal and then less formal.

Addressing One Person

A man

Address:	Mr. Robert F. Crowell
	1415 Grove Terrace
	Winter Park, FL 32789
Salutation:	Dear Sir:
	or
	Dear Mr. Crowell:
Complimentary close:	Very truly yours,
	or
	Yours sincerely,

An unmarried woman

Address:	Miss Charlotte Phillips
Salutation:	Dear Madam:
	or
	Dear Miss Phillips:

Address:	Ms. Marie Garbacz
Salutation:	Dear Ms. Garbacz:

A married woman

Address:	Mrs. Harry Webster
	or
	Mrs. Edna Webster (the form generally used for a married woman in her business capacity or for a divorced woman)
Salutation:	Dear Madam:
	or
	Dear Mrs. Webster:

Addressing More Than One Person

Two or more men

Address:	Messrs. Brown and Holt
	or
	Mr. Jerome Brown
	Mr. Alfred Holt
Salutation:	Gentlemen:
	or
	Dear Mr. Brown and Mr. Holt:

Two or more men of the same name

Address:	Messrs. Hugh and Carl Condon
	or
	The Messrs. Condon
Salutation:	Gentlemen:

Two or more unmarried women

Address:	The Misses Banks and Towne
	or

	Miss Laura Banks
	Miss Frances Towne
Salutation:	Ladies:
	or
	Dear Misses Banks and Towne:
	or
	Dear Miss Banks and Miss Towne:
	or
	Dear Ms. Banks and Ms. Towne:

Two or more women

Address:	Mrs. Arthur Benson
	Mrs. William Lee
	Miss Mary Parker
Salutation:	Ladies:

Correct Order in the Salutation

When the names of both men and women occur in the inside address, the individual whose name appears first should be addressed first in the salutation.

Men and women

Address:	Mr. Paul Betts
	Mr. Horace Betts
	Miss Janet Betts
Salutation:	Gentlemen and Dear Madam:
Address:	Miss Janet Betts
	Mr. Horace Betts
	Mr. Paul Betts
Salutation:	Dear Madam and Gentlemen:
Address:	Miss Janet Betts
	Miss Irene Betts
	Mr. Paul Betts
Salutation:	Ladies and Dear Sir:
Address:	Mr. Paul Betts
	Mrs. Paul Betts
Salutation:	Dear Sir and Madam:
	or
	Dear Mr. and Mrs. Betts:

Punctuation of Salutation

A colon is placed after the salutation in formal writing. In less formal correspondence, a comma is used after a personal name.

Gentlemen:	Dear Henry,
Ladies:	Dear Mrs. Graham,
Dear Senator Hunt:	Mary dear,

8. Subject Line. The subject line, which states briefly the topic of the letter, is typed two lines above or below the salutation in the block or modified block style, and three lines below the address in the simplified letter. In the modified semi-block style, the subject line is centered above or below the salutation. The words *Subject, In re*, or *Re* are unnecessary.

(1)

Dr. H. J. Burton
Personnel Department
Exville College
St. Petersburg, FL 33700

Retirement Pension

Dear Sir:

(2)

The White Insurance Company
19 West 44 Street
New York, NY 10018

Gentlemen:

Policy 10 954 654

9. Body of the Letter. The body of the letter may be written in block or in indented form. If the inside address follows block style, the body of the letter may be either block or indented form. If block form is used, the first line of each paragraph should begin at the left-hand margin; single spacing should be used within paragraphs, double spacing between paragraphs.

10. Complimentary close. In the block and simplified letter formats, the complimentary close appears at the left margin at least two spaces below the last line of the letter or, in a short letter, even four spaces below the message.

In the modified block and modified semi-block styles, the placement of the complimentary close depends somewhat on the length of the signature. It should begin to the right of the vertical center and not extend beyond the right margin. It should be placed at least two spaces below the last line of the letter or, in a short letter, even four spaces below the message.

The selection of the complimentary close depends on the nature and the tone of the letter. The following examples are in order of decreasing formality.

Very truly yours,
Yours very truly,
Sincerely yours,
Cordially,
Sincerely,

The complimentary close should not be preceded by a participial phrase, such as *Hoping to hear from you soon.* Punctuation following a complimentary close depends on the punctuation following the salutation. If punctuation is omitted there, it should also be omitted after the complimentary close.

11. Signature. Placement of the signature should correspond with the style of the heading or of the inside address.

Business Signatures

The name of the organization is not typed after the complimentary close when letterhead stationery is used. When no letterhead is available, the name of the organization is typed in capitals two spaces below the complimentary close.

Four spaces are allowed for the actual signature of the writer. On the line below the signature is the typewritten name of the writer, and on the following line appears his or her official position or rank in the organization.

The following examples illustrate correct forms of signatures:

Yours very truly,

MOUNT GRETNA CEMETERY ASSOCIATION
William Brown [written]
William Brown,
Manager

Yours very truly,
William Brown [written]
William Brown,
Manager

Private Individuals

An individual should use his customary signature for business letters, that is, the first name, a middle initial, and the last name. Or a first initial and a middle name may be used if that is preferred. Some people use initials only, but using a single initial is not recommended. If there is no middle name, the first name should be written out. Confusion could thus be avoided if there happened to be more than one person with that name in the organization.

John F. Whitman *or* J. Francis Whitman
J. F. Whitman *rather than* J. Whitman

Such titles as *Dr.*, *Rev.*, *Prof.* should not precede signatures nor should such degrees as B.A., M.D., LL.D. follow them.

An unmarried woman should not sign herself as *Miss* Elizabeth Jones but should place *Miss* in parentheses before her name if she thinks it necessary.

A married woman must sign her own name; as, *Vera C. Martini.* This may be preceded by *Mrs.* in parentheses or by her married name written in parentheses below the signature.

(Mrs.) Vera C. Martini
  or
Vera C. Martini
(Mrs. Herbert Martini)

A widow should sign her name exactly as she did before the death of her husband; as, *Jane Morrison Ross* or *Jane M. Ross.*

It should be remembered in either case *Jane Morrison Ross* is her *name; Mrs. Herbert Ross* is her *title.* At present it is customary for a widow to retain her husband's title.

Some professional women prefer to keep their maiden names. In such a case, *Mrs. Jane Morrison Ross* would sign her name *Jane Morrison*.

If for any reason she should wish to indicate her married title, the signature would read as follows:

Jane Morrison
(Mrs. Herbert Ross)

A woman who is divorced has the choice of assuming her maiden name with or without *Mrs.*; as, *(Miss) Jane Morrison* or *(Mrs.) Jane Morrison*.

On the other hand, she may retain her husband's surname with *Miss, Ms.*, or *Mrs.*; as, *(Miss) Jane Ross* or *(Mrs.) Jane Ross*. Socially she may be known as *Mrs. Morrison Ross*. She must not use her former title; as, *Mrs. Herbert Ross*.

On checks, a married woman usually signs her own name, not her title; as, *Jane Ross*.

In endorsing checks or signing stock certificates or other legal papers, a woman should be careful to sign as the name appears in the document.

In wills and deeds, a married woman should sign her name, not her title; as, *Jane Ross*, not *Mrs. Herbert Ross*.

Usually on formal programs and announcements, a married woman prefers to use her title; as, *Mrs. Herbert Ross*.

On hotel registers she may sign as she wishes; as, *Jane Ross* or *Mrs. Jane Ross* or the more usual form, *Mrs. Herbert Ross*.

The unmarried woman may sign a hotel register with or without her title; as, *Jane Morrison* or *Ms. Jane Morrison*.

It is desirable for women in signing business or professional letters to indicate the writer's official position. In such cases after the signature the title may be written as follows:

Mary Dawson
Superintendent
    or
Mary Dawson, Superintendent

Margaret Davis
President

For a Private Secretary

Joan MacFarlane
   Secretary to Mrs. Borden
Joan MacFarlane
   Secretary to Mr. James Brown

When the secretary signs the employer's name to a letter, he or she may add his or her own initials or he or she may sign his or her name adding to it *for* with the employer's name.

Henry Newcomb
   J. MacF.
     or
Joan MacFarlane
   for
Henry Newcomb

12. Additional data. The initials of the writer of the letter and those of the typist, notation of enclosures, and distribution of copies (if any) are usually placed at the lower left margin below the signature.

The initials (sometimes the name) of the writer and of the typist may appear in several forms:

FCS:RG *or* FCS:rg *or* FCS/rg
HEC:C *or* Hill E. Case/c

When enclosures are made in the letter, that fact should be noted, below the initials of writer and typist, with *Enc.*, *Encl.*, or *Enclosure.* If more than one enclosure is made, the number should be given: *Enc.* 2. If the enclosure is one of special significance, that fact should be noted: *Enc.* check; *Enc.* Policy N–123456.

When a copy of the letter is being sent to someone other than the addressee, this fact may be noted two spaces below the other notations at the lower left corner of the letter. The abbreviation *cc:* (for carbon copy) is used, whether carbons are addressed to one or more than one person. When the copies are distributed, the name of the recipient of each may be checked with a red pencil to draw his attention and indicate that the copy has been sent to him intentionally. Sometimes the letters *FYI* are added (For Your Information).

13. Postscripts. A postscript is a paragraph added at the end of the letter. In business letters it is not an afterthought but an idea that its writer wishes to stress although it may not fit into the letter itself. The writer's initials are typed below the postscript.

14. Mailing Instructions. When a letter is sent by special delivery, Express Mail, registered mail, certified mail, or by courier, a notation of this fact should be made on the file copy of the letter.

The Simplified Letter

In the simplified letter, sponsored by the Administrative Management Society, all data follow the block form, but the salutation and the complimentary close are omitted. The date appears on the first line, with three or more spaces left below. If *Personal* or *Confidential* is used, this word appears on the next line. The name and address are typed next. (The Society suggests using the abbreviation *Ms.* for addressing a woman when the writer does not know whether or not the correspondent is married.)

Instead of a salutation, a subject line is used, although it is not so labeled. The subject of the letter is typed in full capitals at least three spaces below the address.

The letter is single-spaced without indentation and double-spaced between paragraphs. The name of the addressee is often used in the first sentence or in the first paragraph to make the letter more personal.

The complimentary close is omitted, and at least five spaces are allowed for the signature. The name of the writer is typed in full capitals at the left margin. His title either follows his name or appears on the line below.

If the secretary's initials are used, they appear below the typed signature. Other data, such as *Enc.* or *cc*, appear below the typist's initials. (*See* p. 237.)

Examples of business letters typed in the various styles are reproduced on the following pages.

Block Style

[Letterhead]

January 18, 19—

The Charles G. Nathanson Company
1877 East Main Street
Nashua, MO 64100

Henry Gray

Gentlemen:

The shipment of office furniture (Order No. A877665), which has been en route to you for the past month, was delayed by floods in the St. Louis area. We are informed by the trucking company that delivery will be made to you within the next week. A copy of the bill of lading is enclosed.

We very much regret the delay and the inconvenience to you. We hope that the furniture will please you in every way, and we shall look forward to the pleasure of filling your future orders.

Very truly yours,

John G. Bradley
Manager

JGB:LF
Enclosure

Modified Block Style

[Letterhead]

January 18, 19—

James G. Lamson & Co.
Arcadian Shopping Center
Tarleton Road
White Plains, NY 10600

Purchasing Department

Gentlemen:

Your order for six Smith-Corona electric typewriters, Model XD 7000, has been referred to me. These machines can be delivered this week if you wish.

Do you wish us to bill you in thirty days, or would you prefer to pay in installments? I enclose agreements for payment in ninety days, six months, or one year. There is a service charge of 2 percent per month on the unpaid balance after the first thirty-one days.

Please let me know how you prefer to make payment, and the typewriters will be delivered the following day.

Very truly yours,

John G. Bradley
Manager

JGB:LF
Enclosures 3

Modified Semi-Block Style

[Letterhead]

January 18, 19—

Miss Blanche Horton
25 Carter Place
Carrollton, OH 44615

Dear Miss Horton:

You are cordially invited to attend the luncheon for patrons of the Children's Village, to be held on February 2 at the Old Drover's Inn in Centerville. A reception will be held at 12:30, followed by luncheon in the Carriage Room.

The annual fund-raising drive for the Children's Village will be held in March as usual. We hope you will again be able to direct the drive in Carrollton, Miamisburg, and Germantown. A list of volunteers in previous years is maintained at our office and will be sent to you after the luncheon if you are able to serve.

We hope to have you with us on February 2.

Very sincerely yours,

Raymond C. Hartwood, Chairman
Board of Trustees

RCH:v

Simplified Letter

[Letterhead]

July 6, 19—

Mrs. John Henry Garrison
181 Barlow Street
Staten Island, NY 10308

INSECTICIDE FOR ROSES

We are sending you by parcel post, Mrs. Garrison, two types of insecticide specially developed for use on roses. Please follow the directions on each package, using only one type at a time on any one plant. After one week's use you may wish to try the other type on the same plant, to compare results. We will be glad to have your comments.

The two containers of insecticide are being sent to you with our compliments. Should you wish to order either type, the price is $1.75 per 12-ounce refillable applicator, postpaid.

We hope you will be pleased with the results produced by these new products.

[Signature]

B. F. GARDEY, RESEARCH MANAGER

kjg

cc: Mr. Paul Young

Envelopes and Labels

(Return Address)

The Rocky Mountain Bottling Co.
1214 West Main Street
Fairplay, CO 80440

(To)

CERTIFIED MAIL

Mr. G. C. Ratliff
1888 Norfolk Boulevard
Richmond, VA 23200

(Return Address)

The Smith Paperbox Corp.
53 Valley Avenue
Smithfield, NE 68976

(To)

Jarmon & Jarmon

Manville Road

Pleasantville, NY 10570

(Return Address)

Great Books Publishing Co.
290 Bay View Street
San Francisco, CA 94100

(To)

The Burton Memorial Library

Fourth Street at Ninth Avenue

BOOK RATE   Galveston, TX 77550

Attention, In Care Of (c/o). When either of these lines is used, it may be typed at the lower left of the envelope or in the main part of the address, immediately below the name of the company.

Airmail. Domestic mail need not be marked for airmail, since beyond a specified distance all U.S. mail is automatically sent by air. If airmail service is desired for overseas correspondence or small packages, however, it must be specified on the envelope or label. (Many large firms use telex service if there is a considerable volume of overseas correspondence.) Overseas packages require a customs declaration and are subject to certain restrictions. Customs declaration forms and lists of restrictions are provided at post offices.

Air Express. You should inquire whether your employer or the organization has a preference as to the carrier to be used. If the choice is yours, you can consult the Yellow Pages of the telephone directory for the names of local companies. Ask for rates, expected times of delivery, and whether pickup service is available. The choice can then be made, after considering whether speed or economy is of greater importance.

The United States Postal Service offers Express Mail Next Day Service at a special rate. It will deliver a package weighing up to seventy pounds in envelopes and boxes used by the service to an addressee anywhere in the United States or to a destination Express Mail Post Office. A Next Day Service Directory is provided that indicates which ZIP Codes can be serviced with an overnight guarantee. It is also possible to send packages from post office to post office for pickup at 10 A.M. the following day. (In smaller towns the service may not be available for overnight delivery but might take two days.) Other Express Mail Services include Same Day Airport Service in many metropolitan areas, International Expedited Service to many countries with delivery in three days or less, and custom-designed service when scheduled on a regular basis.

Foreign Countries. Letters sent to foreign countries should bear the name of the country on a separate line, typed in full capitals. Unless the envelope or label is marked AIRMAIL, it will be sent by surface mail, a much slower although cheaper service. (If a telex service is used, *see* Chapter 10).

Large Mailings. If a word processor is used, the envelopes for large mailings can be addressed conveniently and rapidly through the use of a suitable holder attached to the printer.

If no word processor is available, chain-feeding the envelopes into the typewriter makes the job shorter. This may be done from either the back or the front of the cylinder (platen) of the typewriter.

Back of the cylinder: Insert one envelope halfway and then place another envelope behind it, between the first envelope and the paper rest. When the cylinder is rolled forward, the first envelope comes into position to be typed and the second reaches the halfway position. After the first envelope has been addressed, a third is inserted behind the second, against the paper rest. The first envelope is removed by a quick twirl of the cylinder; this brings the second up into position for addressing. The extra twirling needed to insert envelopes separately is eliminated by this method.

To front-feed: The first envelope is rolled into the typewriter and addressed. Before rolling it out backward, place a second envelope behind it, between the envelope and the cylinder. When the first is rolled out, the second moves down into position for addressing.

For an informal mailing, such as to club members or committee members, when speed is more important than formality, self-stick labels may be purchased in sheet form. The individual addresses may be typed on bond paper to correspond with the labels and then copied onto the label sheet using the office copier. If monthly mailings of this kind are made, it will save time to make as many labels at one time as will be needed in the coming months.

Folding and Inserting Letters. A neatly typed letter can lose its attractive appearance the moment it is carelessly folded and crushed into an envelope. When a letter is folded, the edges should meet evenly with no uneven overlapping. The fold should be straight and neatly creased.

Before folding the letter, the size of the envelope must be taken into consideration. The most popular size of business envelope is the No. 6¾, which measures 6½ inches by 3⅝ inches. Either full-size or half-size letterhead stationery may be mailed in this envelope. Full-size letters and those of two or more pages should be placed in a larger envelope, the No. 10, which measures 9½ inches by 4⅛ inches.

Folding for the smaller envelope. The sheet is folded in half from the bottom up, leaving a half-inch margin at the top. Then it is folded from right to left, making the fold slightly less than one-third the width of the sheet. The remaining portion is folded from left to right, leaving a half-inch margin at the right.

The letter is inserted in the envelope with the left creased edge entering first. This will leave the half-inch margin at the right.

Folding for the larger envelope. The sheet is folded from the bottom up, making the fold about one-third the length of the sheet. Next it is folded down from the top, leaving a half-inch margin at the first fold. When the letter is slipped into the envelope, the second fold is inserted first, leaving the half-inch margin near the envelope flap.

Letters should always be placed in envelopes so that when the letter is removed and unfolded, the typed side will face the reader.

Folding for window envelopes. The bottom of the letter is folded up, about one-third the length of the sheet. The upper edge of the letter is folded *back*, so that the top of the sheet is even with the first fold, leaving the letterhead and the inside address on the outside. The letter is then inserted with the letterhead and the address facing the front of the envelope so that the address shows through the window.

Handling Enclosures

Smaller than the letter. If the enclosure is smaller than the letter, it may be stapled to the letter at the upper left corner. The use of pins or paperclips is discouraged by the U.S. Postal Service because the pins may prick the hands of the postal clerks and the paperclips may damage the canceling machines.

Same size as the letter. An enclosure that will fit into ordinary business envelopes may be folded in the same manner as the letter and placed inside the last fold of the letter. When the letter is removed from the envelope, the enclosure will thus appear at the same time and not be overlooked.

Larger than the letter, or folding undesirable. If the enclosure is a booklet or other printed matter too large or bulky to fit into an ordinary business envelope, it is usually mailed in a large manila envelope. Various sizes of manila envelopes are available in stationery stores. A large photograph or document that may not be folded may similarly be sent in a manila envelope, with a cardboard backing of the same size to prevent bending in the mail. The notation PLEASE DO NOT BEND OR FOLD may be typed on the label.

The letter may be placed with the enclosure in the large envelope, and the envelope is then sent first class. Or it may be sent with the merchandise by paying first-class postage on the letter alone, with the notation LETTER ENCLOSED on the label. Photographs may be sent third class, the envelope being closed by a metal or twine fastener but not sealed.

Or the enclosure may be sent separately in an envelope closed by a fastener but not sealed and the letter sent first class in its own sealed envelope.

Or a combination envelope may be used, in which a large outside envelope closed with a fastener but not sealed carries the enclosure and a smaller, attached, sealed envelope carries the letter. Thus, third- or fourth-class postage may be paid on the heavier enclosure and first-class postage on the letter alone, and the letter arrives with the enclosure.

CHAPTER FIFTEEN

Writing Business Letters

Cost of Letter-Writing. Much of today's business is carried on by correspondence. The importance of carefully composed and typed letters is obvious. Yet many firms lose business and the confidence of the public because of the poor quality of the correspondence that goes out on their letterheads. Each letter should be a silent salesman, representing the company to the person who receives it. But a letter that is carelessly typed, with names misspelled and typographical errors uncorrected, gives the impression of inefficiency, which inevitably reflects on the reliability of the company itself. The recipient of such a letter cannot avoid the thought that an office so careless of details cannot be depended on to carry on its business effectively. Millions of dollars spent in advertising a product can be a complete waste if the customer's only personal contact with the company is through the carelessly written letters he receives.

It has been estimated that 5 percent of all business letters are written to correct errors or omissions in previous correspondence. Considering the high cost of stationery and postage, quite aside from the salaries and time of the writer and the secretary, this is a tremendous expense to any firm. The secretary is responsible for careful proofreading of the letters he or she types, as well as for checking price quotations or other figures given in the letters. All computations should be double-checked as a matter of course. Dates given must be accurate. You must *think* as you proofread. You must make sure that enclosures mentioned in a letter are actually enclosed, that material to be sent separately is prepared and sent as promised, that a scheduled follow-up is actually made.

Letters Written for the Employer's Signature. You can relieve your employer by composing many of the answers to routine letters he or she receives. If you are asked to write letters, you should follow the tested principles of good business correspondence. Each letter must be considered an individual case, written to a particular person in a particular set of circumstances. Its purpose is to promote good relations. It can please by its considerate tone—or annoy by its flippancy. It can supply needed information—or irritate by touching on the wrong aspect of the situation. The effectiveness of the letter will be the result of the writer's courtesy, your sincerity, your understanding of the purpose of the letter, and your ability to communicate effectively.

Short Opening Paragraph. An advantage is gained by making the first paragraph of a letter a short one of two or three typewritten lines, four at most. It looks easier to read, and its purpose is to lead the reader into the rest of the letter. It should not be a mere attention-getter without relation to the rest of the letter; it is, rather, a short expression of the reason for writing.

A letter should start at once to agree to a proposal, to issue an invitation, to thank someone for a service, to offer sympathy, and so forth. Whatever the purpose of the letter, you should bear in mind that you are asking for someone's attention. If you cannot say what is on your mind, you are likely to lose your audience in short order.

Pinpointing the Message. Short business letters produce more results than overlong ones. Most letters will not need to furnish much background, and the message can come quickly to the point, specify the action desired, and close with a minimum of pleasantries. If several matters must be discussed, it may be preferable to write more than one letter, so that each can be dealt with separately. With only one or two subjects per letter, there is less chance for confusion about what action is expected. In most cases the recipient will tend to handle the short requests first.

Consideration for Recipient of Letter. As a secretary you often write letters to persons you have not met. Your good manners will guide you to the use of pleasant expressions such as "Thank you for writing us," "We are grateful for the opportunity to be of service," and so forth, rather than simply stopping the letter after the price quotation and losing an opportunity to establish a friendly relationship with a customer or client.

When you must disagree with the customer, the words you put into the letter may soothe the customer or further annoy him. Expressions such as "It so happens that . . . ," "Our records show unmistakably . . . ," and so on, must be used with great care. After all, companies do make mistakes and "our records" may prove to be incorrect after all. You must never appear cocksure or seem to accuse the customer of bad faith. In business relations as in personal affairs, pride often goes before a fall. Everyone is sometimes proved wrong. The tone of the letter should be that of a friendly conversation. If the message has to be unpleasant, let it be stated in sorrow—never in anger. It should truly be a matter of regret that a complaint has been made, and the company must truly care to rectify the matter. Many firms prefer to take a small loss and replace a relatively inexpensive item that may have been broken through the customer's own fault rather than lose the confidence and goodwill of that customer, together with the goodwill of his friends and neighbors. Word-of-mouth advertising can be both favorable and unfavorable.

Written to Order. A good letter is directed specifically to one individual, even if it is addressed to an organization or to a committee. Since one person at a time will read it, the letter must be expressed in the manner most likely to appeal to him.

You should find out as much as possible about the person you are addressing to be sure the letter is appropriately expressed. The tone of the message will differ in a letter to an older person, to a senior officer of a corporation or to a younger, less important one, to an unknown housewife, or to a political figure. The more important the letter, the more care you should take to learn about the person to whom you are writing. The minimum information required is the correct title (Mr., Dr., Professor, Senator, Ms., Miss, Mrs.), the correct spelling of his or her name and address, the correct name of his or her organization, and the correct Zip Code.

Timeworn Expressions. Each word in a letter is important. Consider the effect of these timeworn expressions:

Yours of the 13th inst. received
Your letter has come to hand
Replying to your letter of the 5th we wish to say we have duly noted the
    contents
We beg to announce
Hoping to hear from you soon, I remain
Trusting to hear from you soon
Thanking you in advance for your consideration

Usually there is no need to refer to a letter in the reply. When necessary, the date or a file number or a subject line can be used to refer to such a letter. When giving information requested in a letter, you are obviously answering that letter.

Old-fashioned terms such as *inst.*, *ult.*, and *prox.* are no longer used in business letters, nor are such expressions as "The favor of a reply" and "We beg to inform you." Straightforward language is more effective.

Urgent for Whom? The writer who expresses an urgent need for information or other favors is like a person who enters a room without knocking. Some people will put aside matters of importance to themselves in order to grant an urgent request. More likely, however, that request will be referred elsewhere, ignored, or handled in the routine way.

When asking for a favor, you must consider the effect on the recipient's self-esteem or his pocketbook, his potential enjoyment, his chance for social or business advancement, and (not least) how much time may be required to grant the favor.

Letters That Need Not be Written. Often simple requests can be answered with a few words typed or handwritten on the received letter and then that letter returned to the customer. Neither the letter nor a copy of the reply need fill up the files, and the organization saves time and stationery.

Many businessmen and -women use their business cards, clipped to reports or tearsheets of articles, as an indication of the source of the data. No letter need accompany the report when sent to an acquaintance or to a regular correspondent. If a new client were requesting the information, it of course would be more complimentary to send a letter.

Business Letters of Various Types

Order Letters

Formerly, letters ordering merchandise were probably the most frequently written. Today, with telephone service, easy transportation to stores, and order forms supplied by business houses, order letters are seldom written. On occasion, telephone orders may be confirmed in writing to avoid misunderstanding and to give definite information about the merchandise desired and the shipping orders.

[Letterhead]

June 1, 19—

Smith, Perkins and Co., Inc.
15 East Avenue
Rochester, NY 14603

Gentlemen:

In confirmation of our discussion this morning in regard to furniture for our new offices, I am sending you the order in detail. You have assured me it would be delivered by December 1.

Legal 202WP	6 walnut double-pedestal desks, plastic top 30″ × 66″	@ $850.30	$5,101.80
556WP	1 walnut credenza, 18″ × 62⅝″ brushed chrome legs, walnut wood top		900.80

263	6 walnut armchairs covered in top grain leather, color to be determined	@ 495.00	2,970.00
Board Room 866	1 walnut board table 4' × 12', three sets of legs, laminated plastic top, self-edged		8,000.00
269	12 walnut armchairs, top grain leather	@ 650.00	7,800.00
			$24,772.60

Payment will be made upon delivery and installation of the order.

Yours very truly,
James W. Allison
Office Manager

Business Agreement Letters

[Letterhead]

March 2, 19—

Mr. Eugene Zajic
12 Weatherside Road
Barnstable, MA 02630

Dear Mr. Zajic:

This will confirm the arrangement made in our conversation this morning in my office.

You will provide men and materials to scrape and paint the exterior of my summer cottage in Barnstable, Massachusetts, during the week of April 14, weather permitting, at a cost not to exceed $3,200. Should the weather be bad, you will have the painting done as soon afterward as possible. We agreed that one coat of Sherwin-Williams oil exterior paint will suffice, white for the house and dark green for the shutters and trim.

In addition, you will service the hot-water heater and have two 100-pound cylinders of gas delivered and connected, charging for the gas at current local rates and $25 for the service. You will have the windows washed and the rooms vacuum-cleaned by a competent person at $7.00 per hour. The kitchen and bathrooms should also be thoroughly cleaned. If possible, you will engage the same person to come one day a week during the summer from June 15 to September 15. Otherwise, you will attempt to locate another good worker for the same period.

Please let me know if you agree to these terms.

It was good to see you again, and I feel fortunate in having you to look after the cottage in my absence.

> Very truly yours,
> Elmer G. Richardson

Acknowledgment Letters

Most companies use a standard printed form if acknowledgment is made of orders or payments. Often the order is simply filled or the customer's account is credited, and no acknowledgment is required. On occasion, circumstances do not fit the forms and a personal note is needed. Simplicity and sincerity will convey the message in a brief and cordial manner.

(1)

Thank you for your order for a lace tablecloth in the Venice pattern, 52 inches by 70 inches. However, you did not specify whether you prefer ecru or blue. We will be glad to fill your order as soon as you let us know which color you wish.

(2)

We have received your order for one attic stairway, medium weight. As the shipping weight of this stairway is 80 pounds, it cannot be sent by parcel post and must go by freight. The trucking company will need more detailed information in order to deliver the stairway, since your address includes no street number.

Please tell us the name of some highway, street intersection, gas station, or other local landmark near your house, and explain your location in relation to this landmark. We are holding the merchandise until we receive the necessary information for delivery.

We regret the unavoidable delay and any inconvenience it may have caused you.

Other letters may acknowledge receipt of letters in the absence of the addressee.

(3)

Because Mrs. Hunt is out of town this week, I am acknowledging your letter of August 14. I shall bring it to her attention on Monday, and you may expect to hear from her shortly.

(4)

This will acknowledge receipt of your estimate of the cost of repaving Mr. Stone's driveway. As I know he is anxious to have the work done as soon as possible, I am sure he will get in touch with you on his return to the office at the end of the week.

Thanks for Gifts

Letters to thank donors of money may be brief and simple when the amount is modest. A larger contribution or a more personal gift would require a somewhat more detailed response, as in Letters of Appreciation, pp. 282–283.

(1)

At this time each member of our Fortnightly Club wishes to thank you for the check for thirty dollars you so kindly sent in memory of our dear Mrs. Brookins. We all miss her greatly and share our wonderful memories of her when we gather together. We are adding your check to our Sunshine Fund, as we know Mrs. Brookins would have wished us to do. Thank you again for your gift.

(2)

It is a pleasure to acknowledge with gratitude your contribution to ——— University.

With this most welcome gift we are pleased to enter your name on the roster of those who continue to support the university.

Our best wishes to you.

(3)

Thank you very much for your gift to our College Alumnae Fund.

I'm sure you'll be pleased to know that our drive has been most successful. On the basis of what we have received to date, we think we can project a total somewhere in the vicinity of $100,000.

This will make a gift to the College that our Alumnae Association can well be proud of and that will go a long way toward bridging the gap between tuition income and education costs.

As chairman of the Fund drive, I wish to extend the appreciation of the College.

Sincerely yours,
Alumnae Fund Chairman

(4)

The members of the High Ridge Fire Department wish to thank you for your contribution to our fund-raising drive. Your continued support is most appreciated.

(5)

The Board of Directors acknowledges with appreciation your donation of one hundred dollars toward the support of the Castle Memorial Hospital.

Claim and Adjustment Letters

Letters of complaint are often called claim letters, with the implication that the claim may well be justified. A claim letter must take a positive stand, describing what is wrong and suggesting what can be done to correct the situation. When merchandise has proved unsatisfactory or an error has been made in a statement, the customer should state the facts briefly and honestly, giving all necessary details. He should not threaten anyone or permit himself to discuss personalities. A simple explanation of the difficulty is more dignified and more effective.

Some merchandise can be returned by the customer in person, and no letter need be written. If the item is too bulky or the store is located at a distance, a letter must be written to explain the customer's wishes and arrange for the shipment of the merchandise.

Adjustment. A claim letter should be handled promptly—either the claim settled or the reason for difficulties explained. The customer will be impressed by a quick reply, even if his claim is not acted upon favorably. But a very different impression is created when a claim letter is permitted to lie around on someone's desk or is referred to one or more other departments for action. It is gratifying to receive a long-overdue reply, but the slowness of action will indicate that the matter was not considered of much importance and the customer's goodwill was disregarded. A brief acknowledgment of a claim letter on the day the letter is received will help to mollify the dissatisfied customer, and a delay of several days in settling the claim can then be understood.

While many stores still write courteous notes to disgruntled customers, others simply send replacement merchandise without charge and without correspondence. Because circumstances differ, a small order by an individual could be readily handled in this way. Should further dissatisfaction develop, letters may need to be written. Many complaints and apologies are of course made by telephone. When the buyer in a department learns of a serious difficulty with a good customer, he may pick up the telephone and attempt to straighten out the matter at once.

A manufacturer will also be inclined to take the direct approach, replacing damaged goods by sending a duplicate shipment by express to meet a deadline, using the telephone to speed apologies and maintain customer goodwill.

(1)

129 Eldorado Way
Whitefish Bay, WI 53209
November 6, 19—

Carson & Kitts
453 South Union Street
Milwaukee, WI 53202

Dear Sir:

The watch I bought from you last Friday, November 2, as a birthday present for my husband has just been delivered. Unfortunately, it is not the one I chose, and while I might have been willing to accept it as a substitute, it does not keep accurate time. I shall hold it for the parcel delivery service to pick up. Please inform the service that I shall not be in on Tuesday.

Meanwhile, my husband's birthday has passed, and I have given him something else. Please refund the price of the watch, for which I paid $123, including city sales tax. I do not wish a credit to my account.

Very truly yours,
Bernice Smith
(Mrs. G. R. Smith)

Answer

[Letterhead]

November 8, 19—

Mrs. G. R. Smith
129 Eldorado Way
Whitefish Bay, WI 53209

Dear Mrs. Smith:

We are very sorry to learn that the wrong watch was sent to you and that the one you received does not keep time accurately. We apologize for the disappointment you must have felt.

Apparently the watch you selected was the display model and the only one in stock at the moment. It is not customary to sell the display model, and the salesperson took the liberty of substituting another at the same price, hoping it might be suitable for your husband's birthday present. You should of course have been informed of the situation, and certainly the substitute should have been in good running order.

If the parcel service should call while you are out, a notice will be left at your home and another visit will be made to pick up the watch.

Our check for $123 is enclosed. We regret very much that we were unable to send the watch you ordered in time for your husband's birthday. We hope you will soon give us another opportunity to serve you.

Cordially yours,
Carson & Kitts

(2)

10 Aspen Road
Fanwood, NJ 07023
June 9, 19—

Mr. Ellsworth Barrows, President
Barrows & Company
Indiana, PA 15701

Dear Mr. Barrows:

The four Golden Jubilee peach trees that we ordered from you in March were delivered in April at the right time for planting. Although we followed the planting directions enclosed with the trees, they have not sprouted yet, two months later. It is a disappointment to us to lose an entire growing season, and we wonder if it would be possible to plant other peach trees this late in the year. If so, can they be shipped by express?

If it is too late now for peach trees, will you please give us credit for these four and ship us four more next spring? We like this variety and prefer no substitutes.

We have had excellent results from your shrubs and seeds in the past, and we wonder if peaches are particularly hard to raise.

Sincerely yours,
Carolyn Grant
(Mrs. Henry C. Grant)

Answer

[Letterhead]

June 12, 19—

Mrs. Henry C. Grant
10 Aspen Road
Fanwood, NJ 07023

Dear Mrs. Grant:

We are sorry to hear that the Golden Jubilee peach trees you received from rows & Company failed to grow this season. Actually, we have had this experience before with peach trees shipped with bare roots, despite our use of the best packing and shipping methods. Sometimes weather conditions are unfavorable after the trees are planted, and sometimes the shock of transplanting is too great. In any case, it is now too late in the growing season to plant other peach trees. It is possible that yours may yet show some sign of life if you water them well.

We understand your disappointment, but deciduous trees do best if planted while they are dormant. We will send you a duplicate shipment of four Golden Jubilee peach trees next spring, with our usual guarantee of replacement should they fail to grow.

Cordially yours,
Ellsworth Barrows, President

(3)

16 Maiden Lane
Scioto, OH 46676
October 14, 19—

Belson & Belson
Maple Street at 35th Avenue
Scioto, OH 46676

Gentlemen:

On October 6 I ordered a set of ironstone dinnerware as advertised in the October 5 *Register*, thirty-five dollars for a service for six, including three serving dishes, in the Moonstone pattern. Although it is now October 14, no dishes have yet been delivered to me. I have twice telephoned the China Department, and each time I was assured that prompt delivery would be made.

Will you please fill my order at the sale price. If your supply is exhausted, please let me know so that I may look elsewhere.

Sincerely yours,
Heloise B. Fleck
(Mrs. Robert H. Fleck)

Answer

[Letterhead]

October 16, 19—

Mrs. Robert H. Fleck
16 Maiden Lane
Scioto, OH 46676

Dear Mrs. Fleck:

We are extremely sorry to hear of your disappointment regarding the ironstone dinnerware. We are immediately investigating the reason for our failure to deliver the dishes.

Unfortunately, as you feared, our stock of this particular pattern of ironstone has been sold. We do expect another shipment within a week and could then fill your order at the sale price. The head of the China Department has promised to see to it personally.

We regret the inconvenience and annoyance that you have experienced and hope that you will accept delivery of the dinnerware next week.

Very truly yours,
BELSON & BELSON
(signed)
B. H. Pourtenoy
Manager

Collection Letters

When bills remain unpaid, the customer must be reminded of his obligation. Many companies have printed forms, a paragraph or two in length, that are enclosed with the monthly statement. If no payment is then forthcoming, the next month's reminder may be printed on brightly colored paper, with the name of the collection manager. If the customer is not then moved to pay his bill, a personal letter is written that suggests legal action as the next step.

Various degrees of sternness are shown in the examples following.

(1)

If you have sent a payment within the last few days, our letters must have crossed in the mail. In this event, please deduct what you sent us and remit the balance. If you have paid in full, rest assured that no further bill will be sent to you.

(2)

Perhaps it's just an oversight on your part, but we have not yet received your payment. Unless you mailed it within the past few days, won't you please take the time right now to do so. Just enclose your check or money order along with the invoice in the postage-paid envelope and drop it in the mail today.

Thanks very much for your cooperation.

(3)

Did you overlook our recent reminder of your account? The amount past due for your purchases is $11.92.

Your check at this time will be appreciated.

(4)

Dear Customer:

May we remind you that the terms of your account require payment in full within ten days of receipt of your bill.

If we have made an error that is causing you to delay payment, please let us know. We will be happy to correct the matter for you.

On the other hand, if the statement as rendered is correct, will you please send us your check for the full balance as noted below.

Very truly yours,
John T. Statson
Collection Manager

Amount Past Due $87.45

(5)

Please pardon us . . .

if you have sent us a check for the amount shown below. In the event you haven't mailed it, we thought you would like to know that a charge of 1½ percent of the past-due balance may be avoided if payment is made before your next billing date. If your check is already on the way, please accept our thanks.

Amount Past Due $31.25

Fund-Raising Letters

A successful fund-raising letter must depend on catching the recipient's sympathetic interest the moment he looks at the letter. The number of good causes appealing for help is always large, and everyone has his own favorite organization. Whether the cause is child welfare, conservation of natural resources, the encouragement of cultural activities, or the cure for a disease, the letter must persuade the reader to care and to send money.

Here again, brevity and sincerity are essential. An eye-catching drawing or photograph in the letterhead will help make the message memorable. However, it is the facts behind the need and the reputation of the organization and its backers, as much as the statements about the use to be made of contributions, that will move the reader—or speed the letter into the wastebasket.

Here are some examples of texts of letters that have proved effective.

(1)

Those of us in motion pictures, on the stage, and in television are familiar with the typical story of a physically handicapped person. Almost inevitably the script has a happy ending. But in real life, for many of the ten million crippled men and women in America today, there can be no happy ending without advice, vocational guidance, and employment.

I have accepted the chairmanship of the special gifts committee for Federation of the Handicapped because, in my frequent visits to the Center, I have come to know how Federation has helped and is helping thousands of these handicapped men and women become well-adjusted, self-supporting citizens.

An ever-increasing number need help desperately, but today Federation's shops and classes are filled to capacity. Without additional funds, it will be forced to close its doors to those who come seeking independence.

Twelve hundred dollars per year is the cost of training a handicapped person. Will you help pay for his training today so he can pay his own way tomorrow?

I know that your gift will be multiplied a thousandfold in the assistance it gives to a handicapped person. Won't you send—today—the largest contribution you can?

(2)

My specialty is writing music, not letters. I'm used to drawing musical notes, not pictures. But still this is the way it seems to me.

This is the kind of summer I had as a kid: no place to cool off, no place to play, nothing to look forward to all day long but hot city streets. Hundreds of kids in New York City are facing that kind of summer.

If we—you and I—help Forest House, the kids will be able to jam Morris Playfield daily as they did last year for basketball, shuffleboard, chess, checkers, tournaments, arts and crafts, puppet shows, and other activities dear to youngsters. The boys and girls most urgently in need of sunshine, country air, nourishing food, and rest will be sent to camp. And for the very small fry whose mothers work all day there will be the Forest House Day Camp.

Forest House needs $20,000 to do this job—only $20 a child!

$11,000 to send kids to camp

$3,000 to buy athletic and game equipment for the playground

$6,000 for rest-period cost, hot lunches, and bus trips to beaches

How about providing for ten youngsters—or five—or even one? Confidentially, I think once you've put your check in the enclosed envelope, you'll have a better summer yourself!

(3)

Dear Mr. Swanton:

We are living in an age of rapid change. Change often means progress, but sometimes it brings unfavorable results, too. Such family changes as death of a parent, divorce, or a similar crisis can cause serious emotional disturbances in the children.

The Jennie Clarkson Home provides a residential treatment facility for girls unable to cope successfully with their home environment. The youngsters are given understanding care and affection by trained staff members, treatment prescribed by consulting doctors, and guidance that will help them grow into competent young women who will be assets to their communities.

To finance these services, we depend to a large extent on contributions from the public. Won't you send us your contribution to help us restore girls to successful lives?

(Used by permission of The Jennie Clarkson Home)

(4)

YES, IT'S A FIGHT TO SAVE AMERICA

. . . and we mean that statement quite literally. The strength of our nation rests on many mighty pillars, but without our natural resources we would crumble and fall.

WASTE, GREED, MISMANAGEMENT, AND CARELESSNESS ARE ATTACKING

. . . every day of every year in every state of the union. A stream polluted by greed . . . a bird or animal species forever lost through mismanagement . . . a forest wiped out by a careless fire . . . a wildlife sanctuary or a National Monument swept away by wasteful disregard . . . daily evidences of the strength of these Four Horsemen.

WE STAND ALMOST DEFENSELESS

. . . with our front line troops dangerously thin and hopelessly outnumbered. Our best weapon is Public Opinion, but it is unbeatable only when it is aroused. Our creeping enemy uses Public Indifference with telling effect. You, as an American, care about this destruction, but you'll fight it only when you know the facts.

WE'RE SOUNDING THE BATTLE CRY

. . . we're asking you to pitch in . . . support our campaigns . . . education and information will turn the tide. Convince the American people of the facts . . . and they'll do what has to be done.

We're enclosing a sheet of our Conservation stamps. They help to remind folks what they've got to lose. You're asked to send a dollar . . . or as much as you can afford. Remember what they're doing and what they can do for America, and you'll agree they're worth many, many times more than you could possibly give.

(Used by permission of the National Wildlife Federation)

Letters Regarding Appointments

While most appointments are made by telephone, when someone cannot be reached by telephone a letter is written to suggest a particular date and time. While awaiting a reply, the writer can make appointments at other times on that day.

(1)

Chadwick Place
Biddeford, ME 04006
June 1, 19—

Miss Amanda Clark
40 Peabody Lane
Portsmouth, NH 03801

Dear Miss Clark:

Will it be possible for you to see Mrs. Marcia P. Leslie at your apartment Monday, June 12, at three o'clock to discuss an article she is writing on the restoration of stained glass.

Yours sincerely,
Anne Perkins
Secretary to Mrs. Leslie

Answer

40 Peabody Lane
Portsmouth, NH 03801
June 5, 19—

Miss Anne Perkins
% Mrs. Marcia P. Leslie
Chadwick Place
Biddeford, ME 04006

Dear Miss Perkins:

I am sorry to say that I shall not be able to see Mrs. Leslie on Monday, June 12, as I have made plans to attend the commencement exercises at Dartmouth College on that day. My only nephew is graduating, and I'm sure Mrs. Leslie will understand my wish to be present.

May I suggest Tuesday, June 20, at three o'clock instead? I am certain to be back at my apartment by then, and I shall look forward to seeing Mrs. Leslie and discussing methods of restoring stained glass.

Cordially,
Amanda Clark

(2)

Mr. Cooke has asked me to arrange an appointment with you during your visit in Chicago. Would it be possible for you to see him on Wednesday, December 5, at the University Club, to discuss the matter of foreign speakers for the coming winter?

Answer

I shall be in Chicago on December 5 and shall be happy to meet you at the University Club at four o'clock to discuss the matter of foreign speakers for the coming winter.

(3)

Mr. Galbraith wishes to know whether it would be possible for you to see him at your office Monday, February 15, at ten o'clock, to discuss with him important matters relating to the finances of the Western Shore Beach Club.

Answer

In answer to your letter of February 8, Mr. Hanson suggests that you call next Tuesday at twelve o'clock instead of Monday at ten.

Will you be good enough to confirm this appointment so that Mr. Hanson will definitely set aside this time to see you.

Letters of Refusal

When a letter must be written to decline a chairmanship or some other volunteer post, tact must be used. It is agreeable to be regarded as a responsible leader, even if the honor is not one a person wishes to accept. It is usual to express thanks for the thought and to offer a plausible reason for declining.

When a favor has been asked that must be refused, again the writer must be careful not to be brusque. What might be spoken cannot always be written with the same significance. A letter should spell out what a tone of voice might convey.

One noted adviser to business writers suggests a three-part letter when the message is no. The first paragraph is devoted to saying something agreeable, thanking or complimenting the reader. The next paragraph must say no unmistakably, in as gracious a manner as possible but briefly. The last paragraph is devoted to offering some alternative, and the letter closes on an appropriate personal note.

Examples of firm but friendly refusals follow, but of course each letter of this kind must be adapted to the situation.

(1)

Dear Ted,

Thank you for inviting me to participate in the Berwick Chamber of Commerce Round Table Discussion of New Means for Attracting Light Industry on March 15. I only wish it were possible for me to be with you, for the subject is one I find most challenging.

However, I am scheduled to participate in our spring sales meetings during that same week, and I'm afraid my evenings will be taken up with related events.

Had you thought of asking Fred Howe of the Hannefin Company in Westfield to join your panel? He has served on a similar, successful committee in his own town, and he might have some stimulating comments to make. He is always a popular speaker, and I hope you can persuade him to accept. Please remember me to him if you write to him.

Cordially,

(2)

Dear Miss Gueldensupp:

Thank you for inquiring about the position as my assistant. However, this position has already been filled.

With your permission I would like to keep your résumé on file, since I often hear of openings in other community agencies, and I shall be glad to suggest that you be considered.

We are grateful for your interest in the Greater Norwalk Community Council and wish you success in finding a suitable position.

Sincerely yours,
Edith M. Ward
Executive Director

Letters to Congressmen, Local Officials, Editors

When a citizen becomes aroused about a public issue, he may decide to write to his congressman or senator, to the governor of his state or to a legislator, to the mayor of his city, or to the editor of a newspaper or magazine. He should not write in anger, using insulting or sarcastic language. He should not threaten to work for the elected official's defeat. Instead, he should maintain a courteous, reasonable tone in his letter, attempting to offer constructive criticism. He should also keep the letter as short as is consistent with the points he wishes to make.

As in all writing, a rough outline of the letter should be made and the points to be stressed set down in logical order. The writer of an intelligent, useful letter will try to distinguish between opinion and fact. He must also attempt to avoid sounding stuffy and self-righteous as he offers his advice. Such expressions as "In my opinion," "It seems to me," "Many of us feel," and a generally reasonable tone will help to convince the reader that the message is worthy of attention. The opposite effect is produced by "Everyone knows that," "It is unquestionably true that," "Only an idiot would," and so on.

Letters to officials and editors are usually opened by staff members, and only those from well-known persons are actually read by the addressee. Still, an intelligent letter on a subject of compelling interest probably will be brought to his or her attention. Of the stacks of mail received by persons in public life, much is special pleading or asking favors on matters of limited interest. Letters asking for a congressman's help usually will receive replies, while others giving the writer's opinions may not. However, the writer's name may be placed on a list to receive periodical printed reports from the congressman.

Persons who write to a newspaper or to a magazine editor do not expect an answer. Local newspapers may print most of the letters written to the editor, for this is usually a popular column. But a large metropolitan newspaper or a national magazine will choose only a few of the many received, and sometimes only a portion of the letter is quoted, or the contents may be slightly edited to bring out the points more effectively. Obviously, space limitations would prevent using some letters. Sometimes two letters dealing with the same subject but expressing opposite points of view are printed on the same day. The editor will choose the letters that seem most interesting. If the writer does not wish his name to be printed, he should state that it should be withheld, but he must sign his name. A responsible editor would not print a letter without knowing the identity of the writer, but he would withhold the writer's name if so requested for a good reason. He would of course not print a letter that was primarily a personal attack on an official or was obviously the work of a crank.

(1)

Dear Senator Claghorn:

May I respectfully urge you to vote in favor of S.123, which provides for an increase in the salaries of workers in federally supported day-care centers. This increase can help to keep qualified persons in this important work, and it will also attract others who now find the pay too low for the responsibilities and the training required of these employees.

The large number of working mothers makes good day care essential in today's world. In addition, as you know, more than half of present-day marriages end in divorce, a situation that often leaves single mothers dependent on low-cost day care for their children. Consequently, I believe it is society's responsibility to see that adequate day care is available for all who need the service, at a reasonable cost.

Thus, a decent pay scale for day-care workers can help to provide the necessary safe, wholesome conditions for the many children whose families are seeking good day care.

Very truly yours,

(2)

To the Editor:

Under the newly revised Master Plan, as presently approved by the Planning and Zoning Commission, Norwalk traffic will become ever more congested, the schools will be more sorely pressed to accommodate the students, and the amount of affordable housing will remain as at present—in very short supply.

As a member of the Norwalk League of Women Voters, I am very disappointed to find that changes have been made recently in the density allowed in the Executive Office Zone. Previously, the highest density would have permitted a Floor Area Ratio (F.A.R) of 1.75 for a three-acre tract. The new version permits an F.A.R. of 2.0 on only two acres! And a maximum building height of eight stories is still permitted.

Even greater changes are in store for the planned residential development that will be allowed in the Commercial Zone. Here it is claimed the intent is to provide for the housing needs of small households. However, the developer will be permitted to determine how many units are appropriate within the allowable F.A.R., as long as the requirements for open space, setbacks (already reduced to a minimum), and parking are met. Not only that, but "such development shall be permitted by special permit in the Executive Office, Commercial, and Business Zones." Here we have provision for an unspecified number of condominium units, located on the corridors of Westport Avenue, Connecticut Avenue, or Main Avenue, which are already heavily traveled. There's no suggestion of requiring the developers to contribute to a fund to provide rental housing for persons of moderate income, e.g., the elderly, young working couples, and single persons who cannot afford current condominium prices. I believe this proposed development is not going to benefit the people that the Planning and Zoning commissioners say they are concerned about.

Housing units are great for developers but not so great for the tax rolls. Condominium residents need water, sewerage, police and fire protection, roads—and also schools. While some people believe that no children live in condominiums, that is by no means the case. Families living in one-bedroom condominiums do send children to school, and two-bedroom condominiums certainly can accommodate schoolchildren.

The schools already need additional space for the coming year. When the 475 units planned for the Fox Run area are built and occupied, we shall surely see that many more rooms are required at Fox Run School. Silvermine can expect more students from the 393 units now planned for that area. Cranbury is looking at 265 new units for its area. And so on. Every school can expect an increase.

What is needed is housing for the people now living in Norwalk, units that the residents of apartments can afford to buy, thereby releasing rental units for persons not interested in buying. We need to provide better services for people already living here.

On April 29 the Planning Committee of the Common Council will hold a hearing at 7:30 P.M. at West Rocks School. Residents should come and voice their opinions!

Sincerely yours,

Letters Regarding References

While most prospective employers check on references by telephone, there are occasions when it must be done by letter. The employer mentions the post the applicant is being considered for and asks for information about ability as well as personality.

(1)

Dear Mr. Barnes:

Miss Ida Hailparn has applied to us for a position as secretary and has given us your name as a reference. We understand that she was your secretary for two years before she moved to California, and we shall be grateful for your comments about her work and also about her ability to cooperate with others.
Thank you for your assistance.

Very truly yours,
Ralph Cheney, Personnel Manager

Answer

Dear Mr. Cheney:

Miss Hailparn was my secretary some years ago, and I remember her well. She was an excellent typist and answered the telephone very pleasantly. As I recall, she left because she preferred dictation to the use of the dictaphone.

Yours sincerely,
Roy E. Barnes

(2)

Dear Miss Deland:

Mr. John Battenberg has applied for the position of salesman in our firm. He informs us that he was with your organization during the summer vacations while he was in college. We shall be grateful if you will let us have your impression of Mr. Battenberg, as well as some information about the kinds of work he did for you.

Very truly yours,
Gregory Bedrosian, Sales Manager
Talisman Carpet Company

Answer

Dear Mr. Bedrosian:

Our records show that Mr. John Battenberg started in our mailroom and also helped out in the library during his first summer here. The following year he was a file clerk and also filled in at the retail store during staff vacations. Last year he drove a delivery truck for us.

We have great affection for Mr. Battenberg and have been pleased to watch his progress. He works well with others and is painstaking in completing each assignment. We are glad to recommend him as an ambitious and trustworthy young man who should be an excellent salesman.

Very truly yours,
Marcia E. Deland
Vice President

(3)

Dear Mr. Jenkins:

May I introduce Miss Marietta Robinson, who has been my secretary for the past three years. I hope you will find a place for her in your organization, for I believe it would be very much to your advantage.

Miss Robinson is an excellent secretary. She has the requisite skills and the attention to detail that one would expect. In addition, she is interested in learning the business of the office where she works. She is quick to learn and eager to take on responsibility. Her attitude is unfailingly pleasant, and she is able to deal effectively with potentially unpleasant situations that arise in offices. She is, in short, both capable and energetic, cooperative and firm when the occasion demands.

We are moving to new headquarters in Standish County, and Miss Robinson is unable to commute from her home in Bostwick. I shall miss her agreeable manner and her extraordinary skill.

I hope that your organization can benefit from her availability.

Yours sincerely,

Sometimes an open letter of reference is useful, addressed "To Whom It May Concern." In such a letter, however, the writer would be unlikely to say anything uncomplimentary, and a prospective employer might be inclined to look for what was left unsaid.

(1)

To Whom It May Concern:

It is a pleasure to recommend Miss Mary Burns as an outstanding secretary. My health has made it necessary for me to move to Arizona, and Miss Burns prefers to remain in New York.

I wish to state that her work has been excellent, her manner pleasant, her loyalty unquestioned. She enjoys responsibility and seems to thrive on heavy correspondence, a constantly ringing telephone, and a stream of visitors. During the three years that Miss Burns was with me, she was an invaluable assistant.

I am extremely sorry to lose her.

Anatol Puslowsky

(2)

To Whom It May Concern:

I am glad to recommend James L. Mann of Somers High School for a scholarship. I have come to know him well during the past two years. He has been the managing editor of the school literary magazine, of which I am faculty adviser, and he is now its editor. He is cooperative and persuasive in his work with the staff, while requiring careful prompt work from them all.

He is ambitious and intelligent, with a broad range of interests. Despite the long hours required by his work with the magazine, he stands second in a class of 309, and he seems well prepared for the discipline of college study.

Reminder Letters

Letters of reminder require that all pertinent details be included to ensure that the reminder is complete: date, place, and time when it is an event; sufficient information in other cases, so that appropriate action may be taken.

(1)

Dear Mr. Harrison:

When you wrote to tell me that the convention had been extended to June 5, I wonder if you recalled the weekend invitation from Mr. and Mrs. Greene that you have accepted. You were to leave the evening of the fourth for Northport. If you decide to stay until the end of the convention, I can let Mrs. Greene know as soon as I hear from you.

Yours sincerely,
Catherine Rossbach, Secretary

(2)

Dear Miss Englander:

As we agreed when I telephoned you, I am writing to remind you of your promise to address the Roverton Woman's Club on April 16 on the subject of the theater of the absurd. The time is 2 P.M., and the place is 2409 Central Avenue, Roverton.

We anticipate an interesting afternoon.

Sincerely,
Martha Weinstock

(3)

Thank you for accepting our invitation to speak at the Anniversary Dinner of the Warburton Club on June 3. Mr. Anthony, president of the club, will be here to welcome you at seven, in time to introduce you to some of the members before dinner.

We are looking forward to having you with us at that time.

(4)

Dear Fellow Members:

The Orwell Historical Society is grateful for your continued interest, but it lacks your dues to carry on the projects we have all enthusiastically endorsed. Won't you send a check today before the summer weather and the vacation season prove too distracting?

> Cordially yours,
> George Wimple, Secretary

(5)

Dear Classmates:

Just a note to remind you that our Twenty-fifth Reunion is fast approaching. Save the whole weekend of June 3–5 and plan to bring the family. Accommodations for couples and family groups are being arranged, and we now expect to have all of Redstone Dormitory for our class. Please make reservations now for as many as you hope to bring for our gala weekend. The deadline for reservations is April 15. Don't delay, or you'll need your own sleeping bags!

> Yours,
> Frank Dickey, Class Secretary

Letters Requesting Reservations

Although travel reservations are often made by telephone or through a travel agency, when time permits and a considerable distance is involved, letters may be written to specify the accommodations desired and the dates in question. For further details, *see* Chapter 19, Making Travel Arrangements.

TELEX

57220 Savoy
Firenze
Italy

Please reserve one double room with bath facing courtyard 17/7–23/7 for P. R. Johnson. Confirm soonest.

P. R. Johnson
Harpsam
New York, NY USA

[Letterhead]

Reservation Office
Savoy Hotel
Piazza della Repubblica 7
Firenze 50123
Italy

Dear Sir:

Please reserve a double room with bath, facing the courtyard, from Monday, July 17, through Sunday, July 23, for Mr. and Mrs. P. R. Johnson. They will be arriving by car from Ravenna. Please hold the room for possible late arrival.

Please confirm this reservation and inform me of the amount of deposit required.

Yours truly,

Sarah Smith
Secretary to Mr. Johnson

Letters Requesting Information

When an individual writes for information, he must bear in mind the time and effort that he is asking someone to donate to him. Will that someone benefit from providing the information? In general, requests for information are granted more readily when the giver can hope for new business or in some other way expect to earn goodwill.

The person asking for information should explain how he intends to use it. If he writes to the telephone company asking the rates for speaker phones, jacks, extension phones, and mobile service, he will undoubtedly receive the data. Readily available information is easy to send. But a high-school student who decides to write a paper on services provided by the telephone company would do well to ask for pamphlets and prepared material, since rates alone would not give much background.

A member of a garden club collecting material for a paper on growing roses might write first to the American Rose Society for the annual guide for buying roses. She would not ask for tips on home rose culture, since the society publishes a magazine and other information. She might consult back issues of the magazine for particular articles of value in preparing her study. She could also find the names of home gardeners who might be willing to share their experiences.

A businessman being transferred to a part of the country he knows little about might wish to write to the chambers of commerce in several towns in the area where he will be working to learn what the communities are like before he decides where to live.

(1)

[Letterhead]

June 23, 19—

Executive Secretary
Cape May Chamber of Commerce
Cape May, NJ 08204

Dear Sir:

Would you be good enough to provide me and my family with some information about your community. I have been appointed resident manager of the Marglove Company plant in Spindrift, and I expect to move my family to the area sometime this fall. My wife and I are attempting to learn something about Cape May in advance of our visit three weeks from now, when we hope to buy a house.

May we have a copy of your local newspaper. Although we understand that Cape May is a famous summer resort, we should also like to know something about life in your town after the summer people leave. If it is possible, can you give us a general idea of the relative income of the year-round residents —not their average income, but perhaps an indication of the type of work the majority do. Are most people engaged in some aspect of the tourist trade, or are there nearby small industries that provide employment? Are there many retired people in Cape May?

I hope these questions will not prove burdensome. Perhaps most of the information is already available in one of your brochures. In any case, we shall be most grateful for your assistance in becoming acquainted with your area. When I have been officially transferred to the Spindrift plant, I shall have a chance to drive over and introduce myself to you.

Thank you in advance for any information you can give us about Cape May.

Cordially yours,
Ross K. Lyons

Interoffice Memoranda

Communications within the office are informal in style but as carefully written as other letters or reports. With practice the writer becomes able to organize what he wishes to say. Simple language, clear explanations of the matter at hand, and brief recommendations for action will shorten the writing and reading time. It is safe to say that a situation is not really understood until a straightforward evaluation of what happened and what it means has been written out. Most people simply don't have the habit of thinking through a situation until they have a reason to write it. Doing so seems to focus attention on angles that are otherwise passed over, and in explaining to someone else, the writer finds he has learned something himself.

Promotion Department

9/16/—

To   Mr. T. J. Sullavan

From B. N. Lawrence

I hear from Bill Barnes, the manager of the Billings Hotel in Ransom, that he is not too pleased with the way the redecoration of the grill room was handled by one of our competitors. I know he is thinking of doing over the ballroom and possibly adding a new lounge. You might ask Frank Stoner to drop in to see Barnes the first of the week.

There's another possibility at the Blue Mountain Inn, in Barnet near Ransom. A lot of skiers go there during the season, and the floors are beginning to show the wear caused by ski boots. One of our plastic finishes might interest the Blue Mountain manager, James W. Herrick.

B.N.L.

Social Letters in Business

Many letters written from business offices are partly social or occasionally altogether social in nature. Inevitably, as business matters are transacted, people become better acquainted with one another. Social relationships develop, and ties of friendship and mutual respect grow over the months and years. Occasions arise when the correct and thoughtful thing to do is to send congratulations or condolences or to express good wishes on some personal event that has no direct bearing on the usual business of the day.

Sometimes these personal letters are difficult to write. The most effective letter will of course be written sincerely and simply, without recourse to lists of sample phrases or books of quotations. A kind thought will reveal itself, while no amount of high-flown language will carry a message of regret where none is felt.

The writer of a letter of condolence, for example, should refrain from comments of a religious nature unless he knows that his sentiments are shared by the bereaved person. A well-meant expression can be offensive to someone whose beliefs are different from the writer's.

Similarly, when congratulating an acquaintance on his promotion, the writer emphasizes his hope for success and happiness in the new situation, rather than offering a hint that the event is long overdue. A man may be congratulated on his marriage, but a woman should not be; instead, the writer offers best wishes for happiness.

Consideration for the feelings of others will usually guide the writer of personal letters. Thus, attempts to be humorous must be used sparingly when writing to an acquaintance who may take very seriously a situation that the writer finds amusing.

Dear Bob,

I expect to be in Chicago in a couple of weeks, and I wonder if it would be possible for you to arrange a meeting for me with the head of the Art Museum. I know that Dr. Stone is a busy person, and I rather doubt I could get an appointment without your assistance. I'd like to try for 9 A.M. on January 12.

I'm writing a story on new display techniques in the art museums, and I particularly want to include an interview with Dr. Stone. If he will permit a photograph to be taken of himself in one of the new galleries, it might make a striking lead for the story. Of course, if he's unavailable, I still wish to include the Art Museum. Perhaps Mrs. Kitchener would be willing to talk to me. I haven't met her either.

Many thanks for whatever you are able to accomplish on my behalf. In any case, I count on taking you and Marnie to dinner one night during my stay.

                                        Yours,
                                        Grant

Formal Acceptance

Mr. and Mrs. John W. Jones
accept with pleasure
the kind invitation of
Mr. and Mrs. William K. Petersen
to attend the wedding of
their daughter Anne
on Saturday, the sixth of June
at the Unitarian Church in Concord
at 11 a.m.

Formal Regrets

Mr. Diana Wilensky
regrets she is unable to accept
the kind invitation of
Mr. and Mrs. Nicholas Benyei
for dinner
on Friday, October first.

Letters to Be Handwritten

Most letters and notes may be typed, but certain kinds of letters must be handwritten if at all possible. These include letters of condolence to personal friends and their relatives (but not if sent by the secretary of an organization), invitations to small weddings, replies to formal invitations, and personal letters of congratulation on family events such as the birth of a baby, the engagement of a son or daughter, or the announcement of a private wedding ceremony.

Most letters of this kind should be written by the person who will sign them. The message will be brief but sincere, and what is said may well be less important than the fact that the person took the time to write it himself or herself.

The secretary may write formal acceptances or regrets if she has an attractive handwriting. The form of the invitation should be followed exactly. When accepting an invitation, you should repeat the date, time, and place. When declining, only the date need be mentioned.

Letters of Appreciation

(1)

Broad River Homes
108 New Canaan Avenue
Washington, CT 06777

April 19, 19—

Miss Helen Schwartz
2 East End Terrace
Brookfield, CT 06804

Dear Miss Schwartz:

Through Mrs. Irene Hochheimer I have learned of your recent contribution to our Program Fund. On behalf of the board of directors, I thank you for this generous gift.

As you may know, we are developing a portion of the grounds as an outdoor sitting area for the residents. Your gift will make possible the addition of gas grills, tables for serving, and a water supply. We already have tables, chairs, and umbrellas, as well as planters and boxes for gardening by the handicapped residents. We find that our attractive new space makes outdoor activities more appealing to our elderly residents. Being able to serve food and provide an occasional barbecue will enable us to offer outdoor recreation for many more individuals.

I would be happy to take you on a tour of our facility whenever it is convenient for you. Please call me at 222-4576. And thank you again for your generosity.

Sincerely yours,

Suzanne Hoelzl, Vice President
for the Board of Directors

(2)

We have learned with regret of your illness and resignation. As a sign of our affection, your friends here in the office have deposited to your name at the Bank of Minot the sum of $1,500.

Please accept this as a token of our appreciation of your years of long and faithful service to the firm.

Your many friends hope that you may soon be in the best of health and able to enjoy your well-earned vacation.

(3)

The Committee wishes to thank you for your generous loan of valuable prints and etchings to the Fine Arts Exhibit held at the University in June. We believe that such exhibits have a definite place in education and do much to promote interest in representative arts. Your own personal attitude, as shown by your contributions, should be a great incentive to other members of the alumni to make similar loans if it is in their power to do so.

Be assured that we appreciate your interest in making possible such an opportunity for our students to view your collection of prints and etchings.

(4)

The handsome volume of your collected lectures has just arrived, and I am proud of your inscription to me.

A cursory glance reveals your usual scholarship and graceful expression, and I look forward to reading the lectures. Like most teachers, I feel as proud as a father that one of my students has done well in a field in which he showed such early promise.

I appreciate your thoughtfulness in sending me a copy of your book, and I hope it will be a financial success as well as a critical one.

Letters of Congratulation

To Committees

(1)

May I congratulate you on the way your committee has completed a long and difficult job. The report is a masterpiece, brief but clear, accurate, and complete. It is a pleasure to find all the details in such easily digested form.

(2)

Your committee showed fine spirit and teamwork. Selling tickets these days is no easy matter, but evidently your committee charmed practically all our members into buying tables for the bridge. The evening was a huge success, and the amount of the proceeds a surprise to all.

Please accept the grateful thanks of the Club for your own hard work and extend our appreciation to your committee.

(3)

What a membership committee! Never before have we enrolled so many members or had such enthusiastic support. There is no doubt that this is because of you and your efficient committee, which has worked so hard to interest the citizens of Arden in uniting to improve our township.

The officers wish to express to you and to your committee appreciation of your untiring efforts and wonderful success.

On Appointment to Office

(1)

Sincere congratulations upon your reelection. It is a splendid tribute to your efficient public service.

(2)

Please accept my heartiest congratulations upon your well-merited appointment and my best wishes for your success in your new office.

(3)

Please accept my sincere congratulations and good wishes upon your election. I hope the future will bring you still higher honors and even greater success.

(4)

Your appointment as president is a source of great satisfaction to the alumni and friends of Arona College. At a meeting held last night to raise funds for scholarships and a new science building, I was asked to send you our joint congratulations.

We extend to you our best wishes for your happiness and success in your new work. You may count on the support of the alumni who have watched your career and who are delighted that the College is to have as president a woman of your scholarship and ideals.

On a Speech

Your talk at the annual dinner was a really outstanding one, and I think all of us were delighted to find you a dynamic speaker as well as a tireless worker for the United Fund. In future you are going to be in demand not only in your immediate area but elsewhere as a compelling voice of conscience and a persuasive leader of volunteers.

Have you a copy of your speech? I would be most grateful if you could send me one, for there are a number of neatly expressed ideas that need to be given wider circulation in our organization. You may be sure I will credit the source.

On a Birthday

The approach of your eightieth birthday reminds many of your fellow towns-people of our good fortune in having had you among us for the past forty years. It must be satisfying for you to see the many flourishing organizations and programs that you have helped to start and have continued to support. Both your donations of money and your commitment of time and attention have provided opportunities for healing and growth to hundreds of local residents.

May we join in wishing you many years of continued good health and vigorous activity in public service and private satisfaction.

Best wishes for a happy birthday from all of us at Bishop Memorial Senior Center.

On an Official Anniversary

Dear Father Wiggins:

On behalf of the Green Haven Lions Club, may I congratulate you on the twentieth anniversary of your pastorate at Saint Matthew's Church. We are fortunate indeed to have had a rector of your wisdom, kindliness, and vigor in our town over the years.

Your leadership in civic affairs has contributed in large measure to the progress we have made in adding to the town's recreational facilities as well as to the preservation of historical landmarks. We all owe you a debt of gratitude for your imaginative efforts and your skillfulness in bringing together the service organizations and the town authorities.

We all wish you many more years of success in Green Haven.

Sincerely yours,
George K. De Felice, Secretary
Green Haven Lions Club

On Promotion

Dear Bill,

News has just reached me of your appointment as regional manager of Tip Top. Hearty congratulations! I can't think of a better man for that demanding job. You have always thrived on solving problems, and I know you will meet with great success in your new post.

Cordially,
Jack Lane

On Marriage (business friend)

Dear Ed,

Our mutual friend George Grimm has sent me the newspaper announcement of your recent marriage. All of us here at Allied send our sincere congratulations and best wishes to you and Mrs. Wood.

Sincerely,
John Peters

On the Birth of a Child (personal friend)

Dear Anne and Carl,

We're so happy to hear that it's a girl! We'll be over to see you all and congratulate you in person when you've had a chance to get used to the new member of the family.

Best wishes to you all,
Mary Lou and Hank

On the Publication of a Book

Dear Max,

It was a great pleasure to read the glowing review of your new book in this morning's *Gazette*. It sounds like another of your thoroughly competent biographies, which really bring the man and the period to life. I am looking forward to reading it on my vacation, which starts this Friday.

Don't forget that this coming year marks our twenty-fifth reunion at Kenyon, and I hope we'll have a chance for a real visit then.

Sincerely,
Johnson Flanders

Letters of Condolence

On the Death of Business Associates

(1)

I heard with deep regret of the death of your president, James Knowlton, who has served your company faithfully for many years. The directors wish me to convey their sympathy to you in the loss of a great official and great citizen.

(2)

With regret we read in this morning's *Times* of the death of Mrs. Appleton. The officers of our firm extend to you our sympathy, knowing the sorrow you must feel at the loss of so loyal a friend and so efficient a president.

(3)

The officers and staff of the Benson Company extend their sincere sympathy to the family of Mr. Alfred Benson, Jr. His loss will be felt keenly by his many associates here in the office who have long esteemed him for his integrity of character and his clear judgment in the conduct of the affairs of the company.

(4)

May we express to you our deep sympathy on the death of your daughter, Mary Shipman, who, as a manager for ten years in the Executive Office of the City Bank, commanded the respect and esteem of those she served.

Her devotion to her work and her loyal and intelligent service won for her the regard and admiration of all her associates.

To you, whose loss is irreparable, we send our sincere sympathy.

On the Death of a Mother

We were greatly shocked to hear of the death of your mother, for we had not heard of her illness.

You know how we all loved her for her kindness to us when we visited her. Her welcome was always generous and sincere.

We send our affectionate sympathy and love.

On the Death of a Father

Please accept my sympathy on the death of your father, whose life was so bound up in the progress of the community. He will be greatly missed by all his friends and associates, who admired and loved him.

On the Death of a Husband

News of your husband's death has saddened every member of his department.

His unfailing kindness, his sense of humor, and his constant consideration for others made working with him a privilege.

We offer our sincere sympathy to you in your bereavement.

On the Death of a Sister

I was greatly shocked to learn of the death of your sister, as I had not even heard that she was ill. She will be sadly missed among her wide circle of friends. To you the loss is the greatest, but you will have the comfort of realizing that you did all you could to make her happy. Please accept my sincere sympathy.

Letters of Introduction

Although letters of introduction are rather rare, there are occasions when both business and social situations require them.

(1)

Mrs. Frank B. Long, whose name I am presenting for membership in the Community Club, is an unusual woman who will contribute much interest to our meetings. She is a member of the Boston Woman's University Club and of the Brookline Tennis Club. She is an officer of the Middlesex Society for the Blind and of the Child Welfare Association, and belongs to numerous other organizations of widely different interests.

Charming, humorous, gifted, she would prove, I am sure, a most valuable club member. I consider it a real privilege to propose her name and trust that it will soon be added to our list.

(2)

The bearer of this letter, Mr. Lee Graham, has for several years been organizing camps for underprivileged children. As he is considering locations for camps in Michigan, I have suggested that you are the person to help him, for you know every nook and corner of the state.

I admire Mr. Graham's work, and I shall be happy if you can assist him in any way.

(3)

Andrea A. Bevilacqua has an excellent academic record as well as several years' experience in various aspects of social work. Her dedication to her clients has been repeatedly demonstrated while she served on our staff during the past summer. Her reliability, even temper, and sense of humor have been real assets to our program, quite aside from her unusual competence.

I can recommend her without reservation, having seen her deal effectively with many challenging situations.

Letters of Invitation

[Letterhead]

November 10, 19—

Dear George:

   We are planning to have a dinner in honor of Mr. George E. Chase, Assistant Vice President of Citizens Trust Company, who is retiring on December 31, 19—. As you probably know, Mr. Chase has been with the Citizens Trust Company for about forty-two years and has serviced our corporate account with the bank ever since we placed it there.

   Cocktails and dinner will be served in the company dining room on December 8, 19—, beginning at 6:00 P.M., and I sincerely hope you can attend. If for any reason your plans have changed since you accepted my oral invitation, will you please let me know.

Sincerely yours,
John P. Roberts
Secretary

Mr. George E. Schuster
General Transom & Co., Inc.
644 West 58th Street
New York, NY 10019

Letters of Resignation

(1)

   For eight years I have acted as president of the Middletown Planning Association. Since the time has come when I must retire from active service, I ask that my resignation be accepted. It is with regret that I take this step, as I have enjoyed working with a group that has contributed so much to the happiness and welfare of the community.

   May I express my heartiest good wishes for the continued success of the Association and faith in its plans for further usefulness.

(2)

   It is with regret that I submit my resignation as treasurer of the Arizona Conservation Association. The duties required are more than I can successfully fulfill at present, and I therefore ask to be relieved of them.

   It has been a real pleasure to be associated with the organization and its valuable work, and I regret that my health will no longer permit me to share its responsibilities.

CHAPTER SIXTEEN

Forms of Address

The forms of address, salutation, and complimentary close of letters are affected by the relationship between the writer and the correspondent. As this is the case, no positive directions can be given for all occasions, but the following forms are generally accepted.

In letters to Government officials, the inside address, instead of appearing above the salutation, may be placed at the left margin at the close of the letter. The wording and the spacing on the envelope should agree with that of the inside address.

Honorable. This title is used in addressing the following: the President, ex-Presidents, President-elect, the Vice President, Cabinet officers, congressmen, American ambassadors, under secretaries and assistant secretaries of the executive department, judges (not of the Supreme Court), heads of the independent agencies or commissioners, governors, mayors, and all high ex-officials. (A person once entitled to *Honorable* may retain the title throughout his lifetime.)

In formal correspondence this title is written in full above the name. In less formal correspondence, if the length of the line permits, it is often written in full or abbreviated in the line with the name.

This title is used only when followed by initials or a first name; as, *Hon. Alexander Scott* or *Hon. A. N. Scott,* not *Hon. Scott.* The word should not be abbreviated when preceded by *The.*

The United States Government Correspondence Manual omits the word *The* before *Honorable* and before other titles, such as *Speaker of the House.* It also omits the word *My* before *dear* in salutations.

Note: *The* before *Honorable* is used in this book to conform to the usual style as given in *The Random House Dictionary* and in Webster.

For correct titles of American officials, see the *Congressional Directory*, the *United States Government Organization Manual*, the *Biographic Register of the Department of State*, and the Military Service registers.

Official Usage (U.S.)

The President of the United States

Address:

> The President
> The White House
> Washington, DC 20500

Salutation:

> Dear Mr. President:

Complimentary close:

> Respectfully submitted,
> *or*
> Yours respectfully,

The Wife of the President

Address:

> Mrs. (full name)
> The White House
> Washington, DC 20500

Salutation:

> Dear Mrs. (surname):

Complimentary close:

> Yours sincerely,

The Vice President of the United States

Address:

> The Vice President
> *or*
> The Vice President of the United States
> United States Senate
> Washington, DC 20510

Salutation:

> Dear Mr. Vice President:

Complimentary close:

> Yours respectfully,
> *or*
> Very truly yours,

Speaker of the House of Representatives

Address:

Honorable _____ _____
Speaker of the House of Representatives
or
Speaker of the House of Representatives
Washington, DC 20515

Salutation:

Sir:
or
Dear Mr. Speaker:

Complimentary close: Very truly yours,

*Cabinet Officers (Addressed as "Secretary")**

Address:

The Honorable _____ _____
Secretary of (name of department)
Washington, DC (ZIP Code)

Salutation:

Sir:
or
Dear Sir:
or
Dear Mr. Secretary:

Complimentary close: Very truly yours,
or
Sincerely yours,

*Titles for Cabinet officers are: Secretary of State, Secretary of the Treasury, Secretary of Defense, Attorney General, Secretary of the Interior, Secretary of Agriculture, Secretary of Commerce, Secretary of Education, Secretary of Energy, Secretary of Labor, Secretary of Health and Human Services, Secretary of Housing and Urban Development, and Secretary of Transportation.

Secretary to the President

Address:

The Honorable _____ _____
Secretary to the President
The White House
Washington, DC 20500

Salutation: Dear Ms. _____:

Complimentary close: Very truly yours,

Secretary to the President with Military Rank

Address:

(full rank) _____ _____
Secretary to the President
The White House
Washington, DC 20500

Salutation:

Sir:
   or
Dear (rank) _____:

Complimentary close:

Very truly yours,
   or
Sincerely yours,

Senator or Senator-Elect

Address:

The Honorable _____ _____
The United States Senate
Washington, DC 20510
   (*or* local address)

Salutation:

Dear Sir: *or* Dear Madam:
   or
Dear Senator:
Dear Senator _____: (informal)
   or
Dear Mr. (Mrs., Miss, Ms.) _____:

Complimentary close:

Very truly yours,
   or
Sincerely yours,

Representative

Address:

The Honorable _____ _____
The House of Representatives
Washington, DC 20515
   (*or* local address)

Salutation:

Dear Sir: *or* Dear Madam:
Dear Mr. (Mrs., Miss, Ms.) _____: (informal)

Complimentary close:

Very truly yours,
   or
Sincerely yours,

Commissioner

Address:
The Honorable _____ _____
Chairman, Civil Service Commission
Washington DC 20415

Salutation:
Sir:
or
Dear Mr. Chairman:
or
Dear Mr. _____: (informal)

Complimentary close:
Very truly yours,

Chief Justice of the United States

Address:
The Chief Justice of the United States
The Supreme Court of the United States
Washington, DC 20543

Salutation:
Sir:
or
Dear Mr. Chief Justice:

Complimentary close:
Very truly yours,

Associate Justice of the Supreme Court

Address:
Mr. Justice _____
The Supreme Court of the United States
Washington, DC 20543

Salutation:
Dear Mr. Justice:

Complimentary close:
Very truly yours,

District Judge

Address:
The Honorable _____ _____
United States District Judge
Southern District of New York
New York, NY 12224

Salutation:
Dear Sir:
or
Dear Judge _____: (informal)

Complimentary close:
Very truly yours,

Judge of State Court

Address: The Honorable _____ _____
          Chief Judge of the Court of Appeals
          Albany, NY 12207

Salutation: Dear Madam:
                  or
             Dear Judge _____: (informal)
Complimentary close: Very truly yours,

Governor

Address: The Honorable _____ _____
          The Governor of New York
          Albany, NY 12224

Salutation: Sir:
                  or
             Dear Sir:
                  or
             Dear Governor _____: (informal)
Complimentary close: Very truly yours,

Lieutenant Governor

Address: The Honorable_____ _____
          Lieutenant Governor of New York
          Albany, NY 12224

Salutation: Dear Madam:
                  or
             Dear Ms. _____:
Complimentary close: Very truly yours,

State Senator

Address: The Honorable _____ _____
          The State Senate
          Albany, NY 12224
                  or
          Senator _____ _____
          The State Capitol
          Albany, NY 12224

Salutation:	Sir:
	or
	Dear Sir:
	or
	Dear Senator _____: (informal)
Complimentary close:	Very truly yours,

Member of Assembly

Address:	The Honorable _____ _____
	The State Capitol
	Albany, NY 12224
Salutation:	Dear Sir:
	or
	Dear Mr. _____: (informal)
Complimentary close:	Very truly yours,

Mayor

Address:	The Honorable _____ _____
	Mayor of _____
	or
	The Mayor of _____
	(City, State, ZIP Code)
Salutation:	Sir: *or* Madam:
	or
	Dear Mr. Mayor: *or* Madam Mayor:
	or
	Dear Mayor _____: (informal)
Complimentary close:	Yours very truly,

Military Usage (U.S.)

In official and formal correspondence in the Regular Army and in the Air Force, officers with the grade of captain and above are addressed by their titles.

In conversation and in nonofficial correspondence brigadier generals, major generals, lieutenant generals, and generals are addressed as *General*; lieutenant colonels under the same conditions are referred to and addressed as *Colonel*; fleet admirals of the Navy, full admirals,

vice admirals, and rear admirals of the Navy and Coast Guard, as
Admiral.

General

Address:	General _____ _____, USA
	(Street)
	(City, State, ZIP Code)
Salutation:	Sir: (formal)
	Dear General _____: (informal)
Complimentary close:	Very truly yours, (formal)
	Sincerely yours, (informal)

Major General

Address:	Major General _____ _____, USA
	Fort Myer, VA (Zip Code)
Salutation:	Sir: (formal)
	Dear General _____: (informal)
Complimentary close:	Very truly yours, (formal)
	Sincerely yours, (informal)

Brigadier General

Address:	Brigadier General _____ _____, USA
	Fort Sam Houston, TX (Zip Code)
Salutation:	Sir: (formal)
	Dear General _____: (informal)
Complimentary close:	Very truly yours, (formal)
	Sincerely yours, (informal)

Admiral

Address:	Admiral _____ _____, USN
	Chief of Naval Operations
	Department of the Navy
	Washington, DC (Zip Code)
Salutation:	Sir: (formal)
	Dear Admiral _____: (informal)
Complimentary close:	Very truly yours, (formal)
	Sincerely yours, (informal)

Vice Admiral

Address: Vice Admiral _____ _____, USN
                        U.S.S. (name of ship)
                        San Diego, CA (Zip Code)

Salutation: Sir: (formal)
                        Dear Admiral _____: (informal)
Complimentary close: Very truly yours, (formal)
                        Sincerely yours, (informal)

In written communications, officers of the medical department of the Army and of the Navy are addressed by their military titles regardless of rank.

Captain John Doe, Medical Corps
United States Army

Chaplains are addressed as *Chaplain* regardless of their grade.

Cadets of the United States Military Academy are addressed as *Mister* socially and in conversation, and as *Cadet* officially and in written communication.

Noncommissioned officers are addressed by their titles.

National Guard and Reserve officers on active military duty follow the customs of the Regular Army in the matter of titles and addresses.

MILITARY DISCIPLINE, COURTESIES AND CUSTOMS OF THE SERVICE

In official and formal communications, an officer on the active list of the Navy is addressed as follows:

Lieutenant John Doe
United States Navy

In official and formal communications, officers on the retired list are addressed as follows:

Lieutenant John Doe
United States Navy, Retired

In official and formal communications to officers of the staff, the name of the corps to which any staff officer belongs is written immediately after the name:

Lieutenant John Doe, Medical Corps
United States Navy

In official and formal communications to warrant officers, prefix the title to the name:

Boatswain Jane Doe
United States Navy

Chief Boatswain Jane Doe
United States Navy

In oral address and informal correspondence, officers of the rank of *commander* and above are always called by their rank; "male officers below the grade of commander in the Navy and captain in the Marine Corps may be addressed as 'Mister' and female officers of similar grade as 'Miss' or 'Mrs.,' except that officers of the Medical Corps and of the Dental Corps may be addressed as 'Doctor,' and officers of the Chaplain Corps as 'Chaplain.' "

U.S. NAVY REGULATIONS

"In the Army, the accepted custom is to use the military title, regardless of rank. There is one exception, which has had a steady gain in popularity in recent years, namely, that of referring to physicians whose work brings them in direct contact with patients as 'Doctor' in oral communications. In administrative and field medical jobs, at official functions, and in all written communications, the military title continues as the accepted custom."

U.S. DEPARTMENT OF THE ARMY, OFFICE OF THE SURGEON GENERAL

Official communications to the officers of the United States Coast Guard follow in general the rules of the United States Navy.

Addressing Invitations to Government and Military Officials and Their Spouses

Executives

The President and Mrs. _____
    The White House
The Vice President and Mrs. _____

The Secretary of (name of department) and Mrs. *or* Mr. _____
The Chief Justice and Mrs. _____

Congressmen

On envelope: The Honorable John Smith and
                                Mrs. Smith
                                (home address)

On inside envelope,
as in wedding invitations: Senator (Representative) and
                                Mrs. *or* Mr. Doe

Governors and Mayors

The Honorable John Doe and Mrs. Doe
                    or
The Honorable and Mrs. John Doe
                    or
The Governor (Mayor) of _____ and Mrs. *or* Mr. Doe

Military Officers

General and Mrs. John Doe
            or
General John Doe and Mrs. Doe
Admiral and Mrs. John Doe
            or
Admiral John Doe and Mrs. Doe
Lieutenant and Mrs. John Doe
            or
Lieutenant John Doe and Mrs. Doe

Women Officials

Women officials holding the same positions as men are addressed by
the same titles. In the address the given name without *Mrs.*, *Ms.*, or
Miss should be used: as, *The Honorable Helen Brown*. In the formal
salutation *Madam* for both married and unmarried women is substi-

tuted for *Sir*. In an informal salutation *Mrs.*, *Ms.*, or *Miss* would be used; as *Dear Mrs.* (*Ms.* or *Miss*) *Brown*. Socially a woman official is addressed by her personal title; as *Mrs. John Brown* or *Miss* or *Ms. Helen Brown*.

When a married woman has a title and her husband does not, her name is stated first in business correspondence addressed to both. In social correspondence, the woman's title may be dropped unless she has retained her own name for personal as well as business correspondence.

Business

The Honorable Marilyn G. Hunt and Mr. Hunt
Dear Mrs. (or Governor, Mayor, etc.) Hunt and Mr. Hunt:

Social

Dear Mr. and Mrs. Hunt:

When the maiden name is retained:

The Honorable Marian B. Grant and Mr. George A. Blair
or
Ms. Marian B. Grant
Mr. George A. Blair
Dear Ms. Grant and Mr. Blair:

Diplomatic Usage in Washington

In the address on the envelope and in the inside address, the name and title, if known, should be used. If this is done, the definite article *the* should be dropped in the line that follows, making it read "Ambassador of the French Republic," and so forth.

"The Ambassador of Great Britain" and "The Ambassador of the French Republic" are the exact and official designations, but "The British Ambassador" and "The French Ambassador" are frequently used by the general public and by writers in and outside of Government service.

Address:	His Excellency (Name and title, if known) Ambassador of _____ *or* His Excellency The Ambassador of _____ Washington, DC (ZIP Code)
Salutation:	Excellency: (formal) *or* Sir: (formal) *or* Dear Mr. Ambassador: (informal) *or* Dear Sir: (informal) *or* Dear _____ _____: (title and name, informal)
Complimentary close:	Accept, Excellency, the (renewed) assurances of my highest consideration (formal diplomatic usage) *or* Very truly yours, (formal general usage) *or* I am, my dear Mr. Ambassador, Sincerely yours, (informal)

Ministers from Foreign Countries

Address:	The Honorable _____ _____ Minister of _____ *or* Envoy Extraordinary and Minister Plenipotentiary from _____ Washington, DC (ZIP Code) *or* Mr. _____ _____, (followed by the official title)
Salutation:	Sir: *or* Dear Mr. Minister:
Complimentary close:	(same as for an ambassador)

American Ambassador (man)

Address:	The Honorable _____ _____ American Ambassador (City, Country)
Salutation:	Sir: (formal) *or* Dear Mr. Ambassador: (informal) Dear Sir: (informal) Dear _____ _____: (title and name) (informal)
Complimentary close:	Very truly yours, Sincerely yours,
Address with naval rank:	Admiral _____ _____ American Ambassador (City, Country)
Salutation:	Sir: Dear Mr. Ambassador: *or* Dear Admiral _____: (informal)

American Ambassador (woman)

Address:	The Honorable Jane Doe American Ambassador (City, Country)
Salutation:	Madam: (formal) Dear Madam Ambassador: *or* Dear Mrs. (Miss *or* Ms.) _____:

In Central or South America, the ambassador is styled "The Ambassador of the United States of America."

American Chargé d'Affaires

Address:	_____ _____, Esq. American Chargé d'Affaires (City, Country)
Salutation:	Dear Sir:
Complimentary close:	Very truly yours,

Foreign Chargé d'Affaires

Address:	Baron _____ _____
	Chargé d'Affaires of (Country)
	(City, Country)
Salutation:	Dear Sir:
	or
	Sir:
Complimentary close:	Accept, Sir, the renewed assurance of my high consideration,
	or
	Respectfully yours,
	or
	Very truly yours,

Consul

Address:	American Consul at _____
	or
	_____ _____, Esq.
	American Consul
Salutation:	Dear Sir:
Complimentary close:	Very truly yours,

Excellency

The use of the title *Excellency* in addressing American officials is not in accordance with American custom. However, a few states, such as Massachusetts and New Hampshire, have officially adopted this title in addressing their governors.

According to the U.S. Department of State, "*His Excellency* is the complimentary diplomatic title in addressing foreign presidents, foreign ambassadors, foreign cabinet officers, foreign high officials, and former high officials. *His Excellency* is used in the address; *Excellency* is used in the salutation and (generally) in the complimentary close; and *Your Excellency* is used in the body of the communication."

In ecclesiastical correspondence *Excellency* is used in addressing all Roman Catholic archbishops and bishops (*see* pp. 310–311).

Titles for Members of the Diplomatic Corps

As titles of the Diplomatic Corps may change, it is important to check with the *Diplomatic List* published monthly by the Department of State.

The names and titles of foreign consular officers in the United States may be found in *Foreign Consular Offices in the United States*, published quarterly by the Department of State, and also in the *Congressional Directory*.

The United Nations

The United Nations is an organization of sovereign states. It functions through six principal branches, called *organs* in the language of the Charter, as follows:

The General Assembly
The Security Council
The Economic and Social Council
The Trusteeship Council
The International Court of Justice
The Secretariat

There is considerable variation in the titles of the different representatives. That the title accorded a representative is determined by the position that he holds in his Government's service is generally correct; but his title is to some extent also dependent upon the nature of his position vis-à-vis the United Nations.

EXECUTIVE OFFICE OF THE SECRETARY GENERAL

Communications to the United Nations are addressed to the United States Representative to the United Nations, through the Department of State. Exceptions, which are sent directly to the United States Representative, include those intended for the Economic and Social Council, the Disarmament Commission, the Trusteeship Council, and the delegation to the General Assembly (when it is in session). Direct communication with the United Nations is inappropriate unless exceptions arise. Where it is necessary, the communications should be sent to the Secretary General of the United Nations through the United States Representative by means of a covering letter.

Secretary General of the United Nations

Address:
> His Excellency*
> John Doe
> Secretary General of the United Nations
> United Nations, NY 10017

Salutation:
> Excellency:* (formal)
> Dear Mr. Secretary General:
>   (informal preferred)
>   *or*
> Dear Mr. Doe: (informal)

Complimentary close:
> Accept, Excellency,* the (renewed) assurances of my highest consideration, (formal diplomatic usage)
> Sincerely yours, (informal)

The Assistant Secretary General of the United Nations

Address:
> The Honorable _____ _____
> Assistant Secretary General of the United Nations
> United Nations, NY 10017

Salutation:
> Sir: (formal)
> Dear Mr. _____: (informal)

Complimentary close:
> Very truly yours, (informal)
> Sincerely yours, (informal)

A Foreign Representative to the United Nations with the Personal Rank of Ambassador

Address:
> His Excellency*
> John Doe
> Representative of (country) to the United Nations
> (City, State, ZIP Code, or Country)

Salutation:
> Excellency:* (formal)
> Dear Mr. Ambassador: (informal)

Complimentary close:
> Accept, Excellency,* the (renewed) assurances of my highest consideration, (formal diplomatic usage)
> Yours sincerely, (informal)

*For use of *Excellency*, see p. 305.

The United States Representative to the United Nations

Address:	The Honorable John Doe United States Representative (*or* Acting United States Representative) to the United Nations United Nations, NY 10017
Salutation:	Sir: (formal) Dear Mr. Doe: (informal)
Complimentary close:	Very truly yours, (formal) Sincerely yours, (informal)

Senior Representative of the United States to the General Assembly of the United Nations

Address:	The Honorable John Doe Senior Representative of the United States to the General Assembly of the United Nations United Nations, NY 10017

United States Representative on the Economic and Social Council

Address:	The Honorable John Doe United States Representative on the Economic and Social Council of the United Nations United Nations, NY 10017

United States Representative on the Trusteeship Council

Address:	The Honorable John Doe United States Representative on the Trustee- ship Council of the United Nations United Nations, NY 10017
Salutation, Complimentary close:	The Secretariat of the United Nations employs British usage, not the American, with respect to titles, spelling, and phraseology in formal communications written in the English lan- guage. In formal letters, therefore, the saluta- tion is "Sir:"; the complimentary close is

I have the honour to be, Sir,
Your obedient Servant,

The private individual might use any of the following expressions, depending on the tone of the letter:

Salutation: Sir: (formal)

Dear _____ _____: (title and name)

Complimentary close: Very truly yours, (formal)

Sincerely yours, (informal)

Canadian Officials

Governor General

Address:

If the governor general of a Dominion or Colony is a member of the royal family or of the nobility, he is addressed according to his rank, i.e., duke, earl, viscount, and so forth, preceded by the title *His Excellency*; if without rank of nobility, his name is preceded by *His Excellency The Right Honourable*. If the governor general has a military title, it must precede other titles.

His Excellency
Field Marshal The Right Honourable
The Earl of _____, G.C.M.G.
Governor General of Canada
Ottawa, Canada (Post Office Code)

Salutation:

Excellency:
> *or*

Sir:
> *or*

Dear Governor General:
> *or*

Dear Mr. _____: (*or* title)

Complimentary close:

Believe me, my dear Governor General,
Sincerely yours,

Prime Minister

Address:

Right Honorable
Full name with initials of decorations or orders, if any
Prime Minister of the Dominion of Canada
Ottawa, Canada (Post Office Code)

Salutation:	Sir:
	or
	Dear Sir:
	or
	Dear Mr. Prime Minister:
	or
	Dear Mr. _____:
Complimentary close:	Sincerely yours,

Usage for Officials of the Roman Catholic Church

The Pope

Address:	His Holiness Pope _____ _____
	or
	His Holiness the Pope
	The Vatican
Salutation:	Your Holiness:
	or
	Most Holy Father:
Complimentary close:	Your dutiful son (*or* daughter),
	or
	Respectfully yours,

Cardinal

Address:	His Eminence
	John Cardinal Doe
	Archbishop of _____
	(Local address)
Salutation:	Your Eminence: (ecclesiastical usage)
	Dear Cardinal Doe: (informal)
Complimentary close:	Respectfully yours,

Archbishop

Address:	The Most Reverend Archbishop of _____
	or
	The Most Reverend John Doe, S.T.D.
	Archbishop of _____
	(Local address)

Salutation: Your Excellency:
                                    or
                               Dear Archbishop _____: (informal)
Complimentary close: Respectfully yours,

Bishop

Address: The Most Reverend
                               John Doe, S.T.D.
                               Bishop of Baltimore
                               (Local address)

Salutation: Your Excellency:
                               Dear Bishop _____: (informal)
Complimentary close: Respectfully yours,

Member of the Papal Household
Monsignor (Domestic Prelate)

Address: The Very Reverend Monsignor _____
                               The Vatican

Salutation: Dear Monsignor Doe: (informal)
Complimentary close: Respectfully yours,

Priest

Address: The Reverend Father Brown
                                    or
                               Rev. J. B. Brown
                               (Local address)

Salutation: Dear Father Brown:
                                    or
                               Dear Reverend Father:
                                    or
                               Dear Father:
Complimentary close: Respectfully yours,
                                    or
                               Sincerely yours,

Usage for Protestant and Jewish Clergy in America

Protestant Episcopal Bishop

Address:	The Right Reverend _____ _____ Bishop of New York *or* The Right Reverend John Doe, D.D., LL.D. Bishop of Washington (Local address)
Salutation:	Right Reverend Sir: (formal) *or* Dear Bishop _____: (informal)
Complimentary close:	Sincerely yours,

Dean

Address:	Dean _____ _____ *or* The Very Reverend John Doe (Local address)
Salutation:	Very Reverend Sir: (formal) Dear Dean _____: (informal)
Complimentary close:	Yours respectfully, *or* Sincerely yours,

Methodist Bishop

Address:	The Reverend John Doe, D.D. Methodist Bishop (Local address)
Salutation:	Reverend Sir: (formal) Dear Bishop: (informal) *or* Dear Bishop _____:
Complimentary close:	Sincerely yours, *or* Respectfully yours,

Other Clergy

Address:
The Reverend _____ _____
or
Reverend Dr. _____ _____ (if entitled to a degree)
or
Reverend _____ _____, D.D.
(Local address)

Salutation:
Dear Sir:
or
Dear Mr. _____: (informal)
or
Dear Dr. _____: (if entitled to a degree)

Complimentary close:
Yours respectfully,
or
Yours sincerely,

Rabbi

Address:
Rabbi _____ _____
(Local address)

Salutation:
Dear Sir:
or
Dear Dr. _____:
Dear Rabbi _____: (informal)

Complimentary close:
Yours respectfully,

Usage for Members of Religious Institutions

Superior of a Sisterhood

Address:
Reverend Mother (followed by initials designating order, if desired)
or
The Reverend Mother Superior (without initials of order)
(Local address)

Salutation:
Reverend Mother:
or
Dear Reverend Mother: (informal)

Complimentary close: Yours respectfully,
or
Sincerely yours,

Member of a Sisterhood

Address: Sister Mary Angela (followed by initials of order,
if desired)
or
Sister Mary Angela, Order of St. Dominic
(Local address)

Salutation: Dear Sister:
or
Dear Sister Mary Angela:

Complimentary close: Yours sincerely,

Superior of a Brotherhood (Roman Catholic)

Address: Brother James, F.S.C., Superior
St. John's College
(Local address)

Salutation: Dear Brother James:
Complimentary close: Sincerely yours,

Superior of a Brotherhood (Protestant)

Address: John Doe, S.B.B., Superior
St. Joseph's College
(Local address)

Salutation: Dear Brother Doe:
Complimentary close: Sincerely yours,

The address for the superior of a brotherhood depends on his church affiliation and on whether or not he is a priest or has a title other than *Superior*. A Roman Catholic brother is usually addressed by his Christian name; a Protestant brother is usually addressed by his surname.

Usage for Officials in Universities and Colleges

President of a Theological Seminary

Address: The Reverend President _____ _____
                      (Local address)

Salutation: Dear President _____:
                              or
                      Dear Dr. _____:
Complimentary close: Yours sincerely,

Professor in a Theological Seminary

Address: The Reverend Professor _____ _____
                      (Local address)
                              or
                      Rev. _____ _____
                              or
                      Professor _____ _____
Salutation: Dear Professor _____:
                              or
                      Dear Dr. _____:
Complimentary close: Yours sincerely,

President of a University

Address: (Full name followed by initials for degree or
                          degrees),
                      President of Columbia University,
                              or
                      President _____ _____
                      Columbia University, New York
Salutation: Dear Sir:
                      Dear President _____:
Complimentary close: Sincerely yours,

College or University Professor with Doctoral Degree

Address: Professor _____ _____
                              or
                      Dr. _____ _____
Complimentary close: Sincerely yours,

Dean of a College

Address: Dean _____ _____
                                     or
                            Dr. _____ _____
                            Dear Dean _____:
                            Dear Dr. _____:
                            Dear Miss *or* Mr. _____, (informal)
Complimentary close: Sincerely yours,

CHAPTER SEVENTEEN

Filing

Types of Filing Systems

You may not be expected to set up the office filing system, but you will need to know about the various filing systems. Sometimes you may need to set up new types of files. For example, while an alphabetical system works very well in some circumstances, it may be useful to have a subject file for certain aspects of the organization's business. Or the geographic area may have more importance.

Subject Filing. If subject filing is to be used, select the most important subject title; a general term should be used rather than a particular one. All records for personnel matters would be filed under "Personnel," with subheads for "Recruitment," "Sick Leave," and "Vacation." All labels should be neatly typed in the same color for the same subject. A list of files should be maintained and kept up-to-date. The location of the list of files would be known to those who are authorized to use the files.

Cross-referencing is necessary, so that it is possible to locate needed information quickly. A cross-reference sheet is filed under another heading, so that if correspondence or other data are called for under a different title, they can be found. Perhaps only the name of a company is mentioned. If the needed document has been filed under the subject of the purchase, it would be helpful to have a cross-reference under the name of the company; for example, Brockton Milling Company, *see* Supplies, Hardware.

A cross-referencing index is useful for subject filing as well as other systems. Time can be saved by using the index. While it means looking up all possible headings, it is still easier than looking through the files themselves.

Carpet
   See Interior Furnishings

Dining tables
   See Interior Furnishings

Oil burners
   See Heating

Typewriters
   See Office Equipment

Geographic Filing. In some companies the geographical location is more important than the name of an individual or the subject of the correspondence. For this purpose the name of a city or region would be the main heading, with separate folders for individuals or companies. The same color labels could be used for files placed within each city or region.

CENTRAL REGION

Kentucky
   Murray, A. J.

Illinois
   Johnson, P. R.

Indiana
   Brown, M. C.

Michigan
   Johnson, H. B.

Ohio
   Brown Brothers, Inc.

Here again, a cross-reference file would save the time spent trying to recall which Johnson is located in which state.

Many filing systems combine subjects or letters with numbers. For a fuller discussion of filing systems, *see* pp. 401–402, Filing and Indexing.

Electronic Filing. Using software designed for database management, it is possible to create, store, update, modify, access, and copy information to be used by one or more persons. Using a computer, you follow instructions that appear on the screen and enter information in a prescribed fashion. Each category of information is called a field, and within each field you can insert a given number of characters—whether letters or numbers. Each set of information about one individual, company, product, or other item, is called a record. A collection of all the records of a similar kind is called a file; a file might include personnel records, sales records, an address file, and so forth.

To open a file, you set up a form for the data. Following is a form that is used by a real estate office:

OWNER:	SALE PRICE:	
ADDRESS:		
OWNER PHONE:	RENTAL TERM:	
ACCESS:	BR.:	BATH:
NEGO.:	PHONE:	
TYPE:	EXT.:	ZONE:
BLT.:	ACREAGE:	
BSMT.:		
LR.:	FPL.:	
DR.:	KTCHN.:	
BR/BTH.:		
MBR.:		
BR.:		
BATH:		
ATTIC:	STORMS:	WALLS:
PORCH:	SCRNS.:	WATER:
GARAGE:	COMB.:	SEWER:
OTHER BLDGS.:	STOVE:	WALLO.:
POOL:	DISHW.:	
HEAT SYSTEM:	REFR.:	
WATER SYSTEM:	WASHR.:	DRYER:
OCCUPANCY:	SCHOOL:	ML RATE:
REMARKS:	TAXES:	
NOT INCL.:		
L.O.:	SALESMAN:	
M.L.S.:	SUBAGENT:	DATE:

Using this database, a salesman could retrieve and print out a list of all Colonial or Cape Cod–style houses for rent in a particular section. Or a list could be provided of all houses available in a certain school district. Or all houses with swimming pools and three bedrooms. The convenience of being able to locate certain specifications quickly is obvious.

Having all such information available for all salespeople could save each one from having to maintain a notebook and constantly update it. One secretary in the office could keep the list up-to-date, ready for printing out at any time. The secretary could produce a list of all open houses held in a certain time frame or all houses sold during a particular month.

Electronic filing can save much time and drudgery. The chore of filing can be greatly reduced, given suitable software and the inclination to make it work.

Rules for Alphabetical Filing

General Principles

1. Entries of names of individuals, on cards, lists, and so forth, should always be placed in the following order:

   (1) Surname
   (2) Comma
   (3) Given name (or first initial)
   (4) Middle name or initial
   (5) Title (in parentheses): *Stewart, George D. (President)*

2. Many names are pronounced exactly alike but spelled differently.

   (1) File exactly as spelled
   (2) When spelling differs only at the end of the word, no cross-reference is necessary, since one spelling would follow immediately after the other:

Smith	Conner
Smithe	Connor

   When spelling differs in the beginning of a word, make blanket cross-reference from one form of the name (surname only) to the other:

   Monroe . . . . . *See also* Munroe
   Munroe . . . . . *See also* Monroe
   Conolly . . . . . *See also* Connolly
   Connolly . . . . *See also* Conolly

Illustration of Alphabetical Divisions Found on Filing Guides

25 Divisions	40 Divisions	60 Divisions
A	A	AA-AM
BA-BL	BA	AN-AZ
BO-BY	BE-BI	BA
CA-CL	BL-BO	BE
CO-CZ	BR-BY	BI-BL
D	CA-CE	BO
E	CH-CL	BR
F	CO-CZ	BU-BY
G	DA-DE	CA-CE
HA-HE	DI-DY	CH-CL
HI-HY	E	COA-COP
I-J	FA-FL	COR-COZ-CR-CZ
K	FO-FY	DA-DE
L	GA-GL	DI-DO
MA-MC	GO-GY	DR-DY-EA-EK
ME-MY	HA	EL-EZ-FA
N-O	HE-HI	FE-FL
P-Q	HO-HY	FO-FY
R	I-J	GA-GE
SA-SE	KA-KI	GI-GO
SH-SO	KL-KY	GR-GY
SP-SY	L	HAA-HAP
T-U-V	MA	HAR-HAZ-HEA-
WA-WH	MC	HEK
WI-WY-X-Y-Z	ME-MI	HEL-HEZ-HI
	MO-MY	HO
	N-O	HU-HY-I
	PA-PH	J
	PI-PY-Q	KA-KE
	RA-RI	KI-KY
	RO-RY	LA
	SA-SC	LE-LI
	SE-SK	LO-LY
	SL-SQ	MAA-MAN
	ST-SY	MAR-MAY
	T	MC
	U-V	ME
	WA-WE	MI-MOA-MOO

25 Divisions	40 Divisions	60 Divisions
	WH-WI	MOR-MOZ-MU-
	WO-WY-X-Y-Z	MY
		N
		O
		PA-PEA-PEM
		PEN-PEZ-PF-PH-
		PI
		PL-PY-Q
		RA-RE
		RH-RI-ROA-ROG
		ROH-ROZ-RU-
		RY
		SA
		SC
		SE-SH
		SI-SM
		SN-SQ-STA
		STE-STY
		SU-SY-TA-TE
		TH-TY
		U-V
		WA
		WE
		WH
		WI
		WO-WY-X-Y-Z

3. For convenience and speed both in filing and in research, *Mc* may be filed as though the prefix were spelled *Mac*. This method is used in libraries and in many business offices.

Mackey, Thelma	McMahon, Agnes
McKinney, Louis	McNab, Robert
McLain, Alice	Macnamara, Henry
MacLaren, Frank	McNaughton, Mary
MacLean, Samuel	Macnutt, Albert

Note that telephone directories and some organizations file names beginning with *Mac* before those beginning with *Mc*:

MacBride, Roy
MacDonald, Peter

McBride, Roy
McDonald, Peter

4. When filing a group of one surname in alphabetical order, bear
   the following in mind:

   (1) Nothing stands before something
   (2) Initials always precede names beginning with the same letter.

   Lord, (Mrs.)
   Lord, A. F.
   Lord, A. Frances
   Lord, Augustus

5. Hyphenated surnames of individuals should be indexed under the
   surname as a whole and, when necessary, a cross-reference made
   from the second part:

   Thoburn-Arzt, James
   Quiller-Couch, Arthur T.

   Cross-references:

   Arzt, James Thoburn—*See* Thoburn-Arzt, James
   Couch, Arthur T. Quiller—*See* Quiller-Couch, Arthur T.

Foreign Names

6. Foreign names with *D', da, de, della, di, la, le, van, von,* and so
   forth, are filed alphabetically as they are spelled. The prefix is
   considered as part of the name, not separately.

Da Costa, Carl	Du Bois, Paul
D'Agnostina, Albert	La Barre, Emily
De Kosa, L. A.	La Bell, W.
D'Elia, Louis J.	Le Blanc, Jean
Della Fazia, Anielo	Van Loon, Hendrik
De Stefano, Adolfo	Van Ness, George
Des Verney, Kenneth	Von Bremen, Fritz
De Takacs, Maria	Von Burg, Karl

7. When names beginning with *La* or *Le* are family names (as *Le
   Roy, Le Bolt,* etc.), they follow the foregoing rule. When *La* or
   Le is the equivalent of *the,* index as written.

   La Barre Realty Corp.
   Le Barton Mfg. Co.

When *El* is the equivalent of *the*, index as written: El Caso Apartments.

8. Foreign titles are indexed strictly according to title. Make as many cross-references as may be necessary for identification:

La Société Anonyme des Cycles Peugeot
Make cross-references under *Peugeot* and *Cycles*.

Company Names

9. If a *company* is a customer, enter under the company's title, with name of officer following:

Best & Co.,
    Strickland, W., Manager
Stetson Shops, Inc.,
    Interman, K. M.

If the *officer himself* is the customer, enter under his or her name in care of the company:

Brown, Joseph A.,
    Credit Manager, Stewart & Co.

10. If a company name contains a given name under which it is commonly known, it should be filed under the familiar form:

John Hancock Mutual Life Insurance Company
Marshall Field & Company

But more often company names containing given names are known by the surnames and should be so filed:

Crowell, Thomas Y., Company
Heath, D. C., and Company

11. Arrange all material in A–Z sequence of letters to the last letter of the word, considering each word separately. Consider the second words only when the first words are identical:

Amer, Walter
Amerest Baking Co.
American Can Co.
American Car Co.
Americana Art Co.
Amerman, A.
Ames, E. C.

12. Names that begin with numbers should be indexed as if spelled out:

File
  1st National Bank as
  First National Bank

13. Company names that do not include full names of individuals should be alphabetized under the first name and the names following in strict alphabetical order, with cross-reference from the second name when necessary:

Canadian Pacific Railway Company
Cross-reference:
  Pacific Railway Company, Canadian

14. When there are a large number of titles of the same name, these should be alphabetized according to names of towns in the address:

American Can Company, Allentown, Pa.
American Can Company, Memphis, Tenn.

15. Companies with initials or given names should be filed (1) by surname, (2) by given name or initial, (3) by remainder of title (& Co., Bros., etc.). Small words, such as *and, for, of,* and so forth, should be disregarded in filing.

Ryan, A.   Ryan & Co.
Ryan, B. C.   Ryan, Edward, & Bros.
Ryan, Bernard   Ryan and Jones

16. When companies of one name are followed by the words *Bros., Co., Inc., Sons,* and so forth, the titles are filed as though they were given names:

Patton, Abner   Patton Co.
Patton Bros.   Patton, Inc.

17. Apostrophe *s* (*'s*) or *s* apostrophe (*s'*) is not considered in filing. Strict alphabetical order should be followed.

Stark, Edward
Stark's Grocery Store
Starks, Louise
Starks' Moving Company
Stark's Service Station
Starks, William
Starks Woodyard

Miscellaneous Names

18. When filing material pertaining to a state, county, or city, file under the name of state, county, or city; subdivide by department or bureau:

Washington Assurance Corporation
          "   Candy Corporation
          "   , City of
          "   Public Health, Bureau of
          "   Coffee Co., G. (cross-reference)
          "   , County of
          "   Heights Battery Service
          "   , Martha, Hotel Co. (cross-reference)
          "   Pipe and Foundry Co.
          "   Square Book Shop
          "   , State of
          "   Education, Board of

19. Titles beginning with *Mt.*, *New*, *Pan*, *Rock*, *St.*, *Saint*, *San*, *Santa*, and so forth, are alphabetized as distinct names. Abbreviations are filed as though spelled in full:

Mt. Carmel	St. Agnes Day Nursery
Mt. Vesuvius Lumber Co.	Saint Joseph's Union
Mt. Zion Cemetery	St. Mary's Church
New Lenox Market	Saintsbury, George
New Life Co.	San Francisco Chronicle
Newark Refining Co.	San Joseph, Harold
Pan American Society of U.S.	Sanka Coffee House
Pancoast Co.	Santa Fé Co.
Rock Island R.R.	Santangelo Bros.
Rockefeller, John D.	

20. Churches are filed as the name appears.

Cathedral of St. John the Divine
Cross-reference:
    St. John the Divine, Cathedral of

Corporate Titles

21. Institutions or societies beginning with a given name should be filed under the surname, with a cross-reference from the given name when necessary:

Delgado, Isaac, Museum
Ringling, John and Mabel, Museum

But they should be filed under the given name if that is the generally recognized form:

George Washington University
John Crerar Library
Sarah Lawrence College

22. When titles are composed of two or more names joined by *and*, &, or a hyphen, the connective is disregarded.

American and Canadian Distributors, Inc.
American & Canadian Flour Corporation
American-Canadian Property Corporation
American-Russian Chamber of Commerce

23. When points of the compass are part of the name, index under *north*, *south*, and so forth.

North Chicago, Ill.
South Boston, Mass.

Northwest, Northwestern, and so forth, spelled as one word, are so alphabetized:

North River Savings Bank
Northwest Paper Company
Northwestern Chemical Company

24. Titles beginning with descriptive words should be inverted so that the main entry will come first.

Trustees of Cornell University
      should be
Cornell University, Trustees of

Estate of Chauncey M. Depew
      should be
Depew, Chauncey M., Estate of

CHAPTER EIGHTEEN

Preparation of Reports

Although you may assist in gathering material for the reports your employer prepares and will probably type them for distribution, you may never be asked to compose a report yourself. However, you will constantly be learning details of the work, and in due course you may become an assistant. You might then be expected to prepare rough drafts of your employer's reports.

In any case, good form in preparing a report is important. An attractive appearance has much to do with the attention given the report by those who receive it. The glossy annual reports issued by large corporations reveal the importance they give to color, effective layout, photographs, and easy-to-read charts and tables.

A secretary is expected to be able to organize a report with headings and suitable spacing to display the message in an appealing fashion. Although the keyboard of a standard typewriter does not permit the variation possible with a word processor, it offers a number of possibilities for indicating the main or most important headings and others of descending importance. Following are suggested ways of typing these.

1. THE MOST IMPORTANT HEADING (capitals, spaced, words underscored; two spaces between words)
2. NEXT IN IMPORTANCE (capitals, underscored)
3. THIRD IN IMPORTANCE (capitals, without underscoring)
4. Then Initial Capitals and Underscoring (no capitals for articles or short conjunctions and prepositions)

5. Initial Capitals Without Underscoring
6. Initial capital only

Using an electronic typewriter, you can employ various daisy wheels to create an effective presentation. If you have a word processor, you can be as flexible as your printer allows. Too much variation is distracting, but boldface and other striking typefaces can add emphasis where it is desired. The script styles are not appropriate for most business uses.

Purpose of the Report. In order to include all needed information, the writer of a report should first determine the purpose or aim of the report and what use is to be made of it. A salesman submitting a monthly report of his activities generally need not include the number of miles he traveled, amount of gasoline used, or other such details. The sales manager wants to know on whom he called, the orders he obtained, and the terms of the orders. Similarly, the members of a committee to propose sites for a new hospital will report on feasible sites with pertinent data, mentioning only briefly the unfavorable locations they considered.

Perspective of the Report. A report writer must catch the reader's attention and hold it by offering his material in the right perspective. He presents his points in their true proportion and finds the best arrangement. To do so, he must follow a form that is clear, logical, and easily grasped.

Tone of the Report. The aim of the report and its prospective audience will determine the manner of presentation. The formality will vary with the position held by the writer and the purpose for which the report has been prepared. An engineering report, for example, would differ considerably from the annual report of the president of a women's club. Each report, however, will present briefly the purpose of the report, the proposed solution to the problem or an outline of the writer's accomplishments, and a summary of recommendations or conclusions. Detailed charts, tables, graphs, and the like should be kept separate but easily consulted, as in an appendix.

General Format. In preparing a report, a general format is followed, with the actual contents varying with the type of report. The following outline may be adapted to suit the circumstances:

1. Title page
2. Introduction or preface (or letter of transmittal)
3. Acknowledgments
4. Abstract (if used)
5. Table of contents
6. Summary or synopsis
7. Body of the report (the text or discussion)
8. Conclusion and recommendations
9. Appendix
10. Bibliography
11. Index

Title Page. The title is typed first, about ten lines from the top of the page. On long, formal reports, the title may be supplemented by a subtitle that specifies the scope and purpose of the report. The name of the writer with his position (or the board of directors, commission, or organization making the report) appears below the title. The name of the organization for which the report has been prepared, its address, and the date when the report was submitted are placed at the bottom of the page.

The title page is often omitted from short, informal reports in which the title appears on the cover or as the main heading on page one.

In typing the title page, center each line horizontally, allowing a margin, if the report is to be bound, at least one inch at either the top or the left side. Full capitals underscored may be used for the actual title. Following is a sample title page.

THREE SUITABLE LOCATIONS

FOR MIDDLETOWN'S NEW HIGH SCHOOL

Terrain, Neighborhood, and Cost

of Acquisition of Possible Sites

By the Committee on Site Selection

Middletown Board of Public Education

Prepared for the Board of Public Education

Middletown, Ohio

April 16, 19__

Introduction or Preface For the purposes of a report, the introduction
will be a brief statement of the nature of the report, the scope, the
purpose, and often the circumstances under which it has been made.
If a letter of transmittal is used instead of an introduction, then a preface
may be included to give the circumstances under which the report
was prepared, the background of the authors, and similar pertinent
information about the preparation of the report. The preface may also
be called a foreword.

An example of a preface is as follows.

The capital budget of the City of Newtown has recently exceeded $650
million a year and yet no comprehensive long-range or master plan exists. The
City's annual five-year capital improvement plan lacks legal significance and
is disregarded after its adoption by the City Planning Commission.

With decreasing federal and state aid and with the probability of lowered interest rates, annual capital budgets of $1 billion are nevertheless likely in the near future. Comprehensive planning and effective capital programming are imperative.

It was against this background that the Commission in 19__ asked the author to study capital planning and development in Newtown. The paper was completed late in 19__.

Mrs. Morse was Research Director of the Newtown Department of City Planning from 19__ to 19__, and of the special Newtown Rezoning Study staff from 19__ to 19__. In recent years she has been a consultant for the United Nations, the Norwich Planning Commission, and other agencies, and on the faculty of the Graduate Planning Division of Pratt Institute.

The Commission is grateful for the cooperation received from the City Planning Commission and the Department of City Planning in the compilation of data for this paper.

A different sort of preface appears in a report from the President of New York University on University Research and the City:

Americans today are drawn to their large cities as centers of ideas and opportunities, of business and culture, of political and social life. At the same time they are repelled by the ugliness and decay, both physical and social, of large sections of them.

Few domestic questions are of greater consequence than which of these attitudes toward the metropolis will prevail.

The idea of a civilized, ambitious nation rejecting its cities and leaving them to become jungles of deterioration is, of course, unthinkable—except that we have come very close to doing just that. We have acted as though we found heaven in suburbia and have no further need for the cities. Yet, in reality, increasing numbers of exurbanites long for the more interesting and significant life of the city—if only it were "safe" and if they could afford it.

The plight of our cities frequently prompts the question, "What are our universities doing about the problems of city life?"

New York University, which has been serving New York City for 136 years, is making many contributions to the solution of urban problems. These contributions take two forms.

The first and most important is research leadership, directed at identifying and analyzing major problems and seeking solutions that can be offered to the community for application. This search for knowledge and understanding may take a biochemist to his laboratory, a political scientist to City Hall or Albany, an engineer (in a helicopter) to the smog-filled air above Manhattan.

The second contribution is a by-product of the first. It is service to people, related to research. Thus the clinics of the Medical and Dental Centers supply abundant data for analysis and experimentation and at the same time provide health care for thousands of men, women, and children.

In 19__ – 19__ New York University research involved the efforts of more than 900 faculty members and 1,100 graduate students, postdoctoral fellows and technical assistants. The total cost of this research was $34,000,000.

The following pages describe some aspects of University research that are actual or potential contributions to New York City and its people and to the understanding and improvement of life in urban communities everywhere.

James M. Hester
President

Letter of Transmittal. The introduction may be simply a letter identifying the source of the report.

Dear Mr. Brown:

Here is the report on the proposed expansion of the Tartan plant. Should you wish further details on particular aspects, we shall be glad to furnish more material.

Very truly yours,
George Grant

In the case of a less formal report, the letter of transmittal might be more informative and less stiff.

Dear Fred,

Here is the report you asked for on the Tartan plant expansion proposal. It is the joint work of Bill Jones, Frank Smith, Henry Johnson, and myself. Jones is responsible for the engineering aspects, economical site use, and structural evaluation of the present plant. Smith, as personnel manager, has covered the cafeteria facilities, parking area, employee safety considerations, and other matters having to do with the workforce. Johnson and I looked into the costs of remodeling the present plant and also the estimated cost of purchasing the twenty-acre parcel of land across the highway from the present plant and the probable cost of erecting a new building there.

We have, of course, a mass of data that could not be included in this report. Should you wish further details on particular aspects, we shall be glad to furnish more material.

Cordially,
George Grant

Acknowledgments. The writer of a report will often wish to acknowledge the contributions of colleagues and others not in the text. Such acknowledgments may be presented in the form of a paragraph in the letter of transmittal or placed at the end of the preface.

Such a paragraph might be: "Thanks are due to all members of the

Engineering Department for their careful reading of this report and their many helpful suggestions. Special mention must be made of the contribution of J. B. Greene, who checked all computations and suggested many of the illustrations."

Abstract. Technical reports often include an abstract, which precedes the table of contents, and the summary is omitted. The abstract contains about one hundred words and offers in capsule form the statement of the problem, what studies have been made, and what conclusions or recommendations are made. Some companies make copies of abstracts of reports on index cards for central filing, for a company bulletin, or for circulation to the principal officers of the company. In addition, the company librarian finds abstracts useful in filing the reports and in suggesting useful reports to personnel using the library.

Following is an example of an abstract of a technical report.

<u>Investigation of Foundation Conditions for Proposed Refinery Site,
Seaport, S.C.</u>

Structure design must minimize earthquake, hurricane damage. Subsurface: 400 acres of site investigated intensively, borings at 400' centers. Ground surface Elev. +10 to +22 ft. Subsurface Pleistocene marine terrace 40–80 ft. deep, overlying Eocene marl. Surface sand 28.5 ft. deep. Uppermost safe support for piles: marl and compact overlying sand. Ground water 2–3 ft. below surface. Site grading requires drainage; deep excavation requires cofferdams.

Foundations and locations described for tanks 48 ft. high, over 80 ft. diameter. Foundations for major process units described. Economic site utilization shown. Recommendations included: underwater dredged slopes; bank protection; designs of wharf, mooring and breasting dolphins.

Table of Contents. In long reports a table of contents is often included for ready reference to the parts of the report, and is prepared after the report has been completed. The principal subjects or chapter headings are included, preceded by Roman or Arabic numerals and followed by subtopics or headings within the chapter (subheads) indented from the beginning of the chapter name. Page numbers corresponding to these subjects or chapters are given in Arabic numerals. An introduction of two or more pages might be numbered with lowercase Roman numerals. The numbering of pages as well as of chapter headings and subheads corresponds to usage in the report. If Roman numerals were used in the report, they must be used in the contents.

The first line of the page is Contents or Table of Contents, centered. An inch or more below appears the first line: Introduction, Abstract, or Summary, or the name of the first chapter. If an introduction or abstract precedes the main report, this item is listed first, at the left margin, usually without a number. If there are to be as many as eight chapters and Roman numerals are being used, three spaces must be left at the left margin before typing the "I" for the first chapter. The Roman numeral is followed by a period and three spaces. The name of the chapter or section may be typed in capital letters.

When Arabic numerals are used for the chapters, only two spaces need be allowed for numbering. One space is left at the left margin for the "10" position; the figure for Chapter 1 is typed, followed by a period and three spaces. If desired, paragraphs within the chapter may be numbered to correspond to the chapter number. In Chapter 5, for example, paragraphs would be numbered 5.0, 5.1, and so on. Leaders follow from the chapter headings to the page numbers to draw the eye across the page.

Subheads are indented from chapter headings two or three spaces, and these are typed with initial capital only. In cases where summaries are used under chapter headings, they are indented but period leaders are not used after the summaries.

Following is a sample table of contents:

C O N T E N T S

Summary. A brief summary, following the table of contents, is often included in a report of one hundred pages or more. It is longer than an abstract and is intended to provide an outline of the contents of a nontechnical report. It serves both the reader who skims and persons who will use the report, since it reviews the main points and shows their relationship to one another. It may be divided into sections with subheads such as "Findings," "Recommendations," and "Outlook for Next Year."

CAPITAL DEVELOPMENT AND PROGRAMMING

Summary: Findings and Recommendations

While public capital expenditure in Newtown has increased steadily since World War II and can be expected to continue to grow, no comprehensive long-range or master plan exists to guide this development. The annual five-year Capital Improvement Plan is neither realistic nor based on any rational system of evaluating needs and priorities. With decreasing federal and state aid, and with the probability of lowered interest rates, annual capital budgets of $1 billion are nevertheless likely in the near future. To spend sums of this magnitude without comprehensive planning and with ineffective capital programming would be wasteful and would fail to produce the modern City that its citizens hope for.

Findings

Before the Depression (1924–32) the City was spending (in the equivalent of 1985 dollars) some $775 million a year for capital improvements, or about $128 per capita. During the Depression and War years, fractions of these amounts were spent. It has taken until now just to catch up with the accumulated unmet needs of the 1930s and 1940s. Yet from 1970 to 1985, average annual capital expenditure in 1985 dollars was only $411 million, or $57 per capita.

The processes by which the City's capital programs and annual capital budget are determined have been grossly inadequate to produce rational, orderly development in accordance with any kind of long-range plan. In the absence of an overall development policy and program, capital project decisions are made—indeed, have to be made—on the basis of lists of individual project needs, with their internal priority designations. Requests are submitted by some thirty City departments and then are whittled down by the City Planning Commission to fit within the City's available debt-incurring capacity. There has been little coordination in this procedure between the capital needs of operating departments performing related functions or between the capital programming process and the comprehensive planning and urban renewal activities of the City Planning Commission itself.

Recommendations

Capital budgets currently amount to over $650 million a year. These amounts may be expected to rise. Skillful planning is required to prevent building the wrong things in the wrong places at the wrong times.

The following steps are recommended for more rational and effective planning and programming of the City's capital development:

The City Planning Commission and its staff should formulate a comprehensive development plan and related master plan, which should be officially adopted after public discussion and revision. It should be periodically restudied and revised.

The five-year capital improvement program adopted each year by the Commission should be given official status through a Charter amendment requiring approval by the Mayor, the Council, and the Board of Estimate.

When the Mayor or the legislative bodies adopt amendments or any planning or programming decisions in contravention of the Commission's recommendations, the reasons therefor and the Commission's dissenting opinions should be published.

The role of the City Planning Commission should be clarified and strengthened. It has not, however, used all of its present power. It should not only review departmental requests but should also point out unmet needs and initiate new projects. It should coordinate the City's plans with those of other jurisdictions in the metropolitan area and see that the City utilizes state, federal, and other funds available for capital purposes.

The Budget Bureau should participate in the programming and budgeting process, but it should not delete items from or add items to the Commission's completed programs and budgets.

The Site Selection Board should be abolished. Differences between the commission and the operating departments should be adjudicated not by the Board but by the Mayor and the legislative bodies.

Zoning revisions should be made to accord with the adopted master plan, but continuous erosion of zoning controls by amendments and variances should be ended.

Standing committees should be established for various sectors of the City's capital development—education, transportation, housing, etc. Each should include representatives of the Commission's planning staff, the operating departments concerned, the Budget Bureau, and, when needed, members of the Commission. These committees should formulate programs and budgets in particular areas for presentation to the Commission. This change would eliminate much of the Commission's present staff-type work and permit it to concentrate on the broader aspects of planning.

Body of the Report. The body of the report presents the carefully outlined study of the subjects, logically organized and concisely expressed. The writer uses headings, sideheads, indentations, numbered paragraphs, and other devices to show the relation between main topics and subtopics. He includes maps, charts, tables, and other visual devices to present his facts graphically, but he places aids in an appendix for the benefit of those who will read the entire report. He keeps the body of his report as brief and forceful as possible.

Following is an example of the beginning of Chapter 1 of a report.

I

PURPOSE AND BACKGROUND

This paper describes and analyzes Newtown's capital development in relation to city planning and presents recommendations for improving the planning and programming of the City's capital development.

It seeks to answer these basic questions:

(1) How have the City's capital program and budget been influenced by planning at various periods?

(2) What is the current relationship between the City's capital development and comprehensive planning?

(3) What major problems have arisen that obstruct effective planning and programming of the City's capital development?

(4) What is a reasonable projection of the City's future capital needs, and how can planning provide the most useful framework for setting priorities and coordinating programs within the resources likely to become available?

(5) What specific measures would improve the effectiveness of the planning process in relation to the City's future capital development, private as well as public?

The terms "master planning," "comprehensive planning," "physical development planning," "capital improvement planning," etc., describe related different stages or levels of the planning process and are used in certain specific ways that may need clarification for a thorough understanding of this paper. Definitions will be found in the Appendix (pages 98–100).

Newtown's Capital Development

The Newtown capital plan has been developed over a very long period of time, but only recently, in relation to the sweep of history, have attempts been made to project the City's capital needs in terms of any comprehensive view of its future development.

Conclusion. The conclusion of a report is often the last chapter and bears an appropriate title: "Conclusion" or "Conclusion and Recommendations." It consists of a brief summary of results obtained, of points presented, or of recommendations made. The most important points or recommendations are usually listed first, followed by the less important conclusions, with an indication of what action might be taken and by whom.

RECOMMENDATIONS

On the basis of our three-month study of the Tartan plant, we conclude that a new building will be the most economical and most satisfactory approach to solving the problems of needed repairs and additional space. The existing facility requires major repairs and remodeling to accommodate the present operations, and the prospective addition of a retail sales office will crowd the present site unduly. Parking facilities are already deficient, and additional traffic generated by the retail business will complicate an already difficult situation.

A site of about twenty acres is available across the highway from the present plant. It is now occupied by a soft-drink and ice-cream stand and a pottery sales shop, with vacant land at the rear. Utilities are available, and there is ample access to the site.

A new building can be designed and occupied on a unit basis, with the retail section being opened first.

Options on the property in question should be taken as soon as possible because the convenience to be gained in a nearby location will substantially benefit the Tartan plant. Meanwhile, the activity in light industry in Tartan indicates a constant demand for property in this area.

Appendix. The appendix, found only in long, formal reports, contains supplementary material—bibliographies, maps, charts, graphs, and other visual devices and references—amplifying the statements in the text but too lengthy or digressive or of too special an interest to be included in the main discussion.

The preparation of a bibliography and the style to be followed in typing are explained in Chapter 21.

Index. An index also is found only in long, formal reports. It resembles the index of a book and includes an alphabetical listing of the important topics discussed in the text. Cross-references are used to enable the reader to locate related topics. Care must be taken to give page references accurately if the index is to be at all useful.

Detailed instructions for an index are given in Chapter 23.

Reports in Letter Form

Some reports, such as those to boards of trustees, to the president of a university, to stockholders, and others, often are in letter form.

The body of the report in letter form is organized in much the same manner as that of other reports. It presents the chief features in narration or exposition without too much detail.

The letter report is concluded by appropriate remarks and signed by the writer with his official position. Following are examples of letter reports.

(1)

PRESIDENT'S REPORT

This has been another exciting and productive year for the East Bumstead Community Council and for the many people who, through their efforts with the Council, are succeeding in shaping East Bumstead into a better place in which to live and work.

The Youth Suicide Prevention Committee came into existence this year. One of the Committee's projects has been the establishment of a speaker's bureau that makes available to local agencies and service providers, mental health professionals to speak on the topic of adolescent suicide prevention.

Activity at the Emergency Shelter these days is highlighted by plans to move into the new and larger shelter on Market Street.

The realization of the development of a community residence has brought much satisfaction to all involved with this very worthwhile project.

I would like to take this opportunity to thank everyone involved with the Council, individuals as well as local public and private organizations, who participate in and support the various activities of the East Bumstead Community Council. Special thanks go to the United Way for its continued cooperation and support.

My personal thanks are extended to all who have made my job as President over the past two years such a rewarding experience.

Martha Slayton

(2)

Dear Fellow Alumnus:

In the fifteenth year of the Alumni Fund, a record amount of nearly $65,000 of unrestricted funds was turned over to the College. Three classes set new records for total contributions.

The tenth reunion class, with Bill Kavicky as Reunion Gifts Chairman and

Alice Longley as Chairman of Class Fund-raisers, made the largest reunion gift in the history of the Fund, $16,000.

The Class of 19—, with Jim Atwell and Mary Button in charge, doubled the largest previous fifth reunion gift by contributing $9,500.

The Class of 19—, led by George Waxman and Louise Mulholland, made a notable contribution of $7,500.

These contributions have been the result of the exemplary loyalty and generosity of our alumni and the unstinting efforts of the class fund-raisers, particularly in reunion classes, and of the staff of the Fund here at Plum Creek under the direction of Agnes Murphy.

To all of those who have made these remarkable accomplishments possible, I wish to extend my personal appreciation and thanks for making the job of Chairman a satisfying one. I know that Mark Mulgrew, next year's Chairman, will continue to receive the same support from all of you who have done so much to bring the Alumni Fund to its present position.

                                        Harrison B. Warrington
                                        Chairman

CHAPTER NINETEEN

Making Travel Arrangements

Many corporations have their own travel departments, which attend to making reservations for train or airplane travel and hotel accommodations. In other firms all reservations are handled by an outside travel agency. The travel specialists maintain up-to-date files of all airline and railroad schedules and of facilities at major hotels. The agent will make travel and hotel reservations, prepare the tickets, arrange for a rental car if desired, prepare an itinerary, and see to many other details. If your organization does not use a particular travel agency, it may be necessary for you to choose one. The names of travel agents may be found in the classified pages of the local telephone directory or in the directory of the nearest city. Membership in the American Society of Travel Agents, Inc. (ASTA), is usually designated in the agency advertisements. While there are many good agents who are not members of the society, those who are members are credited with a high standard of ethics.

Agents are aware of the latest rates and schedules of both major and regional airlines, as well as visa and immunization requirements in foreign countries, travel times to principal cities around the world, luggage limitations, air freight rates, and so forth. They can sometimes arrange for tickets to theater, opera, or other events abroad.

In making your choice of agency, you can inquire whether the agency can provide corporate rates and whether they will deliver tickets or pick up unused tickets for refund. Is there a toll-free number to be used when calling from out of town when reservations must be changed?

You may find that convenience and savings are possible with one or more agencies. Billing is prearranged between the travel agent and the client, either using the client's individual credit card or a credit card issued by the corporation for the individual's use on company business. Employees who travel frequently for the company are issued air travel cards, and these are used for billing. (Similarly, telephone credit cards can be used by company representatives for long-distance calls from outside the office.)

Client Profile. Large travel agencies use a profile card for frequent travelers. This card is used to record personal information and preferences so that whenever the agency is asked to make reservations for transportation or hotel accommodations, the data is at hand, either on the card or in the computer. Knowing a person's preferences makes it possible for the travel agent to request the traveler's choice of seat, the airline he or she prefers, the nonsmoking area, or the corner hotel room. The concierge floor, for example, provides extra amenities much appreciated by someone who must travel frequently. Some of these features are separate check-in, separate elevator, complimentary breakfast and newspaper, perhaps an honor bar and refrigerator, a hair dryer, toiletries, and so forth. The extra charge for the concierge floor may ensure a restful night for an employee who is constantly traveling. Consideration of personal preferences can help to make the difference between a successful trip and an unsuccessful one. A traveler who arrives exhausted and spends an uncomfortable night in a hotel where the food is poor will not be an effective representative of the company.

Among the data requested for the profile card are:

Credit card numbers: American Express, Diners Club, MasterCard, Visa, and so forth;

Company policy on cost of air travel, hotels, car rentals, and other items, and corporate numbers, if any;

Air travel: airline preference and frequent flier membership information;

Seat assignment preference (smoking/nonsmoking, window/aisle, first class, business class, coach);

Meal preference: dietary restriction, vegetarian, fish, fruit plate, and so on;

Car rental: credit card number and any special membership number. Type and make of vehicle preferred;

Hotel: chain preference, membership if any;

Room preference: corner, courtyard, high/low floor, concierge floor, and so forth;

Any special needs, for example, nonsmoking room, bedboard, queen-size bed;

Address for bill to be sent;

Company regulations on hotels, if any. Corporate number if any;

Train: smoking/nonsmoking; sleeper accommodation preference.

If your company does not have a travel department, you should establish a personal relationship with the person at the agency who handles your company account. You should provide the information listed above so that it can be on file or recorded in the agency computer. Then whenever you ask for reservations, it will be unnecessary to specify your employer's preferences in order to ensure a comfortable trip. You will of course keep a copy of this information for future reference. When necessary you will update it and provide the information to the travel agent—changes in company policy, changing health conditions, or simply your employer's wish to do something differently.

Whether your company has a travel department or an outside agency is making the arrangements for a trip, you should ask your employer for the following information for each place to be visited: date and preferred time of arrival, and departure date and approximate time of departure.

Some executives like to allow extra time for the trip to the airport or railroad station. Others expect to make every trip as if only they were using the highway. Some even expect to have an airplane wait until they have boarded. It is unlikely that this can be done; therefore, be sure to allow sufficient time when scheduling a limousine to take your employer to an airport, for example. Traffic will be heavier at rush hour, slower in bad weather. For overseas flights, passengers are required to check in *a minimum of two hours* prior to departure. And on some domestic flights a person using a discounted airfare may not be permitted to "pre-reserve" a seat and will have to stand in line for seat assignment after arriving at the air terminal. In these cases you must allow sufficient time when arranging transportation to the airport.

Some employers wish to be reminded of early departure even when leaving from their own homes. You can judge how to handle this aspect of your employer's travel from your knowledge of his or her habits and temperament.

When you know what cities your employer plans to visit, you will ask the travel agent to book all the flights at one time. It is cheaper, for example, to book a flight from San Francisco to Dallas with an additional flight to Austin than to take the flight to Dallas and then book the flight to Austin. There are three advantages to booking the entire trip at once. First, the traveler is then holding a ticket issued and priced for the total trip at the lowest price consistent with the firm's travel policy. Second, the firm has been able to take advantage of the lowest price of travel. Third, should your employer be unable to leave when scheduled, he or she would still be holding a prepaid ticket to his or her next destination.

When the first reservation is made, you should find out when the tickets must be picked up (to hold the reservation) and also arrange for delivery or pickup of the tickets well in advance of departure. It will be preferable to have the agency deliver the tickets, but that may not be possible.

The company library may have timetables for airlines and railroads as well as hotel guides. You may be able to get an airline pocket guide for your own use. It is useful to know which airlines have flights to the places your employer needs to visit and what hotels are located there. Sometimes there are attractive smaller hotels that make a pleasant change from the usual commercial ones, but make sure your employer approves before making such a reservation. The names of hotel guides and airline guides are given in Chapter 25, in the section on Travel Guides.

Travel by Car. If your employer is a member of the American Automobile Association or another travel club, you can request information for him or her regarding hotel and motel accommodations as well as highway routes and road conditions. Special maps can be prepared for automobile trips, showing the selected route and listing recommended dining places and overnight accommodations.

Hotel Reservations

If you yourself are making hotel reservations, you should always telephone rather than write a letter. Most hotels that are members of chains have toll-free numbers to be used for making reservations. By telephoning you will know immediately whether you can get the desired reservation. Should you be told there is no room at the hotel where your employer always wants to stay, you can try calling the hotel directly and ask to speak to the reservations manager. Often a special arrangement can be made for a regular guest at a hotel.

Reservations for Conventions. If you are going to make arrangements for your employer to attend a convention, you should ask him or her for the literature dealing with procedure that the organization sponsoring the convention has sent him or her. Usually arrangements with an airline and one or more hotels are made for the convention attendees by a travel agent who specializes in conventions. You should provide the travel agent with the information concerning airline and hotel reservations and the fact that your employer is a member of the organization; the agent can then check on those rates. It is sometimes possible to get a better rate by booking independently. On the other hand, a last-minute reservation may not be possible except through the convention arrangement. In any case the agent will need to know that your employer is entitled to the special rate set up for the convention.

Calling for Reservations. If you are personally telephoning the toll-free number of a hotel, you will ask for the reservation desk and say, "This is Diane Johnson of So-and-So Corporation calling. Will you please reserve a single room at the corporate rate for Mr. John Smith of this firm, arriving in Denver on September 5 and checking out on the seventh, two nights, on the concierge floor, with a king-size bed." The clerk will say, "Yes, we do have—," and he repeats the information. You then give your employer's credit card or hotel membership number, and you ask, "Are you giving mileage credit with any airline? How can Mr. Smith have this stay credited?" He may say, "He should inquire when checking in." Or perhaps no credit will be given.

You then state that the room is guaranteed for late arrival. The charge will be applied to your employer's credit card or, if it is the company's policy, the request is guaranteed by the company. You must ask, "What is your cancellation policy?" and also, "May I have the specific address and local telephone number of the ———— Hotel." With this information, which you will type on the itinerary, your employer will know he or she must call before 6 P.M. (or whatever time is given) to avoid a charge, in case he or she is unable to arrive before the stated hour. For example, you will note next to the name of the hotel, "Cancel prior to 6 P.M. day of arrival." You ask for the name of the reservation clerk and for the confirmation number of the reservation you have made. If there is no number, he may say, "Use my name, Mr. Brown, and today's date." You then ask, "Please send me written confirmation of this reservation." When this confirmation arrives, you will place it in a file you have set up for all matters dealing with arrangements for this trip. Later it can be clipped to the itinerary.

Itinerary. If the airline tickets have been generated by a computer, a printout will show the seat assignment and any requested meal. A handwritten ticket may not have the flight information typed out. If the travel agent makes the hotel reservations, you should get a typed confirmation of those reservations.

When you receive the tickets from the travel agent, you should photocopy them, so that you have all the information in case the tickets should be lost. You will then prepare a detailed itinerary, including time of departure for the airport or railroad station, name of the airport or railroad station, flight or train number, hour of departure, destination, seat number, and whether a meal is included. Then you will note the hotel name, address, and local telephone number, the dates of stay, time and date of departure, and all data on the next mode of transportation. (*See* the sample schedule.) A separate list of appointments during the trip with name, date, time, place, address, and telephone number for each should be prepared and given to your employer at the same time. Reminders to reconfirm plane reservations where necessary should be included.

Itinerary for Mr. John Smith

Date	Departure	Destination	Via	Hotel	Address
4/16	Lv. Pittsburgh 8 A.M.	Arr. Philadelphia 8:50 A.M.	Continental Flt. 802	Barclay Plaza	1400 Court Sq. Tel. 215 523-6500
4/17	Lv. Philadelphia 8 A.M.	Arr. Atlanta 9:43 A.M.	Delta Flt. 529	Regency Hyatt House	1230 Park Place Tel. 404 396-3400
4/18	Lv. Atlanta 9:15 A.M.	Arr. New York (Newark) 12:57 P.M.	United Flt. 690	—	
4/18	Lv. New York (La Guardia) 6:20 P.M.	Arr. Pittsburgh 7:30 P.M.	Continental Flt. 335	Home	

Appointments for Mr. John Smith

Place	Date	Time	Name	Address	Telephone No.
Philadelphia	4/16	9:30 A.M.	Henry Timmons Brown Brothers	8714 South St.	215 221-6530
	4/16	12 M.	Frank Smith	Bandbox Café	215 367-8420
	4/16	2 P.M.	W. R. Jones Arpex Corp.	1880 So. 13th Ave.	215 165-7630
Atlanta	4/17	10:30 A.M.	B. W. Elkus Canso Co.	2993 Peachtree St.	404 854-2198
	4/17	3:30 P.M.	J. W. Prince (lunch)	Regency Hyatt	404 396-3400
	4/17	6:30 P.M.	K. G. Stovall (dinner)	1376 97th St. Stone Mountain	404 238-5799
New York	4/18	2 P.M.	P. D. Quill Arpex Corp.	1821 Seventh Ave.	212 708-8743

You should make sure all materials needed for the trip are carefully assembled: speeches, agreements, contracts, agendas for meetings, samples, videotapes—whatever the various meetings require. Manila folders labeled for each appointment may help to organize the materials. Your employer may prefer to pack the briefcase personally, but you should be aware of what may be needed and assist as much as possible.

If formal events are scheduled, you should remind your employer of needed evening attire, including cuff links and shirt studs for men.

Short Trips. Many employers make short trips, visiting one city for only a day or two. Several airlines offer shuttle service or commuter service between cities having considerable daily business travel of this sort. No reservation is required, and passengers are taken on a standby basis, but you should check flight numbers and departure times. For trips along the Northeast corridor and some other areas of the United States, taking the train is often preferred to the plane, since the railroad stations are centrally located in the cities and weather conditions seldom affect the schedules. However, seat reservations are required on the high-speed trains.

If your employer is visiting a branch office or working with a client in another city, it often happens that hotel reservations are made for him or her in the other city. You will, of course, always know where to reach the employer.

Cash for the Trip. You may be asked to arrange for cash for your employer's trip, and you should be familiar with the procedure followed in your office. When you know the amount needed, you type the request if the accounting department is to provide a cash advance. Your employer signs or initials the request, and you present it at the accounting department. Or you may be asked to take a personal check to his or her bank to be cashed. In either case, when you receive the money, you should ask for at least ten single-dollar bills and a couple of five-dollar bills to be used for cab fare or other incidentals. If traveler's checks are needed, the employer must buy them and sign them personally.

Foreign Travel. In addition to all of the above, a passport is needed for leaving or reentering the United States, except for Canada, Mexico, and the Caribbean. However, proof of citizenship, such as a birth certificate with a raised seal, a valid passport, or a voter's registration card should be carried for travel in those countries. In addition, Mexico requires a Mexican tourist card, which can be supplied by your travel agent.

Note: frequent travelers will have a valid passport. Others should keep several copies of their birth certificate (with raised seal, not photocopies) on file; they are obtainable for a small fee from the city or town of birth. The only copy should not be carried around because of the inconvenience of replacing it if it should be lost. A voter's registration card is readily obtained, free, from the registrar of voters in the traveler's hometown. These are used for travel in the Caribbean only.

Obtaining a Passport. Anyone who expects to travel abroad should apply for a passport several weeks before the proposed departure. An application form for a passport can be obtained at passport agencies in large cities or at post offices. Evidence of citizenship must be submitted; either a previously issued passport or a birth certificate with raised seal is required. Two photographs taken within the past six months must also be submitted. These should be two inches square. Either black-and-white or color photos are permitted. In addition, the person must appear with the application and proof of identification, such as a previously issued passport, driver's license, or a certificate of naturalization. Otherwise, the applicant must be accompanied by someone who has known him for at least two years. Credit cards and social security cards are not acceptable. The fee is forty-two dollars for adults and twenty-seven dollars for someone under eighteen, and the passport is good for ten years for adults, five years for someone under eighteen.

Vaccinations and Immunizations. Before a person visits some countries, certain vaccinations and immunizations are required. You can find out from your travel agent or the local, county, or state health department what is required for travel to each country. Some shots are given only by official health departments, while others can be given by a private physician. A person traveling to a country that requires certain immunizations should call his own physician and tell the physician where he is going. Because of his medical condition, some shots might not be advisable. He should discuss the situation with the physician. Because some information may need to be held in confidence, the employer should attend to the matter personally and receive appropriate treatment. Necessary shots should be given well before the trip, since some cause discomfort and time should be allowed for recovery. Doing so can avoid unnecessary delay at the time of departure.

Certificates of vaccination and immunization should be placed with the passport for presentation when entering a country where such certificates are required.

Tourist Information. Many useful guides are available for the enjoyment of visitors. The tourist information bureaus of each state can provide free information about the special attractions of their state, while many guidebooks are available for the traveler outside the United States. Some of these books are listed in Chapter 25 in the Travel Guides section.

In addition, there are tourist information bureaus in New York for most European, South American, and Asian countries, as well as New Zealand and Australia. Special events and suggested itineraries are described. Some business travelers find they can combine a business trip with a vacation, so that tourist information will increase the pleasure of a trip.

Visa Requirements. Visas are being required for entry and exit in more and more countries. You should inquire of the travel agency when you call in the employer's itinerary whether there are visa requirements. It may be necessary to check with consulates of particular countries and start work on securing the visas. There may be forms to fill out, extra photographs needed, and so on. You could ask the travel agency for the name of a visa service, which will handle such details for a fee. In large corporations there may be an in-house specialist who deals with these matters, so you should inquire before seeking outside help.

CHAPTER TWENTY

Preparing a Manuscript

Style Matters

A manuscript submitted to an editor, publisher, or printer should be carefully and attractively typed. Busy editors and literary agents react more favorably to legible manuscripts that are free from typographical errors and look as if they have been produced by an experienced writer. Actually, many professional writers have their final drafts copied by expert typists. If the substance of an article or a book is worthy of attention, it deserves a good presentation.

Editing. Before the final typing, the author should edit the manuscript critically to be certain that it contains no incorrect usage, that punctuation is exact and consistent, that nothing essential has been omitted, and that all footnotes are correctly placed and numbered. The paragraphing should be clear and effective, the grammar correct, and the facts verified. Uniformity of spelling, punctuation, capitalization, and abbreviation should be maintained. (*See* Chapter 6 for guidance in expressing numbers in text.)

Paper. The manuscript is typed on only one side of the paper, which should be good-quality bond typing paper. Cheap paper not only is less attractive but tears easily, and erasures are likely to leave holes.

Typing. The manuscript should be typed on an electric typewriter or word processor for best appearance. The typeface should be a conventional one, not full capitals or imitation script.

A book manuscript might be submitted on disks, if the word processor used is compatible with the equipment used by the publisher. The author would be able, of course, to print out the manuscript if the disk could not be submitted. Unsolicited manuscripts, however, should never be submitted on disks.

Title Page. The first page of the manuscript is the title page. It bears the name of the work and the author's name and address. The name of the article or book is centered about one-third down from the top of the page, with the author's name about eight spaces below it. Whether "by" appears on the same line as the author's name is a matter of individual preference. Neatness and legibility are the principal criteria.

The author's name, address, and Social Security number should be typed at the upper right-hand corner of the title page, with a statement of estimated length of the manuscript if it is a magazine article.

Estimated Length. To estimate the length of an article, add the number of words in six lines. Divide this number by six, to get the average number for one line. Multiply the average by the number of lines on the page, disregarding lines having no more than two or three words. This result is the average number of words on one page. For the estimated total length of the article, multiply the average number of words per page by the total number of pages.

Contents. Nonfiction book manuscripts should include a table of contents, listing the preface (or foreword or introduction), the chapter titles, the bibliography (if any), and the index. Some types of books lend themselves to a fuller table of contents, which will include the topics discussed in each chapter, but this treatment is mainly suited to textbooks and how-to books.

Chapters. The division of the subject matter by sections, parts, chapters, and so forth, should be clearly shown in typing, particularly in technical books. Each chapter should begin at the top of a new page.

Walter B. Fredston
120 Willard Street
Burlington, NJ 00000
Soc. Sec. # 202-15-3333

Estimated length: 900 words

PHYSICISTS TRY
TO LIBERATE
QUARKS AND GLUONS

by

Walter B. Fredston

The word *chapter* is often omitted, but all chapters should be numbered consecutively (either in Roman or Arabic), whether or not they are given individual titles.

Some books of a technical nature are improved by the use of sideheads within the chapters, to permit quick reference to the contents of these paragraphs. The sideheads may consist of a few descriptive words set off in italics (underscored in typing) or placed a line above the paragraph at the left margin.

Typing Style. Manuscripts should always be double-spaced on one side of the paper only. No extra line should be left between paragraphs.

The margins of a page of text should be: top, two inches on the first page of each chapter, one and a half inches on subsequent pages; left, one and a half inches; right, one inch; bottom, one inch. The manuscript is more attractive if the same number of lines is typed on all pages, and doing so facilitates the quick and accurate computation of the length of the manuscript.

Paragraphs should be uniformly indented. Five spaces are usual (*see* p. 357).

Division of Words. Words should be divided by syllables at the ends of the lines. (Any dictionary indicates where words may be divided.) However, the last word on a page should not be divided but carried into the margin if it is a very short word. A long word is carried over to the following page. It is preferable to avoid dividing the last words on two or more consecutive lines.

Page Numbers. All pages after the title page should be numbered consecutively. The page numbers should be typed either in the center of the fifth line from the top or on that same line at the right-hand margin. On manuscript going to the printer, it is advisable to include the author's last name or a key word from the title on the same line as the page number. In this case the page number would be centered and the name or key word would be typed at the right margin.

Insertions. No insertions should be made in short manuscripts being submitted for publication. Instead, the manuscript should be retyped. In the case of book-length material, insertions may be typed on separate pages numbered to correspond to the pages where they are to be

3. INFLUENCES OF THE MANNHEIM SCHOOL

During the classical period the leading orchestra of Europe was not in Paris, Berlin, London, or Vienna. It was in the small city of Mannheim in southwestern Germany, at that time under the jurisdiction of Elector Palatine Karl Theodor.

Many composers had their symphonies and other works performed at Mannheim. By the 1750's the city had become a most important musical center. Composers Toeschi, Flitz, Holzbauer, and Cannabich formed a group which has become known as the Mannheim School. The leader of this school was Johann Stamitz, who also served as concertmaster of the orchestra.

The strength of the new style was its characteristic dynamics. "The Mannheimers had a wealth of tone-gradations between extremes of fortissimo and pianissimo, and abrupt dynamic contrasts formed an essential effect of their art, which they exploited to the point of abuse and deliberate disregard of the natural accent of music."[1] The orchestra at Mannheim gained recognition with its world-famous crescendo. This concept of crescendo was rather new, for the old style distinguished only between forte and piano. In the new style, the crescendo and diminuendo comprised the chief composition technique.

Neither Haydn nor Mozart made use of the crescendo as did the composers at Mannheim. The works of these masters were far nobler and more

---

[1]Alfred Einstein, A Short History of Music (New York: Alfred A. Knopf, 1954), p. 153.

Sample Manuscript Page

inserted and lettered in sequence: a lengthy addition to page 8 would appear on pages numbered *8a, 8b,* and so forth. A note in the left margin on page 8 at the point where the insertion is to be made will state, "Insert pp. 8a–8b," with an arrow to indicate exactly where the material should be added. The added pages are placed after page 8.

Deletions. Deletions spoil the appearance of a manuscript. Shorter manuscripts should be retyped if material is removed. In a book-length manuscript from which a page or more has been deleted, the number or numbers of deleted pages are added to the preceding page to avoid renumbering all following pages. For example, if pages 31, 32, and 33 have been removed, page 30 would be marked "30–33" and page 34 would then follow page 30.

Quotations. Short quotations may be placed within the text and enclosed in quotation marks. When short lines of poetry are quoted in the text, the lines are separated by a virgule (/).

> and we can say with Goldsmith, "by sports like these are all their cares beguiled, / The sports of children satisfy the child." And yet in sports . . .

If quotations are six or seven lines of typewritten material, they should not be separated from the text. Longer quotations are set in smaller type and indented. The typist double-spaces below the text, indents four spaces from the left margin and types the quotation across the page, with the right margin even with the text. Single-spacing is used, with double-spacing between paragraphs of quoted matter. (If the manuscript is to be typeset, however, double-spacing should be used.) Paragraphs are indented eight spaces from the margin in such quotations, and quotation marks are omitted.

> Mozart showed the world how to use the clarinet in the orchestra, although Haydn and Gluck and others had been certain of themselves in handling this new voice of the orchestra. At first these composers considered it as a kind of substitute for the oboe and flute, or at least only an addition or reinforcement for the oboe and the flute. Gluck hesitated to use the clarinet as a solo instrument and confined himself to using it as a harmony instrument. Haydn had two clarinets in his Eisenstadt orchestra between 1776 and 1778, but he did not understand their possibilities until some years later, after Mozart had demonstrated their great resources.
>
> Mozart was attracted by the clarinet when only a child, having written a symphony for strings, bassoons, and clarinets in 1765 while on a visit to London. This raises the interesting possibility that Mozart . . .

When quoting, the typist must follow the original exactly in wording, spelling, punctuation, and capitalization. If a word is inserted in a quotation as a correction or explanation, it should be enclosed in brackets. For example, "The company was founded here [in Scranton] in

1908." When the quotation contains an obvious misspelling or other error, the Latin word *sic* is enclosed in brackets to indicate that the error appeared in the original. "I will and bequethe [*sic*] all my worldly goods to my wife, Eleanor."

The source of a quotation is often placed in parentheses after the quotation to avoid the use of footnotes in informal writing. In scholarly works with many references to source material, footnotes are sometimes numbered consecutively within each chapter and placed at the end of the chapter or at the end of the book.

In many cases, however, the source of the quotation is given in a footnote at the bottom of the page where the quotation begins. When permission to quote is required, the credit line appears in a footnote on the same page. (*See* below for details on typing footnotes.)

Permission to Quote. Quotations of more than a few words of previously published material may require the written permission of the owner or copyright holder. Although copyright law is very complex, some generalizations can be made: all published song lyrics, illustrations, and lines of poetry must be used only with the owner's written permission, and the credit line must be given in the manner he requests. In addition, written permission must be obtained to use passages of one hundred words or more, or for quoting any complete unit, such as an anecdote, except in book reviews. Critical essays may quote somewhat more extensively for purposes of analysis, provided acknowledgment to the source is made. A letter addressed to the publisher of the desired material will be referred to the owner of the copyright. If permission to use such material is denied, it must not be used.

The author of the book or magazine article containing the quotation is responsible for obtaining permission to quote. All permission letters will be checked before the book or article can be published.

Footnotes. There are three reasons for using footnotes: to acknowledge the source of quoted materials, to introduce an explanation of the text in cases where inclusion in the text might be intrusive, and to provide a cross-reference to another passage in the manuscript. The readers of scholarly works are more accustomed to numerous footnotes than the general reader. In informal writing, therefore, the source of a short quotation is briefly stated and included in the text with the publisher's name in parentheses (in the case of a book), unless the publisher requires a particular form of credit line. In the latter case, the length of such a line will usually prevent its inclusion in the text, and using a footnote becomes preferable.

An example of an abbreviated credit line follows:

> As Maya Pines states in *Revolution in Learning* (Harper & Row), "When reading instruction is begun early, it often provides the only clue to some serious visual disabilities—lumped under the term dyslexia—which can be largely corrected if caught in time, but otherwise can poison the child's life." Studies of Maori children in New Zealand bear out this contention, as does the work of Dr. Louis B. Noiseaux at the Institut pour la Recherche sur les Enfants. . . .

Similarly, cross-references can be included in the text without interrupting the train of thought:

> As illustrated by the discussion of telephone-computer links used by the Lincoln National Bank (Chapter 2), the opportunities for saving time and man-hours are only now beginning to be exploited in many large organizations. The willingness to experiment and to invest the necessary capital is of course a key factor. We predict that within the next five years most . . .

Typing Footnotes. When a footnote is to be used, its presence is indicated by a number typed after the word or sentence requiring a further explanation or at the end of the quotation, following the punctuation mark. (Footnotes are numbered consecutively within each chapter.) An ordinary figure is used, typed half a line above the text. By using the variable linespacer you can resume typing on exactly the same line after inserting the footnote number.

If you are using a word processor, you probably will have a program that handles footnotes automatically. You will need only to follow instructions and the footnotes will print out at the bottom of the pages where they are desired. If such a program is not available, you might group all footnotes at the end of the document. Then when you are paginating the document, you can allow space on the pages where footnotes are needed and move them from the end to the proper location. You should underscore across the page or at least ten spaces on a blank line above the footnote matter and leave a blank line to separate the footnotes. Thus a two-line footnote would require three lines, and two footnotes of two lines each would require six lines.

If you are using a typewriter, you must plan ahead to allow sufficient space at the bottom of the page. In addition to the lines required for each footnote, you must allow for the blank line and underscoring below the text.

To type the footnote, you double-space below the text, underscore across the page, and single-space below the underscoring. After indenting five spaces, you type the number of the footnote half a space above the line. The carriage is returned to the line, and the first letter of the footnote is capitalized with no space between number and letter. The footnote matter is single-spaced across the full width of the text if necessary. Second and successive lines of the footnote begin at the left margin. A blank line is left between footnotes, and the next footnote follows.

When the footnote is placed within the text, a second line of underscoring follows on the line below the footnote. After double-spacing, you continue the text.

A single footnote to explain the text would be typed as follows:

---

[1]This map was prepared from original sources, which Mitchell found in East Falmouth and which were later destroyed by a fire.

To acknowledge material quoted from a magazine or newspaper, the following form may be used:

---

[1]Bernard Plimmer, "Silence Does Not Give Consent," Harper's Magazine, March, 1900, pp. 39 ff.

The author's name is followed by the title of the article or story, enclosed in quotation marks, followed by the name of the publication, underscored. The date of the issue and the page on which the article appears complete the credit line.

The data needed for crediting a quotation from a book include the author's name as given on the title page and the full title of the book, underscored; then in parentheses directly following are stated the place of publication, the name of the publisher, and the date of publication. Lastly, the page number or numbers on which the quotation appears are stated. The author's name, with first name or initials first, is followed by a comma. The title of the book is not followed by a comma. Within the parentheses, the place of publication is followed by a colon, the publisher's name by a comma and the date of publication; the closing parenthesis is followed by a comma. A period follows the last page number. (*See* footnote 2, p. 362.)

For second and later references to the same work, if no other references intervene, the abbreviation *ibid.* (from the Latin *ibidem,* "in the same place") is used.

---

²H. A. Calahan, The Sky and the Sailor (New York: Harper & Row, 1952), p. 151.

³Ibid., p. 275.

If a number of manuscript pages separate the two references to the same book, it is preferable to repeat the footnote information in the shortened form of footnote 4, below.

When a footnote refers to a work already cited but not just previously, it should give the author's last name, the title of the work, and the page reference. *Op. cit.* and *loc. cit.* were formerly used for this sort of footnote, but modern practice favors the shortened version of the previous footnote, as shown in footnote 4, below.

---

²H. A. Calahan, The Sky and the Sailor (New York: Harper & Row, 1952), p. 151.

³J. L. Buttolph, Twin Falls in 1910 (Barclay, Idaho: Barclay Publishing Company, 1980), p. 18.

⁴Calahan, The Sky and the Sailor, p. 167.

When quoting by permission from a published work, if no particular form of acknowledgment is requested, the following may be used:

---

¹Reprinted from (title of book) by (author's name), by permission of (name of publisher). Copyright (correct date, shown on copyright page) by (holder of copyright).

Legal Citations. The preferred style for legal citations is that described in *A Uniform System of Citation,* published by the Harvard Law Review Association (*see* p. 393, Modern English Usage). Because of its specialized nature, no attempt is made here to cover this subject.

Reference to Periodicals. Spell out the names of periodicals in the first reference; thereafter shorten the title. For example, *Harper's Magazine* in the first reference becomes *Harper's* later.

In general, the month and year of the periodical provide sufficient identification of the source, but with technical journals the volume and number should be given as well.

Illustrations. All charts, plates, graphs, drawings, and photographs should be numbered. If they have captions, the number is given first, followed by the caption. Tables are given consecutive numbers; drawings are numbered separately from photographs or other kinds of illustrations, and again the numbers must be consecutive. The captions for each type of illustration are typed on a separate sheet so that the proper caption can be placed with each illustration. A copy of each caption should be pasted on the back of each illustration, to eliminate any possibility of confusion.

The approximate location of each chart, graph, drawing, or photograph should be indicated in the left margin of the manuscript. The illustrations should be numbered on their backs to correspond to the caption. When numbering photographs, care must be taken to write lightly in order not to mar the right side.

All illustrations and captions should accompany the manuscript, carefully packed with cardboard to prevent them from being folded or otherwise damaged.

Bibliography. Instructions for preparing a bibliography are found in Chapter 21.

Index. The index of a book is made after galleys have been corrected and page proofs come from the printer; *see* Chapter 23.

Proofreading. After the final typing, the manuscript must be carefully proofread before it is submitted for consideration. Small errors due to careless copying or failure to check the source might spoil the chances of an otherwise promising manuscript. The omission of a word or sentence could make whole passages incomprehensible. If a manuscript has considerable technical detail, it will be helpful to have another person read aloud the correct version to ensure that the final typing is correct in all details.

Mailing the Manuscript. The pages of a manuscript should never be pinned, stapled, or clipped together. If consecutively numbered, as they should be, the pages could always be reassembled if they should get out of order.

All manuscripts should be mailed flat in a box or heavy envelope with cardboard enclosures the size of the paper to ensure protection in the mail. The author should enclose return postage if submitting the manuscript for publication, or put a self-addressed postal card in the box. The card can then be sent him for notification if the manuscript is to be picked up from the publisher or agent by messenger. The author's name and address should appear both on the title page of the manuscript and on the outside of the package.

Typewritten material must be sent by first class or third class (educational rate). The manuscript should be sent by certified mail, if not delivered by hand. If original artwork or photographs are included, the manuscript should be registered.

The original or a good copy should always be submitted to an editor or publisher. A copy of the manuscript should be retained by the author for reference and as a protection against the loss of the original.

Formal Papers. Each college and university has its preference in typing style, and some even specify the paper to be used for typing theses and dissertations. For other formal writing, detailed instructions for typing may be found in *A Manual for Writers of Term Papers, Theses, and Dissertations* by Kate L. Turabian (*see* p. 393, Modern English Usage).

CHAPTER TWENTY-ONE

Compiling a Bibliography

A bibliography is included in a book or research paper to show the reader what source material was consulted by the writer in preparing the manuscript. Although footnotes give credit to the work being quoted, a list of books, magazine articles, and newspaper stories or even letters, pamphlets, and interviews reveals the extent of the author's research and preparation for his present work. In a very full bibliography the author may not have read all the works listed, but he is likely to be aware of the general contents of each and includes only what is applicable to his subject and general approach.

There are, of course, varying degrees of completeness in bibliographies. The simplest kind would include only books or magazine articles that have been listed in footnotes in the work. A somewhat more detailed bibliography would also list each publication the author has examined and been influenced by to some degree. A really exhaustive bibliography might be almost a book in itself, listing every item of any relevance that the author has turned up in the course of his research.

The most useful bibliography for general purposes is the somewhat detailed type, which includes only material actually examined and used by the author. It permits the interested reader to locate the original sources and read them himself.

The forms used for entries in a bibliography may differ in details, such as capitalization and punctuation of titles and of authors' names, the order of listing the various parts, and punctuation between the parts. However, the data to be included always consist of three basic parts: (1) the author's name, (2) the title of the work, and (3) the facts of publication—place, publisher, and date (in the case of periodical articles, the name, date, and paging of the magazine). Once a style of listing is decided upon, it should be followed consistently.

The style recommended here is mainly based on the *Manual of Style* and Cecil B. Williams's revision of *A Research Manual* (Harper & Row). A basic entry would be:

Allen, Robert G. Creating Wealth. New York: Simon and Schuster, 1983.

Author. Enter the author's last name first, followed by the given name or names or initials. Write out a single given name, as in Ehrlich, Blake. In the case of Churchill, Winston Spencer, the name might also be given as Churchill, W. S., or Churchill, Winston S. Titles or degrees should be omitted. If the entry requires more than one line, indent these so that the author's name will stand out clearly.

If there are two authors, use both names (surnames first) connected by *and*: Robb, David M., and Garrison, J. J. If there are three or more authors, use the name mentioned first on the title page, followed by *and others*: Benton, Clarence E., and others.

When listing more than one work by the same author, do not repeat the name but use a long dash (three-em dash) to represent it as follows:

Collier, Jesse. Fundamentals of Shipbuilding. New York: W. W. Norton & Co., 1980.
———. Landlubbers Aboard. New York: Harper & Row, Inc., 1979.

Collections. A compilation of plays, stories, essays, or poems by several authors should be entered under the name of the editor or compiler; as, Maxton, Emory, ed.

A collection of letters, papers, and so forth, that have been edited is listed according to the author's name, followed by the title and the name of the editor: as, Hamilton, Alexander. The Papers of Alexander Hamilton, ed. Harold C. Syrett and Jacob E. Cooke.

Publications or Organizations. Books issued by an association or reports of a business firm should be entered under the name of the association or firm responsible for the publication.

The Child Study Association of America. Annual Report. New York, 1985.
Optics, Inc. Seeing Is Believing. Brownsville, Vt., 1982.

Government Publications. Books issued by a department of a government should be entered under the name of the country, followed by the name of the department issuing such material.

United States Government Printing Office. Manual of Foreign Languages. 1984. Smithsonian Institution. Annual Report. Washington, 1987.

No Author Named. Reference works, such as encyclopedias and yearbooks, and anonymous classics are entered under their titles.

Encyclopaedia Britannica Who's Who in America
Grove's Dictionary of Music and Bhagavad-Gita
   Musicians

Title. List the title exactly as it occurs on the title page. The chief words in titles may be capitalized (*see* p. 65, Capitalization, paragraph 55); as, Guide to Understanding World Affairs. Underscore the title in typing, to indicate italics. If a subtitle follows, separate it from the title by a colon and do not underline the subtitle; as Bits: Their History, Use, and Misuse.

Editions. If the work in question is other than the first edition, this information should be included, following the title: Guide to Reference Books, 7th ed.; The Shaping Years, Rev. ed.

Place, Publisher, Date. This information may be given in various ways, but it is customary to give the place name first, the publisher's name next, and the year of publication last. If the place is not a known publishing center or the best-known city of that name, include the state or country: London, Ont.; Berlin, N.H.

The facts of publication generally appear on the title page, but the copyright date is given on the page following the title page. The latest date of copyright is the one to list in the bibliography, since earlier dates refer to previous publications of material included in the present book. If more than one city is given as the place of publication, the first named is usually the home office of the publisher and should be used in the entry.

No publisher, no date. On occasion no publisher's name or date of publication can be discovered. This lack can be noted as *n.p.* for "no publisher found" or *n.d.* for "no date given."

Hiler, Hilaire. From Nudity to Raiment. London: Simpkin Marshall, n.d.

Unpublished Material. Bibliographies often include unpublished sources of various kinds: theses for academic degrees, letters, personal interviews, speeches, radio and television interviews. These sources should be adequately identified and are listed under the name of the writer or speaker. Following are some examples.

Flexner, Abraham. Letter to the author, November 15, 1956.
Harrington, Donald. Sermon at Community Church, New York, December 5, 1965.
McKinney, Stewart B., on WNLK Morning Show, September 4, 1986.
Marton, Margaret G. "Literacy in the Virgin Islands." Unpublished Master's thesis, University of Montana, 1986. 185 pp.

Periodicals. If the source is a periodical, the information is given in the same order as for a book: author, title, facts of publication. However, the titles of articles or short stories are given in quotes, not underscored, and the facts of publication are handled somewhat differently. The name of the magazine or newspaper is stated first, then the volume number, then in parentheses the date of the issue, and last the pages covered by the article or story. The volume number and date may be found on the cover of a periodical or with the statement of ownership or on the contents page.

Cloonan, James B. "The Worth of Voting Rights," American Association of Individual Investors Journal, Vol. VII, No. 5 (May, 1985), p. 31.
Russell, George. "Manic Market," Time, Vol. 128, No. 19 (November 10, 1986), pp. 64–70.

The name of the periodical is underlined to indicate italics. Note that the place of publication is not given in the case of periodicals.

In entries that include a newspaper reference, the name of the city is not ordinarily considered part of the name of a newspaper and is not underscored.

Los Angeles Times   White Plains Reporter-Dispatch
Exceptions: The Times (London),
   The New York Times

The page reference is not given for newspaper entries, except for a signed article or editorial or within a special section such as a Sunday magazine or book review section.

Schumer, Fran. "Lovers, Enemies and Other Dedicatees," New York Times Book Review, September 28, 1986, pp. 1, 38–39.

When citing unsigned articles from newspapers or magazines, list first the title of the article and then the usual credit.

"Are Your Exercises a Waste of Time?" Redbook, Vol. 167, No. 6 (October, 1986), pp. 148–149.
"Tornado Wipes Out Camp Meeting." St. Louis Post-Dispatch, September 14, 1962.

Legal References. Citations of legal documents and publications must follow standard forms. A case citation should indicate what court decided the case, either in the name of the report or in parentheses with the date.

United States v. Whiteside, 5 U.S.C.M.A. 541, 13 C.M.R. 97 (1962)
Henry v. Blanton, 254 N.Y. Supp. 889 (App. Div. 1959)

For correct form in citing statutes, see *A Uniform System of Citation,* 14th ed., pp. 24–25. This booklet also lists general style rules for legal work in more detail than in the *GPO Style Manual;* annual supplements are published.

Punctuation. Periods are used after the name of the author, after the title of the book, after the date, after the number of pages and after the price (when given). A period also follows each abbreviation.

Commas are used to separate the names of authors, when more than one name is given; after the place of publication; and after the name of the publisher. In citing periodicals, a comma is used after the name of a publication to separate it from the volume number.

Commoner, Barry. "Nature Under Attack." The Columbia University Forum, Vol. XI, No. 1 (Spring, 1968), pp. 17–22.

A colon may be used instead of a comma following the place of publication or to separate a title from the subtitle.

Use no punctuation between a volume number and the date.

Reading Lists

The secretary may be asked to prepare a reading list. If all the material is readily available in the local library, the addresses of publishers need not be included. If books or periodicals must be ordered, however, it will be useful to include both the mailing addresses of little-known publishers and the price.

Each entry should list the name of the author, the title of the article or book, and the facts of publication in the style outlined above. It is preferable to separate books from periodicals in the reading list. The mailing addresses of periodicals may be grouped at the end of the list to avoid repetition and to simplify the entries. A sample reading list follows.

The Uniform Marital Property Act

Books

Card, Emily. Staying Solvent—A Comprehensive Guide to Equal Credit for Women. New York: Holt, Rinehart and Winston, 1985. $15.95.

Follis, Anne Bowen. I'm Not a Woman's Libber—But. Nashville: Abingdon, Parthenon Press, 1981. $8.75.

Reppy, William A., Jr., and Samuel, Cynthia A. Community Property in the United States, 2nd ed. Charlottesville, Va.: The Michie Company, 1982. $25.00.

Takas, Marianne. Child Support: A Complete, Up-to-Date Authoritative Guide to Tackling the System and Winning. New York: Harper & Row, Inc., 1985. $12.45.

Periodicals

"Yours, Mine, Ours." Consumer Reports, Vol. 51 (January, 1986), pp. 48–50.

Gerd, A. "When Money Comes Between Couples." Redbook, Vol. 164 (January, 1985), pp. 42–43.

Graham, Janis, and others. "Sylvia Porter: Wives & Husbands' Credit." Good Housekeeping, Vol. 201 (November, 1985), pp. 56–88.

Nelson, S. "For Richer—for Poorer." Nation's Business, Vol. 73 (September, 1985), pp. 24–26.

Rhoads, S. R. "Getting Credit When Credit Is Due—the New Legal Options for Women." Vogue, Vol. 175 (April, 1985), pp. 175–177.

Willis, C. "One Marriage, Two Checkbooks." Money, Vol. 14 (December, 1985), pp. 106–109.

CHAPTER TWENTY-TWO

Proofreading

Proofreading requires accuracy, alertness, and judgment. Errors should be carefully sought out and corrected in the first reading. You should be familiar with commonly accepted marks of proofreading and with their actual use on proofs.

Kinds of Proofs

Galley proofs, about the length of a newspaper column, are the first proofs made by the printer. They are usually revised and cleared of all apparent errors before being sent to the author.

An author's proofs are those corrected and revised from the first galley proofs and sent to him for correction.

Page proofs are those made from the galley proofs as they are to appear in regular page form. These should be corrected with great care, as any changes are at additional cost. The proofreader should observe closely the headings, subheads, numbering of pages, footnotes, and other parts of the page to be sure that all are correct.

After corrections have been made by the author on the page proofs, the pages are then locked up for the press.

The plate proof is the final proof furnished to the publisher but not usually sent to the author.

Marks Used in Correcting Proofs

Standardized marks and instructions to the printer are used in correcting galley or page proofs. On proofs, notations of some of these are written in the margins beside the line in which the change or correction is to be made, as well as marked in the text.

The same or equivalent marks are used in proofreading or correcting typed manuscripts; these are written within the text immediately above or below the line, without marginal notations.

Following are the marks used in correcting galley proofs or page proofs, with the equivalent used in the text and in manuscripts in parentheses:

℈	delete (cross out)
℈	delete and close up
∧	caret, to indicate where insertion is to be made
stet	let it stand; change was wrong (. . . . . dots below line)
☐	indent one em
⊂⊃	join together; no space
⊏	bring matter to the left
⊐	bring matter to the right
#	make a space
space out	move words farther apart
¶	make a paragraph
no ¶	run on without paragraph indentation (connecting line)
tr.	transpose ( )
l.c.	lowercase, i.e., not capital (/)
√ √ √	space words evenly
rom.	use roman type (circle word)
ital.	use italic type (_____ underscore)
w.f.	wrong type font—size or style
‖	type is uneven at sides of the page; align it
═══	type is uneven within the line; straighten it
×	broken letter
⊓	raise word or letter
⊔	lower word or letter
⊙	period
,	apostrophe
,/,	comma
=	hyphen
"/"	quotation marks
'/'	single quotation marks

(/)	parentheses
[/]	brackets
$\frac{\vert}{M}$	em dash (—)
$\not{\hat{N}}$	en dash (-)
$\not{V}$	superscript (number or letter)
caps	capital letters ($\equiv$)
s.c.	small capitals ($=$)
$\sim\!\sim\!\sim$	boldface (heavy) type
$\downarrow$	push down lead
sp.	spell out
] [	center

General Directions for Proofreading

1. Read all proofs slowly, letter by letter, in order to detect every error.
2. Read through the proof several times with a definite point in view. Consider carefully the punctuation, correct usage, typographical errors, general alignment, spacing, general effect.
3. Make all corrections in a color contrasting with that used by the professional proofreader.
4. Put all corrections in the margin near the word marked. If several are made, place them in the order of their occurrence with a slanting line between them; as, *w.f./tr./s.c./*.
5. Do not erase a correction made that you have found unnecessary. Draw a line through the correction and write *stet*, which means *let it stand*. If necessary, rewrite a correction.
6. Underline three times a word or words to be written in large capitals and write *caps* in the margin; underline twice to indicate small capitals and write *s.c.* in the margin.
7. When a word is incorrectly capitalized, draw a line through the letter and write *l.c.* in the margin to indicate "lowercase."
8. Underline a word once to indicate that it is to be italicized, and write *ital.* in the margin.
9. Place a circle in the margin around a period or colon to be inserted. To indicate a comma write ,/ or , ; to indicate an apostrophe write ' ; to indicate quotation marks write " "
10. To indicate that a word or expression should be removed draw a line through the word or expression and write in the margin the sign $\mathcal{S}$ (dele), which means *take out*.

11. Write in the margin all new material to be inserted and indicate by caret (∧) where it is to be placed.
12. Write in the margin a double hyphen (=) to show that a hyphen is to be placed where indicated by a caret sign.
13. Use the sign # to indicate that more space is needed where indicated by the caret.
14. Use the sign ⌣ to indicate that space between letters of words is to be eliminated.
15. Answer all queries made by the printer's proofreader. To indicate your approval, cross out the question mark and allow the correction to stand. To show disapproval of the correction suggested, cross out the question or answer it in full.

Proof Showing Corrections

cap

ADDRESS AT GETTYSBURG

Fourscore and seven years ago our fathers brought forth on this continent a new nation, conceived in liberty, and dedicated to the proposition that all men are created equal. Now we are engaged in a great civil war, testing whether that nation or any nation so conceived and so dedicated, can long endure. We are met on a great battlefield of that war. We have come to dedicate a portion of that field as a final resting-place for those who here here gave their lives that that Nation might live. it is altogether fitting and proper that we *should* do this.

But, in a larger sense we cannot dedicate—we cannot consecrate we cannot hallow this ground The brave men, living and dead, who struggled here, have consecrated it far above our poor power to add or detract. The world will little note nor long remember what we here say, but it can never forget what they did here. It is for us, the living, rather, to be dedicated here to the unfinished work which they who fought

(Address at the dedication of the Gettysburg National Cemetery, Nov. 19, 1863. Reprinted, by permission of The Macmillan Publishing Company, from Abraham Lincoln, the Man, the People, by Norman Hapgood.)

Corrected Proof

ADDRESS AT GETTYSBURG

Fourscore and seven years ago our fathers brought forth on this continent a new nation, conceived in liberty, and dedicated to the proposition that all men are created equal.

Now we are engaged in a great civil war, testing whether that nation, or any nation so conceived and so dedicated, can long endure. We are met on a great battlefield of that war. We have come to dedicate a portion of that field as a final resting-place for those who here gave their lives that that nation might live. It is altogether fitting and proper that we should do this.

But, in a larger sense, we cannot dedicate—we cannot consecrate—we cannot hallow—this ground. The brave men, living and dead, who struggled here, have consecrated it far above our poor power to add or detract. The world will little note nor long remember what we say here, but it can never forget what they did here. It is for us, the living, rather, to be dedicated here to the unfinished work which they who fought here

(*Address at the dedication of the Gettysburg National Cemetery, Nov. 19, 1863*. Reprinted, by permission of THE MACMILLAN PUB-LISHING COMPANY, from "Abraham Lincoln, the Man of the People," by Norman Hapgood.)

CHAPTER TWENTY-THREE

Making an Index

The purpose of an index is to provide a means of ready reference. If the indexer is not the author, he or she must read the book carefully before attempting to prepare the index. Not only names and topics used in the book but cross-references and sometimes terms not given in the book must be included, so that as many approaches to a subject as possible are provided. The usefulness of an index depends upon the good judgment of the indexer.

Preparation of an index involves a series of procedures carried out systematically. The following directions will serve as a guide.

1. The first step is to read the page proofs carefully, from beginning to end, so that the entire work is understood and the indexer becomes familiar with the substance of the book and the terms and names used.

2. Next, starting with Chapter 1, underline all subjects suitable for entries, including subentries and in general any topic the indexer considers useful. The weeding out of unnecessary entries will be done later. It is easier to cover too many subjects than to be obliged to start over because an important category has been omitted. When an idea should be included, a short name for it may have to be supplied and can be written in the left margin at this time. Continue through all the proofs, reading through the entire text. (Appendices are not generally indexed.)

376

3. Entries should include all important subjects, chapter headings having a general meaning, subheads, and the names of most persons, places, countries, books, organizations, and so forth, unless they have only a passing interest. Adjectives should not be used as entries, but sometimes an adjective phrase used as a noun may be; as, *public opinion, natural science, gold rush.*

4. Abbreviations used throughout a book may be used as entries; as, *NASA* or *XIX Corps.* (In alphabetizing, such entries are treated as if spelled out.) Terms used less often may be spelled out with the abbreviation in parentheses after the entry: Space Technology Laboratories (STL).

Do not abbreviate *Professor, Senator, Company,* and so forth, in the index. The names of states may be abbreviated in subentries.

If reference is made to a footnote, state the entry as follows: University of Colorado, 21 *n.*

Use *f.* following a given page number to refer to material continued on the following page. Use *ff.* to refer to what follows on several pages.

    coal mines, 31 *f.*
    secession, 129 *ff.*

5. Headings that are too general are almost useless. Such an entry as *Wars,* with *American Revolution, Civil War,* and so on, listed under it would require too many subheads. It is preferable to enter each war separately and to cross-index from the general term; as, *Wars, see name of war.* Some special subjects might present exceptions, but the indexer should always be as specific as possible.

6. Page numbers alone have little or no value for the reader. Wherever possible, subdivide an entry rather than list more than five or six page numbers. Words from the text will usually suggest subentries, or the indexer may supply appropriate terms.

Poor:
Hooker, General Joseph, 20, 65–66, 67–68, 93–97, 138–139, 144–156, 161–166, 167, 255, 260, 262, 386

Preferred:
Hooker, General Joseph, 65–66, 386; at Chancellorsville, 144–156; and Chattanooga campaign, 255, 260, 262; as Commander of Army of the Potomac, 67–68, 93–97, 138–139; at Fredericksburg, 20; and Gettysburg campaign, 161–166; relieved of command, 167

7. Avoid using more than one indentation under the main heading. Never use more than two. Change the subentry and use others so that the reader can more readily locate the reference desired.

Poor:	*Preferred:*
California, 111, 167, 403	California, 111, 167, 403
preprimary endorsements, 353	civil rights, 158
rights, civil, 158	preprimary endorsements, 353
water, 112	real estate taxes, 349
taxes, real estate, 349	sales tax, 113
sales, 113	school taxes, 129
school, 129	water rights, 112

8. Using 3-by-5-inch index cards, write each entry near the top, starting at the left, with a comma after the entry and followed by the page number or numbers. Use whole numbers; as, *123–124,* not *123–4.*

Place the most important word first, as, *Water, conserving,* not *Conserving water;* or *Equity, loss of,* not *Loss of equity.* Use a separate card for each entry and subentry unless a chapter is brief and the material fairly simple. Otherwise, cross-referencing might be overlooked and important entries omitted.

A separate entry is made for each individual's name:

Roosevelt, Anna Eleanor, 126
Roosevelt, Franklin Delano, 155–167

9. Cross-index as needed, using *see* or *see also.* To conserve space, the page numbers are placed with the entry most likely to be sought by a reader, with the *see* following the less common term. *See also* is used when actual page references have been given and additional information is found under another entry.

Nazis, 63–73, 87
  See also Fascists
Russia, *see* Soviet Union

Cross-indexing may also include references to related material, as:

Furniture, *see* Chairs, Sofas,
  Tables, *etc.*

10. Sort the cards and arrange alphabetically. Subentries in a biog-

raphy or history may be arranged either chronologically or alphabetically, but the latter is more usual in the United States.

In alphabetizing, ignore the words *and, as, at, by, for, from, in, of, to, with,* and so forth, when used as the first word of a subentry.

Democracy, in Asia, 33
    background of American, 27–33
    basic principles of, 4–20, 86–87
    civilian command in, 65
    and civilization, 64
    and Communists, 4
    dispersal of power in, 89
    in Greece, 63
    as way of life, 283

In general follow the principles of alphabetizing, on pp. 320–327.

During the sorting, the indexer should watch carefully for possible omissions of page numbers or cross-references.

An example of an index in the chronological manner follows.

Connecticut: protests stamp tax, 254, 270–271; export trade, 457–458
Continental Army: John Adams moves for in Congress, 526–528; voted by Congress, 529–533; generals leave for North, 534; Congress provides for, 536–537; difficulties of building, 543–544, 546, 549–550; dysentery epidemic, 545; growth and influence of, 577
Continental Association, 496–498, 501, 503; opposition to, 505–506, 509–510

11. Consolidate all page numbers for each entry on one card. If slightly different terms for the same idea have been used as subentries, choose the best term and use that. Tighten the index as much as possible by eliminating entries that prove to be of small significance.

12. Type the index from the cards on 8½-by-11-inch bond paper, double-spacing throughout. It is essential that all cards be in the desired order (subentries either alphabetical or chronological). Before typing, the indexer or typist should find out from the editor or person in charge of the publication the number of pages and

the number of lines allotted to the index in the publication. The number of lines will determine whether the index should be typed full width on the page or half-width (for two columns). An index in two columns is the more usual form, and in typing, the length of the line should not exceed thirty-five characters.

The run-on style may be used, in which the entry word is typed (capitalized) at the left and subentries follow on the same line, with continuation indented two spaces: *see* example in **6**. Or each subentry may be typed (indented two spaces) on a separate line, for easier reference, if space permits: *see* example in **7**. In this case, continuation is indented four spaces.

13. After the index is typed, check it against the cards to catch omissions or errors in typing. If space is very limited, a dozen or more possible deletions may be noted by making a light pencil mark at the left of such entries.

CHAPTER TWENTY-FOUR

Taking Minutes of a Meeting

If you are regularly assigned to take the minutes of an organization, you should of course be prepared with extra pens and notepads. In general, the duties of the recording secretary are as follows:

1. To attend all meetings of the executive board and of the organization and to record their transactions in the minutes with the exact wording of each motion that was seconded, who made the motion, and whether it was lost or carried;

2. To keep the minutes of all meetings and to read the minutes of the previous meeting at the general meeting;

3. To see that the president is provided with a copy of the minutes of the last meeting at least one week before the next meeting and, if requested, to provide an agenda for the president;

4. To file all reports with dates and signatures of the committee chairmen or officers making the reports;

5. To record and file the names and addresses of all members and of standing committees and special committees with their chairmen;

6. To bring a copy of the constitution, bylaws, and standing rules to each meeting for reference and, in some organizations, to bring minutes of the past year's meetings as well;

7. In the absence of the president and the vice president, to call the meeting to order and to conduct it until a temporary chairman is appointed;

8. At the end of the year to present a report of the year's work if the organization so requires.

Preparation of Minutes. Minutes are records of meetings and of the action taken in them. They are written by the recording secretary of the organization or, in the case of a committee or workshop, by a committee member who agrees to act as the secretary. Minutes are often consulted in confirmation of an action, as a source of information, or as records. They must therefore be written accurately, clearly, and concisely.

Because keeping the minutes of an organization is so important, you should make full notes of *all* business transactions of a meeting. When the minutes are prepared, you will omit mention of discussions on which no action was taken as well as irrelevant discussion. Meetings often fail to follow the prepared agenda, and therefore you must sift your notes and record only the actual events of the meeting. The full notes should be preserved in case a question regarding the minutes arises later on.

The language of minutes is formal and follows traditional lines. Generally, definite forms are used and strictly observed. Minutes often conform to the following order, although not all organizations make use of the complete list.

Name of body holding meeting
Type of meeting (regular, annual, special, etc.)
Time, date, and place
Name of presiding officer
Names or number of those present
Approval of previous minutes
Unfinished business and reports of committees of investigation
Action taken on unfinished business; digest of business pending
New business, such as motions both lost and approved. Those
    withdrawn without vote may be omitted. Names of the pro-
    posers of all main motions should be given.
Date of next meeting
Adjournment and time of adjournment
Approval and signature of minutes

Tone of the Minutes. You should prepare the minutes as soon as possible after the meeting has been adjourned, while you can recall details of discussion and the background of what may be hastily written notes. The tone of the minutes should be objective, without adjectives expressing personal opinion (such as an "inspiring" address, an "interesting" meeting, a "delightful" hour). The minutes should be typed, with a copy for the president's use.

Distribution of the Minutes. In the case of meetings of executive committees and other small groups, it is often desirable to have the minutes duplicated and circulated before the next meeting. When this is to be done, the minutes should first be presented to the presiding officer for a check of their accuracy and completeness. They may then be duplicated for distribution to all committee members. Thus absent members are informed of actions taken at the last meeting, each member is reminded of the job he or she undertook, and an impression of the activity and efficiency of the group is given. The report is more likely to be read while the meeting is still fresh in everyone's mind. If errors in the minutes are discovered, corrections can be made immediately and distributed to all or announced at the following meeting.

All members thus have time to think over the discussions and can bring useful comments and information to the next meeting. The work of the group is expedited, and there is then no need to spend time reading the minutes at the next meeting. Each member brings his or her own copy, and the minutes may be approved as distributed or as corrected.

Approval of the Minutes. When the minutes have not been distributed, they are read at the next meeting of the organization for approval. After the minutes have been read to the assembly, corrections may be suggested. If these are accepted, they should be inserted in red ink. When this is done and the minutes have been approved, they should never be changed or rewritten. The secretary should then sign his or her name, followed on the same line or on the line below by the word *Secretary* (or *Secretary pro tem* in the case of a temporary secretary). The expression *Respectfully submitted* is not used today. The word *Approved*, with the date, should be written at the left margin on the line below the signature, followed by the secretary's name and also by that of the president if the organization requires it.

Secretary's Signature. Whether married or single, you sign your first name, middle initial (if any), and surname.

Mary Ann Smith   William B. Chelminwicz

Recording Motions. The name of the person making a motion should be given in the minutes, but that of the seconder is usually omitted. Whether the motion was carried, lost, referred to a committee, or tabled should be recorded. A motion that is not seconded is not recorded. In some cases it may be advisable to tell how the motion was voted upon, that is, by show of hands, by standing, by voice, by ballot, or by roll call. If the vote was by ballot or by roll call, the number voting, the number for the affirmative, and the number for the negative should be stated.

Committee Reports. These may be entered in the minutes in one of the following ways, depending on the importance of the subject or on the wish of the organization.

1. A summary of the report with the name of the chairman
2. A copy of the entire report as submitted by the chairman
3. Reference to the subject of the report when the entire report is filed separately and therefore available in the files

In some organizations, committee reports are prepared in triplicate: one copy for the president, one for the recording secretary, and one for the committee records.

When a resolution contained in a report has been adopted by an organization, it should be included in the minutes exactly as it was worded.

Types of Meetings. The following types of meetings will be found recorded in minutes of organizations: regular, special, annual, and possibly adjournments of one or more of these. The examples given illustrate the form and phraseology that may be used in the minutes of such meetings.

Regular Meetings

In the following example, sideheads giving the subject of each paragraph make it easy to locate each item of business given in the minutes.

The regular meeting of the Pleasant Valley Civic Association was called to order by Andrew Nash, president, at 2:30 P.M. on February 20, 19—, at the Chamber of Commerce, forty-three members being present.

Correction of Minutes

Following the roll call, the minutes of the meeting of January 24 were read. Priscilla Rankin called attention to the fact that the name of the speaker was Amelia Howe, not Amelia Howell. The minutes were approved as corrected.

Treasurer's Report

The report of the treasurer, showing a balance of $2,875.23, was read and placed on file.

Hospital Landscaping Appropriation

Charles White, chairman of the Hospital Beautification Committee, reported that a plan for landscaping the hospital grounds had been submitted on February 6 by John Briggs of the Greenway Landscape Company. This plan called for the planting of 10 trees and 8 shrubs at a cost of $1,800. Mr. White then asked for an appropriation from the association to cover the cost of this project. Alexander Lawson moved that the sum of $1,800 be appropriated. The motion was seconded and carried.

City Planning Committee

It was moved by Alice Graham and duly seconded that a committee be appointed to work with the City Commissioners on City Planning. Action on the motion was postponed until the next meeting.

Annexation of Goodwin Estates

Ralph Hadley moved that the association go on record as opposed to the annexation of Goodwin Estates to the city of Pleasant Valley. The motion was seconded. A standing vote was taken, resulting in 6 affirmative, 37 negative. The motion was declared lost.

Address by Horace Blake

Horace Blake, city manager, addressed the meeting on the importance of city planning. He was accorded a vote of thanks for his presentation of the subject.

The meeting was adjourned at 4:15 P.M.

Harriet Jackson
Secretary

Approved March 20, 19—, Harriet Jackson, Secretary

Special Meeting

A special meeting of the Pleasant Valley Civic Association was held at the Chamber of Commerce at 2:30 P.M. on March 10, 19—, with Andrew Nash, president, in the chair. Fifty-six members were present.

Mr. Nash reported that the following notice, in accordance with the bylaw requirements was mailed to every member of the Association on March 5: "Notice is hereby given that a meeting of all members of the association will be held on March 10 at 2:30 at the Chamber of Commerce for the purpose of determining what action the association wishes to take regarding the proposed recreation center on the plot of land between Magnolia Avenue on the east, Lakeview Road on the west, Glencoe Street on the north, and French Boulevard on the south."

Thalia Wentworth read the following resolution and moved its adoption:

WHEREAS, converting the plot of land between Magnolia Avenue on the east, Lakeview Road on the west, Glencoe Street on the north, and French Boulevard on the south would depreciate the property in the neighborhood, and

WHEREAS, land bordering on a busy thoroughfare, such as French Boulevard, is not suitable or safe for a recreation center, therefore

RESOLVED, That it is the sense of the Pleasant Valley Civic Association that this plot of land shall not be converted into a recreation center, and

BE IT FURTHER RESOLVED, That this resolution be spread upon the minutes of the association and a copy be sent to the Mayor.

The motion was seconded and carried.

On motion of Florence Merrill, the meeting was adjourned at 3:10 P.M.

HARRIET JACKSON, Secretary

Minutes in Report Style. Traditionally written minutes are prepared for a legal record or to fulfill formal requirements. Many groups do not require this form of minutes and would actually benefit from a newer kind, written in the style of a report or a news story. A chronological record of a meeting can be made for the benefit of those who feel it is the only proper form, but with it can be sent a report of the meeting, which will be more readable and may contain more information because it is not confined to the standard format. If the members find the report more useful, the traditional minutes may not be needed. The secretary does not propose the change, but another member may do so.

In the report type of minutes, the order is rearranged. The decisions reached, the actions taken, the plans that have been made, and the projects undertaken are listed first, followed by enough of the discussion concerned with these steps to enable absent members to understand what occurred.

The president can readily prepare an agenda from report-style minutes, with such a list of the accomplishments of the previous meeting.

Unless there is a particular requirement for formal minutes, the report style can be used for minutes of meetings of executive boards and for committee meetings as well. They require more skill in summarizing, but their added usefulness should recommend them to recording secretaries as well as to the membership.

Following are examples of report-style minutes.

Annual Meeting

At the annual meeting of the Friends of the Longworth Public Library, held May 16, 19__, in the Memorial Room of the Library, President Nathan Atkins welcomed the gathering of more than seventy-five members. He explained the purpose of the Friends of the Library and the ways in which membership dues are used. He then presented a résumé of the past year's activities.

Programs of 19__–19__ Season

Some of the programs that have been initiated or continued by the Friends are as follows:

Lending Library of Phonograph Records and Video Cassettes
Lending Library of Reproductions of Paintings and Sculpture
Continuation of the Children's Summer Reading Program
Continuation (for the fifth year) of the Drama Group
"Meet the Author Night" with Ms. Jane Bronson, noted lawyer and writer
Spring Production: Actor Lawrence Ringgold in an evening of readings

Treasurer's Report (attached)

Membership Dues

A motion was made by Marshall Collins that the $5.00 membership fee be abolished so that in future the lowest membership fee will be $10.00. The motion was seconded and carried.

Officers for 19__–19__

George Flandrau, Chairman of the Nominating Committee, presented the following slate of officers for the coming year:

President: Frank G. Boardman
1st Vice President: Flora Button

2nd Vice President: Cheryl Flint
Recording Secretary: Edward Flougel
Corresponding Secretary: Anne Nylander
Treasurer: Harkness P. Stevens
Nominating Committee: Lester B. Frink, Chairman
                             Joyce Silvers, George M. Riley

Nelson Dillingworth moved that the election be by voice. The motion was seconded and carried unanimously. Robert Keyser moved that the slate presented by the Nominating Committee be declared elected. This motion was seconded and carried unanimously. Mr. Atkins then declared the slate elected. He congratulated the new officers and turned the meeting over to Mr. Boardman, who took the Chair as the new President.

Speaker of the Evening

William Adelson, Program Chairman, introduced the speaker of the evening, Dr. Brooks Stringfellow of the Museum of Natural History. Dr. Stringfellow spoke on conquering the sea, describing the possibilities of deriving protein from tropical fish, ranching on the ocean floor, extracting minerals from the water, and describing his own experiences as a scuba diver.

A short discussion period followed the talk, and the meeting was adjourned at 11 P.M.

> Helen J. Blackwell
> Recording Secretary

Minutes of Directors' and Committee or Workshop Meetings. Most boards of directors and committees keep minutes of their meetings, both as a record of the discussions and for the information of absent members. Keeping the minutes may be the job of one of the newer members, who will probably have fewer comments to make than the more experienced participants. Keeping accurate notes can prevent the secretary from taking an active part in the discussions, but it is good training for a new member. Learning to take good notes helps to focus on the main issues and the actual accomplishments of a meeting. When you are sifting your notes to write the minutes, you will find that many of the comments had little to do with the topic under discussion.

Minutes of committee or workshop meetings need not and should not resemble a tape recording of all that was said. Useful minutes record the principal subjects discussed, the conclusions reached, and the assignments given to each member of the group.

Sometimes a meeting comes to a close without a vote being taken or any definite summary of the discussion being made by the leader. In such cases, the manner of expressing in the minutes what was discussed may suggest the beginning of the next meeting. The general agreement felt by the committee members will be implied, so that at the following meeting they need not go over the same ground again.

(1)

The Board of Trustees of the Millerville Union Church met in the Parish House at 8:15 P.M. on April 21, 19___. Present were Lloyd Barbell, John Coxeter, Martha Crawford, Marijke Maarten, Henry Peterson, Richard Pillsbury, Stephen Slater, Frederic Waggoner, Walter Walters, Kenneth Wilson, and Rev. Franklin Lawrence. Absent: Marvin Klinger.

Election of Officers

Mr. Slater, last year's vice president, served as temporary chairman and opened nominations for secretary for the Board of Trustees for the coming year. Mr. Waggoner nominated Mrs. Crawford. The nomination was seconded. There were no further nominations, and she was elected unanimously.

Mr. Peterson nominated Mr. Walters for president. The nomination was seconded, and Mr. Walters was elected unanimously.

Mr. Barbell nominated Mr. Wilson for vice president. Mr. Wilson's nomination was seconded, and he was elected unanimously.

Mr. Coxeter nominated Mr. Pillsbury for treasurer. The nomination was seconded, and there were no further nominations. He was elected unanimously.

As president for the coming year Mr. Walters conducted the remainder of the meeting.

Assistant Treasurer's Post Eliminated

Mr. Pillsbury stated that he would like to eliminate the post of assistant treasurer and handle both incoming and outgoing funds himself. If the job becomes burdensome, he will call for assistance. This procedure was approved by the trustees.

Responsibilities of Committee Chairmen

Mr. Wilson asked what procedure was followed and who was responsible for obtaining committee chairmen. On being informed that this was a Board function, Mr. Wilson suggested that the Board reexamine its responsibility for the purpose of delegating more work, thus leaving the Board free for more discussion and communication with the various committees.

Board to Get Copies of Bylaws and Charter

Mr. Barbell recommended that each Board member receive a copy of the bylaws and charter. Mrs. Crawford will obtain copies and distribute them.

Proposal for Reviewing Past Discussions of Policy

Mrs. Maarten suggested an agenda item for the next meeting: The Board will reopen and review past discussions on policy matters.

The next meeting was set for Monday, May 19, 19__ at the Parish House at 8:15 P.M. The meeting was adjourned at 10:30 P.M.

Martha Crawford, Secretary

Approved as Circulated: May 19, 19__, Martha Crawford, Secretary

(2)

The Housing Workshop of the Dunston League of Women Voters met in the Parish House of the Dunston Union Church at 8:30 P.M. on December 3, 19—, with twenty-five members and six visitors present.

The following actions were taken:

A subcommittee was formed to investigate housing surveys made by other Leagues.

A project was undertaken to study local housing in a limited area and to publish the findings in dramatic fashion.

Housing Workshop Chairman Marianna Marlow presided and discussed briefly the aims of the Workshop, namely, to study conditions in Dunston with a view to drawing the attention of the public to the large number of substandard dwellings now in use. She will appear at the village hearing on rent supplements on December 10 to state that in general the position of the Dunston League of Women Voters is that rent supplements are at present desirable in Dunston due to the lack of alternative housing.

After discussion of possible studies by several members, Margaret Opel suggested the intensive study of some rundown block or area. Terry Topliff emphasized that such preparation would be needed before any visits could be made to tenants—not only of workshop members but of the public—to explain the purpose and reasons for questions and interviews.

A committee to investigate the methods of other leagues that have conducted similar surveys was named: Daphne Shoup and Margaret Opel will secure and sift data from national and state organizations of the LWV, including information about how the investigation was set up, what questions were asked, in what order, how the groundwork was laid beforehand, how the area was selected, etc. Mrs. B. Greenaway of Blackbury will be consulted by M. Marlow about the experience of the Blackbury League in making a survey in that town. Pat Carswell will contact Glenn Raymond, chairman of Somerset Housing Council. Claire Jarrett will inquire into the experience of Tanglewood and North Tanglewood in surveying their housing situation. Terry Topliff will consult Mrs. Gary Fan on Jellicoe's experience in securing low-rent housing and will also get data from a Pennsylvania housing survey she once worked on. Louella Brown will get information regarding surveys from the Council on Social Agencies in Greene County and from a Stubbs College professor whom she knows. All are to secure sample interview sheets and any other pertinent material available.

The Workshop determined to engage in a project with the following aim: to study a limited area in depth in order to make the community aware of present conditions and needs and to publish our study in dramatic fashion.

Committee responsibilities assumed were as follows:

Hospitality chairman: Pat Carswell

Telephone chairman: Anne Stevenson with Mae Sanders, Dorothy Bull, Helen Dixon, and Catherine Culpepper assisting

Village Board Meeting observers: Margaret Carney, chairman, with Gloria Rasmussen and Grace Worthy assisting

The next full Workshop meeting will be on January 7, the place to be determined and the members to be notified by the telephone committee. M. Marlow will meet in the interim with the committee gathering information.

Daphne Shoup, Secretary

CHAPTER TWENTY-FIVE

Sources of Information for Secretaries

Sometimes a secretary is asked to locate information in a completely unfamiliar field. Even if you have access to a well-stocked library, you may not know how to use all its facilities. The following sources of information are offered as a beginning in your research. Of course, much more is available in your company's library or in the local public library. There are databases that you may be able to access from your computer. If possible, ask the reference librarian to make suggestions. It can save you time and provide a wide background to select from.

Unabridged Dictionaries

The American Heritage Dictionary. Boston: Houghton Mifflin Co., 1984. Abbreviations, biography, and geography in the main part of the book.

The Random House Dictionary of the English Language. New York: Random House, 1987. Abbreviations, biography, and geography listed in the main part of the book. Supplementary material: atlas of the world, gazetteer of place names, dictionaries of French, German, and Italian.

Webster's Third New International Dictionary of the English Language. Springfield, Mass.: G. & C. Merriam Co., 1971. Preliminary pages on spelling, plurals, capitalization, punctuation. Abbreviations in main alphabet.

Abridged Dictionaries

Funk & Wagnalls Standard College Dictionary. New York: Thomas Y. Crowell, 1977. Biography and geography listed in main part of book.

Webster's Ninth New Collegiate Dictionary. Springfield, Mass.: G. & C. Merriam, 1985. Abbreviations, biography, and geography listed separately.

Modern English Usage

Barnet, Sylvan. *Barnet and Stubb's Practical Guide for Writing,* 5th ed., paper. Boston: Little, Brown, 1986.

Bernstein, Theodore M. *The Careful Writer.* New York: Atheneum, 1965.

————. *Dos, Don'ts & Maybes of English Usage.* New York: Random House, 1977.

Evans, Bergen, and Evans, Cornelia. *A Dictionary of Contemporary American Usage.* New York: Random House, 1957.

Follett, Wilson. *Modern American Usage,* ed. Jacques Barzun. New York: Hill & Wang, 1966.

Fowler, H. W. *A Dictionary of Modern English Usage,* 2nd ed. Rev. by Ernest Gowers. New York: Oxford University Press, 1965.

Harvard Law Review Association. *A Uniform System of Citation,* 14th ed. Cambridge, Mass.: Harvard Law Review Association, 1986. Correct legal style.

The McGraw-Hill Style Manual. New York: McGraw-Hill Book Company, 1983.

Morris, William, and Morris, Mary. *Harper Dictionary of Contemporary Usage,* 2nd ed. New York: Harper & Row, 1985.

Safire, William. *On Language.* New York: Times Books, 1980.

Turabian, Kate L. *A Manual for Writers of Term Papers, Theses, and Dissertations,* 4th ed. Chicago: University of Chicago Press, 1973.

U.S. Government Printing Office. *Style Manual.* Washington, D.C.: Government Printing Office, 1984.

University of Chicago Press. *Chicago Manual of Style,* 13th ed. rev. Chicago: University of Chicago Press, 1982.

Zinsser, William. *On Writing Well.* New York: Harper & Row, 1980.

Synonyms and Antonyms

Roget's II: The New Thesaurus. Boston: Houghton Mifflin, 1980.

Webster's New Dictionary of Synonyms. Springfield, Mass.: G. & C. Merriam Co., 1984.

Special Dictionaries and Directories

American Dental Directory. Chicago: American Dental Association, 1981. Lists members of the Association, state dental organizations, and agencies, including character of practice.

American Medical Directory, 30th ed. Chicago: American Medical Association, 1986. Lists physicians in the United States and Canada, hospitals, medical societies, and colleges giving degrees in medicine.

Black's Law Dictionary, 5th ed. St. Paul, Minn.: West Publishing Company, 1979.

Black's Medical Dictionary. New York: Barnes & Noble, 1981.

Directory of Directories, 4th ed. Detroit: Gale Research Co., 1986.

Dorland's Illustrated Medical Dictionary, 26th ed. Philadelphia: W. B. Saunders Co., 1981.

Martindale-Hubbell Law Directory. Annual. Summit, N.J.: Martindale Hubbell. Lists members of the bar of the United States and Canada with law digests.

Social Services Organizations and Agencies Directory. Detroit: Gale Research Co., 1982.

Directories and Handbooks of the U.S. Government

Official Congressional Directory for the Use of the United States Congress. Washington, D.C.: Government Printing Office. Authoritative information on all legislative, judicial, and executive departments in Washington; biographical data on members of Congress and the judiciary; lists of foreign diplomatic and consular officers in the United States; lists of ranking diplomatic and consular officers in the United States Foreign Service. Revised for each session of Congress.

Official Register of the United States. United States Civil Service Commission. Lists of persons occupying administrative and supervisory positions in the legislative, executive, and judicial branches of the U.S. Government.

United States Government Organization Manual. Office of the Federal Register, National Archives and Records Service. A useful outline of the functions and personnel of the various agencies within the legislative, executive, and judicial branches with brief histories of agencies abolished or transferred since 1933. Revised annually.

Biographical Information

Concise Dictionary of Scientific Biography. New York: Charles Scribner's Sons, 1981. More than five thousand scientists included.

Contemporary Authors. New revised series. Detroit: Gale Research Co., 1987. 17 vols.

Current Biography. New York: The H. W. Wilson Co., 1940 to date. This publication gives sketches, with portraits of persons prominent in the news of the day. Monthly, with yearly cumulations.

Dictionary of American Biography. New York: Charles Scribner's Sons, 1928–1958. An important set in twenty volumes, plus index volume and supplements, containing authoritative accounts of noteworthy Americans no longer living (through 1940). *The Concise Dictionary of American Biography* (Scribner's, 1964) is a one-volume abridgment.

Dictionary of Canadian Biography. Toronto: University of Toronto, 1982, 11 vols. 1000 to 1890.

Ewen, David, ed. *Composers Since 1900.* New York: The H. W. Wilson Co., 1978.

———. *Great Composers, 1300–1900.* New York: The H. W. Wilson Co., 1966.

Kunitz, Stanley J., and Haycroft, Howard. *American Authors: 1600–1900.* New York: The H. W. Wilson Co., 1938. More than one thousand biographies and four hundred portraits.

———. *British Authors Before 1900.* New York: The H. W. Wilson Co., 1952. With 650 biographies and 200 portraits.

———. *British Authors of the Nineteenth Century.* New York: The H. W. Wilson Co., 1936. One thousand biographies and 350 portraits of authors of the British Empire, including Australia, Canada, New Zealand, and South Africa.

————. *Twentieth Century Authors.* New York: The H. W. Wilson Co., 1942. Supplement by Stanley J. Kunitz. The H. W. Wilson Co., 1955. In addition to biographies, these volumes include many portraits.

The McGraw-Hill Encyclopedia of World Biography. 12 vols. New York: McGraw-Hill Book Co., 1973.

Van Doren, C., and McHenry, R., eds. *Webster's American Biographies.* Springfield, Mass.: G. & C. Merriam Co., 1975.

Who Was Who in America. Chicago: Marquis–Who's Who, Inc. 3 vols. A biographical dictionary of persons whose names appeared in *Who's Who in America* and whose deaths occurred between 1897 and 1976.

Who's Who. London: Adam Charles Black; New York: St. Martin's Press, Inc. Annual. A biographical dictionary of notable persons in Great Britain.

Who's Who in America. Chicago: Marquis–Who's Who, Inc. Annual. A biographical dictionary of well-known contemporary men and women in America.

Who's Who in Canada. Annual. Toronto, Ont.: International Press Ltd.

Williams, E. T., and Nichols, C. S., eds. *Dictionary of National Biography.* 1961–1970. New York: Oxford University Press, 1981. The basic source for the lives of prominent persons of the British Empire and earlier eras.

Yearbooks

Canadian Almanac and Directory. Toronto, Ont.: Copp Clark Pitman, Ltd. Annual. Sections on broadcasting and communication, commerce and finance, education, geography, health and hospitals, history, tourism, and so forth. *The directory.*

CQ Almanac. Washington, D.C.: Congressional Quarterly, Inc. Covers each session of Congress. Reports on agriculture, appropriations, foreign policy, health, education, voting records, and so forth.

Information Please Almanac, Atlas and Yearbook. Boston: Houghton Mifflin. Annual. Statistics on sports, literature, theater, education, government, and so forth.

The Statesman's Year-Book. New York: St. Martin's Press. Published since 1864. Annual. Information and essential facts about political, economic, and social conditions of the world. Chronology of world events in past year.

Whitaker's Almanack. London: Whitaker, 1869 to date. Annual. Statistical data relating particularly to Great Britain.

The World Almanac. New York: Pharos Books. Annual. Facts and statistics on sports, history, current events, population, ZIP Codes, area codes, personalities, and so forth.

Educational Directories

Fiske, Edward B., and Michalak, J. M., *Best Buys in College Education.* New York: Times Books, 1985.

Lovejoy's College Guide, 15th ed. New York: Simon and Schuster, 1981. A complete reference book covering nearly three thousand American colleges and universities.

Patterson's American Education. Chicago: Educational Directories. Revised annually. Private, public, and denominational schools, with names of heads.

Atlases and Gazetteers

National Geographic Atlas of the World. Washington, D.C.: National Geographic Society, 1981.

The Statesman's Year-Book Gazetteer, 3rd ed. New York: St. Martin's Press, 1986.

Webster's New Geographical Dictionary, rev. ed. Springfield, Mass.: G. & C. Merriam Co., 1984.

New York Times Atlas of the World. New York: Times Books, 1985.

Business and Financial Guides

Business Organizations, Agencies and Publications Directory, 3rd ed. Detroit: Gale Research Co., 1986. More than twenty thousand entries. Includes banks, convention facilities, hotels/motels, information services, periodicals, and so forth.

Kelly's Manufacturer's and Merchant's Directory. London: International Publications Services. Annual.

Million Dollar Directory. Parsippany, N.J.: Dun and Bradstreet Corp. Annual listing of 160,000 U.S. businesses worth over $500,000.

Moody's Bank Finance Manual. Annual. New York: Data on three thousand American banks, as well as savings and loan associations, federal agencies, insurance company data, real estate, and so forth.

Reference Book of Corporate Managements. Parsippany, N.J.: Dun & Bradstreet. Annual. Information about corporate officers and directors of twelve thousand companies.

Standard & Poor's Register of Corporation Directors and Executives. 1928 to date. New York: Standard & Poor's. Annual data on forty-five thousand corporations, including Canadian firms. Annual sales, types of business, officers and directors, and so forth.

Thomas Register of American Manufacturers, 76th ed. New York: Thomas Publishing Company, 1986. 21 vols. Lists manufacturers classified by product, subdivided by state and city; includes trademarks, trade names, and trade associations.

Wall Street Journal Index. New York: Dow Jones & Company, Inc. Monthly. Corporate and general news, profit and dividend reports, and so forth.

The following companies offer basic and current information on corporations, stocks, and bonds: Dun & Bradstreet, Moody's Investors Service, Standard & Poor's Corporation (all with main offices in New York). Much of this information is available on online databases.

Postal Guide

United States Postal Service. *Post Office Directory* (with ZIP Codes). Available in all U.S. post offices. Annual. Lists all post offices, branch post offices, and stations, Army and Fleet post offices and stations. May be purchased for nine dollars by mail from Superintendent of Documents, U.S. Government Printing Office, Washington, DC 20402-1575, GPO Stock No. 039-000-00264-7, or at twenty-six bookstores maintained in twenty major cities, listed in the back of the directory.

Guides and Indexes to Books and Periodicals

Access. Evanston, Ill.: John Gordon Burke Publisher, Inc., 1983 to date. Covers magazines not included in *Reader's Guide* and reviews books, concerts, dance performances, and so forth. Author and subject indexes. Includes general magazines as well as regional ones.

Applied Science and Technology Index. New York: The H. W. Wilson Co., 1958 to date. Monthly. Formerly the *Industrial Arts Index* (1913–1957), this covers a wide list of engineering and technical journals.

Books in Print. Vol. I, Authors; Vol. II, Titles; Vol. III, Publishers. New York: R. R. Bowker Co., 1948 to date. Annual. Lists books available from twenty thousand American publishers.

Business Periodicals Index. New York: The H. W. Wilson Co., 1958 to date. Annual. Covers periodicals in all business and related fields.

Cumulative Book Index. New York: The H. W. Wilson Co., 1898 to date. Monthly (except August). Contains the names of all books published during the year in English; a supplement to the *United States Catalog*, which listed all books in print in 1899.

Guide to Reference Books, 10th ed. Chicago: American Library Association, 1986.

New York Times Index. New York: The New York Times Company, 1913 to date. Monthly. References to articles, events, and names recorded in *The New York Times*, with date, page, and column number.

Paperbound Books in Print. New York: R. R. Bowker Company, 1955 to date. Biannual. Indexes by title, author, and subject.

PAIS Bulletin. New York: Public Affairs Information Service, Inc. Monthly. Indexes library materials in six languages worldwide. Public policy matters, with emphasis on factual and statistical information.

Reader's Guide to Periodical Literature. New York: The H. W. Wilson Co., 1900 to date. Semimonthly. An index to cultural and scientific articles in a selected list of general magazines.

The Standard Periodical Directory. New York: Oxbridge Publishing Co., 1964 to date. Biennial. A guide to more than sixty-five thousand periodicals in the United States and Canada.

Subject Guide to Books in Print. New York: R. R. Bowker Co., 1957 to date. Annual. Follows the headings assigned by the Library of Congress. Mainly nonfiction, listed under sixty-five thousand headings plus cross-references.

Ulrich's International Periodical Directory. New York: R. R. Bowker Co., 1932 to date. Annual. Periodicals from many countries, classified by subject. Includes list of periodicals no longer published since previous edition.

Many indexes are available online as electronic databases.

Computers and Databases

Cane, Mike. *The Computer Phone Book.* New York: New American Library, paper, 1983. A guide to electronic mail, online systems, and so forth.

Directory of Online Databases. New York: Cuadra/Elsevier. 1979 to date. Quarterly. Current available information on more than three thousand databases.

Grayson, Fred N. *The Secretarial Handbook for the Modern Office.* New York: Perigee Books, 1985. Handling telecommunications; the uses of computers.

Katzan, Harry. *Office Automation: A Manager's Guide.* New York: American Management Association, 1982.

Lewell, John. *A–Z Guide to Computer Graphics.* New York: McGraw-Hill Book Company, 1985. More than 1,750 entries with information about corporations, products, terminology and techniques.

The North American Online Directory. New York: R. R. Bowker Company, 1985. Information products and services, library networks, companies, and associations.

Sippl, Charles J., and Sippl, Roger J. *Computer Dictionary and Handbook.* Indianapolis, Ind.: Howard W. Sams Co., Inc., 1981.

Webster's New World Compact Directory of Computer Terms. New York: Simon and Schuster, 1984.

Wight, Scott F., ed. *Software Reviews on File.* New York: Facts on File, Inc. 1985 to date. Monthly. A guide to choosing the right software for business, personal, or educational use.

Quotations

Bartlett, John. *Familiar Quotations.* 15th ed. Boston: Little, Brown and Co., 1980.

Flesch, Rudolf. *The New Book of Unusual Quotations,* rev. ed. New York: Harper & Row, 1966

Safire, William, and Safir, Leonard. *Good Advice.* New York: Times Books, 1982. Two thousand quotations.

Stevenson, Burton, ed. *Home Book of Quotations, Classical and Modern,* 10th ed. rev. New York: Dodd, Mead and Co., 1984.

Etiquette

Baldridge, Letitia. *The Amy Vanderbilt Complete Book of Etiquette,* rev. ed. New York: Doubleday & Co., 1978.

————. *Letitia Baldridge's Complete Guide to Executive Manners.* New York: Rawson Associates, 1985. Corporate protocol and interpersonal relations.

Post, Elizabeth, ed. *Emily Post's Etiquette,* 14th ed. New York: Harper & Row, 1984.

Business Letters and Reports

Effective Reports. New York: Barnes & Noble, 1982.

Mullins, Carolyn J. *The Complete Writing Guide to Preparing Reports, Proposals, Memos, etc.* Englewood Cliffs, N.J.: Prentice-Hall, 1980.

Nauheim, Fred. *How to Write Business Letters That Work.* New York: Van Nostrand Reinhold Co., 1982.

Poe, Roy W. *The McGraw-Hill Guide to Effective Business Reports.* New York: McGraw-Hill Book Co., 1982.

Schell, John. *Writing on the Job: A Handbook for Business and Government.* New York: New American Library, 1984.

Weaver, Patricia C. *Persuasive Writing: A Manager's Guide to Effective Letters and Reports.* New York: Free Press, 1977.

Webster's Secretarial Handbook. Springfield, Mass.: G. & C. Merriam Co., 1976.

Filing and Indexing

Diamond, Susan Z. *Records Management: A Practical Guide.* New York: American Management Association, 1983.

Finkel, LeRoy. *Data File Programming in BASIC.* New York: John Wiley and Sons, 1981. File organization. Programmed instruction.

Stewart, J. R. *Progressive Filing*. New York: McGraw-Hill Book Co., 1980.

Thomas, Violet, et al. *Filing Systems for Information Management*. New York: John Wiley and Sons, 1983.

Getting a Job

Camden, Thomas M., and Fleming-Holland, Susan. *How to Get a Job in Chicago*. Chicago: Surrey Books, 1986.

————. *How to Get a Job in Dallas–Fort Worth*. Chicago: Surrey Books, 1984.

————. *How to Get a Job in Los Angeles*. Chicago: Surrey Books, 1985.

————. *How to Get a Job in New York*. Chicago: Surrey Books, 1986.

Gowdy, Eve. *Job Hunting with Employment Agencies*. New York: Barron, 1978.

Lareau, William. *The Inside Track: A Successful Job Search Method*. Piscataway, N.J.: New Century Publishers, 1985.

Lonngrenn, Betty, and Shoff, Gloria J. *Starting Your Own Secretarial Business*. Paper. Chicago: Contemporary Books, 1982.

Salmon, Richard D. *Job Hunter's Guide to Eight Great American Cities*. Cambridge, Mass.: Brattle Publications, 1978. Paper. Also guides to job hunting in Atlanta, Rocky Mountains, the West, and the Sunbelt.

Smith, Michael H. *The Résumé Writer's Handbook*. New York: Harper & Row, 1987.

Travel Guides

Airlines

Official Airline Guide, North American edition. Oak Brook, Ill.: Official Airline Guides, Inc. Published twice monthly. All flight information for all cities in the United States, Canada, and U.S. possessions. Also gives information on the availability of car rental service or air taxi service for each city.

Official Airline Guide, Worldwide edition. Oak Brook, Ill.: Official Airline Guides, Inc. Monthly

Pocket flight guides are available, including *Frequent Flyer*, by subscription.

OAG Travel Planner Hotel/Motel Guide. Quarterly. Editions for *Official Airline Guide,* North American edition. Oak Brook, Ill.: Official Airline Guides, Inc. Published twice monthly. All flight information for all cities in the United States, Canada, and U.S. possessions. Also gives information on the availability of car rental service or air taxi service for each city. Pocket flight guides are available, including *Frequent Flyer* on subscription.

Official Airline Guides Electronic Edition. The online version.

Automobile Travel

AAA Road Atlas for the United States, Canada and Mexico. Falls Church, Va.: American Automobile Association. Annual.

American Automobile Association. Falls Church, Va. Members are given lists of approved hotels and motels in the area of the trip being planned, as well as a strip map showing the best routes to follow.

Rand McNally Road Atlas. New York: Rand McNally & Company. Revised annually. Complete road maps of the United States, Canada, and Mexico, including a mileage and driving-time map of the United States.

Mobil Travel Guides. Revised annually. Ratings on food and lodgings in seven volumes dividing up the United States.

Railroads

New York: National Railway Publication Co. Issued bimonthly. This guide lists schedules and fares of passenger rail lines, including suburban services, connecting bus/ferry services, and rail tour operations.

AMTRAK issues a system-wide timetable. Reservations may be made using toll-free numbers listed in local telephone directories.

Hotels and Motels

The Berkshire Travellers Travel Shelf. Country Inns and Back Roads in North America, Britain and Ireland, and Europe. Stockbridge, Mass.: The Berkshire Traveller Press.

Leahy's Hotel-Motel Guide and Travel Atlas. Chicago: The American Hotel Register Co. Annual.

Official Hotel Red Book and Directory. New York: American Hotel Association. Annual.

Guidebooks

Among the many good guidebooks for foreign travel are the Fodor's series, published in New York by Fodor's Travel Guides and available for most European countries, Southeast Asia, South America, the Soviet Union, and so forth.

The Michelin Red Guides provide maps of areas and cities, and rate hotels and restaurants in detail. The Michelin Green Guides include history, notable sights, suggested touring routes, and distances between places, hours when buildings and gardens are open to the public, and so forth. Detailed maps are available. The Michelin Guides are published in London by Michelin Tyre Co. and are available in most bookstores.

APPENDIX

Signs and Symbols

´	acute accent
*	asterisk, a mark used to denote a reference
@	at, about; as, velvet @ $10 per yd.
[ ]	brackets used to enclose matter incidental to the thought of the sentence or to enclose material not a part of the original being quoted
˘	breve, a mark used to indicate a short vowel; as, *ĭll*
c/o	care of
^	caret, a sign inserted below a line between words or letters to denote an omission
͵	cedilla, under a *c* (ç) to show it is pronounced like *s*
¢	cent or cents
√	check
″	ditto
÷	division
$	dollar or dollars
=	equals
°C.	degrees Centigrade or Celsius
°F.	degrees Fahrenheit
′	feet; as, 16′; also minutes; as, 6′
`	grave accent
>	greater than

∴   hence, therefore

=   hyphen

″   inches; as, 11′ 4″ (eleven feet, four inches); also means second(s) when using ′ for minutes; as, 6′4″ (6 minutes, 4 seconds); a dictionary mark indicating secondary accent

<   less than

‾   macron, a mark used to indicate a long vowel; as, *īce*

—   minus

×   a sign denoting multiplication; a sign denoting *by* in dimensions; as, 3 ft. × 3 ft.; a character used instead of a signature by one unable to write his name

number; as, #7; pounds; as, 7#; also a printing mark used to indicate a needed space

¶   paragraph

‖   parallel to

%   percent

+   plus

£   pound; as, £6 (English money)

˜   tilde, a mark placed over *n* in Spanish words to denote the addition of the sound of *y*; as *cañon* pronounced *canyon*

§   section

Symbols for Foreign Currencies

The symbol for pounds, not available on most American machines, can be made using the capital L with a hyphen typed over it: Ł. Similarly, the symbol for yen is the capital Y, with or without the equals sign typed over it: ¥.

Country	Currency Name	Symbol
Argentina	peso 100 centavos	$
Australia	dollar 100 cents	$A
Austria	schilling 100 groschen	S *or* Sch
Belgium	franc 100 centimes	F *or* BFr
Brazil	cruzeiro 100 centavos	$ *or* Cr$

Canada	dollar 100 cents	$ *or* $Can
Chile	peso 1,000 escudos	amount followed by *Chilean pesos*
China, People's Republic of	renminbi 100 fen	$
China, Republic of, *see* Taiwan		
Colombia	peso 100 centavos	$ *or* P
Cuba	peso 100 centavos	$
Czechoslovakia	koruna 100 halers	Kčs
Denmark	krone 100 öre	Kr *or* DKr
Egypt	pound 100 piasters	£E
Finland	markka 100 pennia	M *or* MK
France	franc 100 centimes	F *or* Fr
German Demo- cratic Republic	mark *or* ostmark 100 pfennings	M *or* OM
Germany, Federal Republic of	deutsche mark 100 pfennigs	DM
Great Britain, *see* United King- dom		
Greece	drachma 100 lepta	Dr
Holland, *see* Netherlands, The		
Hong Kong	dollar 100 cents	HK$
Hungary	forint 100 filler	F *or* Ft
India	rupee 100 paise	Re (*pl.* Rs)
Ireland	pound 100 pence	£ or amount fol- lowed by *Irish pounds*

Israel	shekel	I£
	100 agorot	
Italy	lira	L
	100 centesimi	
Japan	yen	Y or ¥
	100 sen	
Korea, Republic	won	W
of South	100 chon or jeon	
Korean People's	won	W
Democratic Re-	100 jun	
public		
Mexico	peso	Mex$
	100 centavos	
Netherlands, The	gulden or guilder	Dfl or Fl or G
	or florin	
	100 cents	
New Zealand	dollar	NZ$
	100 cents	
Norway	krone	Kr or NKr
	100 öre	
Pakistan	rupee	Re (pl. Rs) or PRe
	100 paisa	(PRs)
Philippines	peso	₱ or P
	100 centavos or	
	sentimos	
Poland	zloty	Zl or Z
	100 groszy	
Portugal	escudo	$ or Esc
	100 centavos	
Romania	leu	L
	100 bani	
Saudi Arabia	riyal	R or SR
	20 qursh or 100	
	halala	
Singapore	dollar	S$
	100 cents	
South Africa	rand	R
	100 cents	
Spain	peseta	Pta or P (pl. Pts)
	100 centimos	
Sweden	krona	Kr or SKr
	100 öre	
Switzerland	franc	SFr or F

	100 centimes *or* rappen	
Syria	pound	£S *or* LS
	100 piasters	
Taiwan	dollar	NT$
	100 cents	
Thailand	baht	Bht *or* B
	100 satang	
Tunisia	dinar	D
	1,000 millimes	
Turkey	lira *or* pound	£T *or* LT *or* TL
	100 kurus *or* piasters	
Uganda	shilling	Sh
	100 cents	
Union of Soviet Socialist Republics	ruble	R *or* Rub
	100 kopecks	
United Arab Emirates	dirham	DH
	100 fils	
United Kingdom	pound	£ *or* amount followed by *Pounds Sterling*
	100 pence	
Uruguay	peso	$
	100 centesimos	
Venezuela	bolivar	B
	100 centimos	
Yugoslavia	dinar	Din
	100 paras	
Zaire	zaire	Z
	100 makuta (sing. *likuta*) *or* 10,000 sengi	
Zimbabwe	dollar	Z$
	100 cents	

Index

Apostrophe(s) *(cont.)*
  possessive singular, 87
  of-phrase and, 89
Articles, 24, 36–37

Bad and *badly,* 34
Bibliography(ies), 365–70
  anonymous works, 367
  author, 366
  collections, 366
  government publications, 367
  legal references, 369
  periodicals, 368
  place, publication, date, 367–68
  publications or organizations, 366–67
  punctuation in, 369
  reading lists, 370
  title, 367
  unpublished material, 368
Brackets, 97
  enclosing words independent of
    sentence, 97
  no punctuation with, 97
  sic and, 97
Business letters (forms), 218–47
  air express and, 244
  airmail and, 244
  appearance, 218
  attention line, 226, 244
  block style, 220, 239
    example of, 239
  body of, 233
  cc (carbon copy), 237
  complimentary close, 234
  confidential, 223
  continuation pages, 219
  date, 222
  enclosures, 237, 246–47
  envelopes and, 243, 245–46
  extra copies, 219–20
  file number for, 222–23
  folding and inserting of, 245–46
  foreign countries and, 244–45
  format, 220–21
  forms of address. *See* Forms of address
  headings, forms for, 222
  in care of (c/o), 244
  initials of writer or typist, 237

inside address, 223–26
  business titles, 225
  Messrs., 224
  professional titles, 225–26
  titles in, 224
labels for, 243
large mailings, 245
mailing procedures, 238, 243–47
modified block style, 220, 240
  example of, 240
modified semi-block style, 220, 241
  example of, 241
parts of, 221–38
  arrangement, 221
personal, 223
postscripts, 237–38
salutations, 227–33
signature, 234–37
simplified letter, 220–21, 238, 242
  example of, 242
subject line, 233
titles in inside address, 224–26
typing instructions for, 218–20
See also Forms of address; Letter(s)
  (generally); Salutations

Capitalization, 45–68
  academic degrees and titles, 46–47
  abbreviations and, 66–67
  adjectives from proper nouns, 67
  administration, 51–52
  Bible and, 59
  books, plays, reports, programs,
    compositions, display lines, etc.,
    65–66
  cabinet, 51
  church, cathedral, synagogue, temple,
    and chapel, 58–59
  code references on number in letter,
    64
  colons, word following, 61–62
  committee, 51
  commission, 52–53
  commonwealth, etc., 52
  constitution, 52
  courts, 51
  deity, 59–60
  divisions in a work, 64